Japan, Alcoholism, and Masculinity

Japan, Alcoholism, and Masculinity

Suffering Sobriety in Tokyo

Paul A. Christensen

LEXINGTON BOOKS
Lanham • Boulder • New York • London

Published by Lexington Books
An imprint of The Rowman & Littlefield Publishing Group, Inc.
4501 Forbes Boulevard, Suite 200, Lanham, Maryland 20706
www.rowman.com

Unit A, Whitacre Mews, 26-34 Stannary Street, London SE11 4AB

British Library Cataloguing in Publication Information Available

Library of Congress Cataloging-in-Publication Data Available

∞ ™ The paper used in this publication meets the minimum requirements of American National Standard for Information Sciences Permanence of Paper for Printed Library Materials, ANSI/NISO Z39.48-1992.

Printed in the United States of America

Contents

Acknowledgments

Writing about alcoholism, addiction, suffering, illness, loss, and the countless other afflictions that surround these topics is trying. Yet my struggles with gathering data, even when the subject matter was raw and unsettling, or fashioning that bulk of information into a coherent piece of scholarship, is nothing when compared to the struggles of the alcoholics introduced in the pages to follow. For this reason I owe an enormous debt to all the members of Alcoholics Anonymous, Danshūkai, and the doctors and staff at the hospitals and clinics I visited in Tokyo, Kōchi, Kagoshima, and other locales across Japan. Everyone's unfailing patience and unhesitating assistance allowed me to write something I hope is insightful and valuable to Japan's alcoholic community and beyond. Deepest thanks to the members of the Central Group, Ohashi Danshūkai, and Kōchi Danshūkai, for graciously inviting me into your meetings and allowing me to observe all that transpired without reservation or hesitation. I can only hope to capture a degree of the emotion and power that transpired in those meetings. Finally, particular thanks to Aki, Yoshi, Gen, Toru, Masa, Hiroka, Yuka, Nakamura, Kazu, Toshi, and Ryota. Rarely have I met such an amazing collection of individuals who have overcome so much and work tirelessly every day in the service of others. Without your time, words and patience this book would not exist.

At the University of Hawai'i I benefited tremendously from numerous friends and colleagues within and outside the Department of Anthropology and the Center for Japanese Studies. Christine Yano is the best doctoral advisor, friend, and academic mentor anyone could wish for. Sincerest thanks and *mahalo* as well to Ty Tengan, Eirik Saethre, Andy Arno, Deb Goebert, William Wood, Bob Huey, Gay Satsuma, Alex Golub, Geoff White, Eric Cunningham, Kelli Swazey, J.D. Baker, Hirofumi Katsuno, Satomi Fukutomi, Toru and Naomi Yamada, and Adam Lauer. Elsewhere, Laura Miller, Ted Bestor, Nicolas Sternsdorff, Merry White, Alvaro Jarrin, Linda Cool, Jennifer Matsue, Nancy Campbell, and Joyce Madancy all gave welcome and insightful comments and feedback on elements of the project. In Japan specific thanks to David Slater for his guidance and commitment to an intellectually vibrant anthropological community in Tokyo. Thanks as well to Anne Allison, Richard Chenhall, and Tomofumi Oka for insight and guidance while on the ground in Tokyo.

This work was supported initially through funding from the Monbukagakusho Scholarship, sponsored by the Government of Japan and administered in Hawai'i through the Consul General of Japan at Honolulu and the Center for Japanese Studies at the University of Hawai'i. Later work was funded by the Association for Asian Studies and the Union College Faculty Research Fund. I remain flattered that so many saw merit in my work and helped foster its growth and development over the years.

My family has never wavered in their support along my long and winding path to an academic career. Mom, Dad, Amanda, Jonnie, Sam, Abby, Madilyn, Emma, Jackson, Lucy, Lucia, and Angela—I am so fortunate to have each of you, thank you for everything. Especially to my mom and dad, thank you for fostering an intellectual curiosity in all of us that even you might not fully realize. Finally, Ana and Caetano, the long process of taking this project from an idea to a book has coincided with much of our life together (plus one arrival!). You both are my inspiration and I love you immensely. Thank you for so much patience, help, and wonderful companionship.

Introduction

In August 1995, I was seventeen years old and working for the summer as an English teacher in Fukuoka, the major city on the southern Japanese island of Kyūshū. It was during this summer that I drank my first beer. I and the other teachers, high school students and undergraduates from Washington State and Wisconsin, were down to our final weekend after spending six weeks in Japan. Our collective thirst to do something we believed rebellious had peaked, so we ventured out into a warm Fukuoka evening armed with limited Japanese and the hazy knowledge that being under the legal drinking age in Japan (20) and the United States (21) mattered little, if at all. Despite our collective linguistic limitations, we managed to find Oyafukō-dori (the street of disrespectful children), with its expected wealth of drinking establishments.[1] As mugs of beer arrived without incident and passports remained unchecked in pockets and purses we marveled at the casualness surrounding alcohol consumption in Japan and the impossibility of our sanctioned drinking upon return to the United States in a few days.

That evening I also took mental notes and blurry photographs to induce jealousy in my friends at home. I imagined their astonishment at vending machines that in exchange for a few coins spit out cold beer and sake. Although I did not consider it then, this was the first time I paid attention to the structures and patterns that surround drinking alcohol in Japan. Return trips in the ensuing years fed my growing interest in the topic, particularly how alcohol was consumed and regulated, as well as the surprising (at least to me) frequency with which the consequences of overconsumption—vomiting on train station platforms, public intoxication, and passing out almost anywhere—were typically met with indifference, and perhaps a mop, from others.

Yet out of this early interest grew the gnawing feeling that an important component was missing from the prevailing perception of drinking in Japan, as if something had been left absent from the frame or positioned carefully outside the commonly perceived scene. While drinking is important in Japan, and there are many who have said why and how they think it is important, the unremarked position is that such a stance is rarely challenged or questioned. Drinking is everywhere in conversations about Japan, nonchalantly noted in popular and academic texts, films, and countless other accounts. As the only nation in the world where beer is widely available from vending machines, these same machines have earned ubiquitous mention in travel guides and other accounts of Japan by foreign observers. Yet the prominence of Japan's alcohol consumption also renders it culturally banal to most, and the victim of trite conclusions by others. That first beer I had in Fukuoka did more than satisfy my thirst for youthful insolence, it set in motion a scholarly interest that in this book brings the backstage complexity surrounding drinking and, more importantly, *not drinking* in Japan out into the light. It allows me to ask why drinking is given such cultural importance in Japan and, more importantly, what then are the implications for those who do not drink.

FROM BARS TO MEETINGS

I am not an alcoholic—not "in the program," as the question is typically phrased by Alcoholics Anonymous (AA) members in the United States. While that may seem an odd statement, especially at the book's onset, it is necessary to an understanding of how the subject of alcoholism in Japan is broadly significant and what contributions I, an American anthropologist, can offer on the topic. The long jettisoned beginning to this research project was a look at alcohol consumption in Japan, how drinking retains a prominent place among men in contemporary Tokyo despite economic and social shifts that, since the bursting of Japan's economic bubble in the early 1990s, have changed the imbibing landscape in meaningful ways. My early months of fieldwork in Tokyo during the spring of 2007 were spent in pursuit of bars amenable to such efforts, or in conversation with individuals excited to discuss their devotion to alcoholic beverages as a culturally meaningful pursuit.[2] Yet within these conversations on drinking was the persistent question of where and how alcoholism, as well as addiction generally, fit into the picture—how were these conditions understood and experienced in Japan? What of the individual, particularly a man, who has elected not to drink or determined that his drinking has become destructive? While Japan's alcoholics are often invisible to their countrymen (sometimes deliberately so), as a group they have a tremendous amount to say concerning how alcoholism is generally understood, as well as meaningful insights into notions of disease, illness, addiction, and appropriately gendered conduct in Japan and beyond.

The severing of my research agenda from questions of alcohol consumption occurred three months into my time in Tokyo, on August 20, 2007. On this typically hot and muggy summer day I attended my first AA meeting. Walking to the meeting from Ikebukuro Station, an always crowded jumble of converging train and subway lines, I remember feeling self-conscious about sweating, feelings that proved unfounded as everyone else was equally flushed from the dense blanket of August humidity spread across Tokyo. Instead, the heat became the topic of general conversation, allowing me an opportunity to casually engage group members as we waited for the meeting to begin.

This particular meeting was held in a building that had previously been a junior high school and now served as a community center. I walked first to the Japan Service Office (JSO), AA's headquarters in Japan, to meet Toshi and Aki, the first Japanese AA members I met and who feature prominently in the pages to come.[3] They had invited me to the evening's meeting several days prior during an earlier visit I paid to the JSO. After quickly finishing their work for the day the three of us walked the short distance over narrow side streets from the JSO office to the meeting and arrived a few minutes early. Once everyone assembled, I observed for the next hour and a half what would gradually become a complex ethnographic setting rife with cultural borrowings, deeply revealing discourses, and maddening inconsistencies on the nature and structure of alcoholism and addiction as a highly individualized category of personal identity.

Fitting comfortably into the large room that evening were seventeen people—twelve men (including myself) and five women. Meeting attendees ranged in age from their late twenties to retirees in their sixties and seventies. Some dressed in suits, having come directly from work to the 8:00 pm meeting; others wore jeans and similarly casual attire. One man, likely in his early forties and dressed all in black, with long hair that extended to the middle of his back, was the antithesis of the white-collar "salaryman" image (Dasgupta 2013). In short, beyond individual admissions of alcoholism, few overt ties linked this diverse group together. Before taking their turn speaking, each participant introduced themselves by giving the customary AA greeting, a single name they used in meetings followed by "alcoholic." Many used the word *aru-chū*, a colloquial term that shortens the transliterated Japanese word for "alcohol" and combines it with the kanji for middle or center, implying that one is engulfed in alcohol.[4] Several others used the medical term *arukoru izonnsyo* or "alcohol dependency syndrome" that is popular in AA's Japanese literature.[5] I return to the choice between these two terms of identity as an alcoholic in chapter 7, as it reflects individual member feelings on the nature of alcoholism and its role in their recovery. Many speakers also elected to use a nickname, with English names being popular, instead of their given names when introducing themselves. Not knowing what to say when called on to speak, I introduced myself as "Paul, a cultural anthropologist" which caused first Aki and then everyone else to chuckle at my attempt to use AA's linguistic conventions.

This was a "book meeting," meaning each attendee read aloud a portion of the Big Book, AA's primary text, and then spoke on how this passage was personally meaningful to their experiences with alcohol and sobriety.[6] The meeting's theme was family and friends, and each attendee took their turn reading several sentences from the designated section of the text. After reading, members then spoke of feelings these passages elicited related to their family and friends. Throughout the meeting I remained struck by the depth of feeling and emotion the gathered members voiced. Japanese men in particular are not stereotypically known for frequent and public, or in the context of the meeting semi-public, expressions of intimate feelings, frustrations, and shortcomings. In fact, alcohol consumption is often cited as necessary in order to freely express oneself, allowing Japanese men to forge a bond that sobriety and its accompanying social boundaries render impossible. Yet the male majority filling the meeting room that evening all reflected on their past drunken memories and transgressions, declaring for all in attendance to hear that it had been the conduct of a sick individual now trying to live "in recovery" without alcohol.

I left my first sobriety group meeting feeling excited, almost overwhelmed. The terminology of AA and alcoholism are topics not typically covered in Japanese language courses or daily conversation, and at times it had been a challenge to follow what was said in the meeting. However, the meeting also indicated that this was fertile ground for understanding how an aspect of life often overlooked in Japan and elsewhere is lived. And while not something I found immediately evident, going to meetings also enables here a look at how major medical concept seemingly rooted in biomedical certainty, alcoholism as well as addiction, are individually experienced in widely differing and culturally influenced ways that weigh heavily in dictating how recovery is experienced. Looking back, much of the initial meeting's content came slowly into focus during the remainder of my time in Tokyo. In my notes after this initial meeting I wrote that "talk therapy seems like an exercise in filling the hours and reminding members of the difficulties they had while drinking. I guess I'm perplexed that the meetings alone are capable of helping someone stay sober." As I wish to convey here, the contrary is true, as for many members the sobriety group meeting is a richly textured and necessary social ritual revealing the broader and frequently gendered implications surrounding the contemporary definitional apparatus of alcoholism and addiction.

To help readers navigate the pages to follow, I offer here an outline of the book's chapters. Alcoholism and recovery are unquestioningly complex notions that in areas remain hazily understood despite decades of research from numerous fields of study. Additionally, the complexity I emphasize comes from the individual negotiations of recovery made by Japanese men, and I cannot stress enough the individuality of each recovery journey. While these narratives provide deeply interesting and often tragic accounts of personal struggles with alcohol, loss, and recovery, they also necessitate the casting of a particularly wide net in order to account for the profusion of contributory factors that go into shaping alcoholism as an aspect of lived identity for Japanese men.

In chapter 1, "Drying Out," I further introduce the topic, emphasizing the historical trajectory of alcoholism and recovery. The history of alcoholism in the United States, particularly the neat parallels with temperance and prohibition movements in the early part of the twentieth century, helped shape global definitions of addiction and the extent of possible recovery options for afflicted individuals. This history, firmly rooted in a Judeo-Christian worldview, continues to dominate the definitional framework surrounding contemporary diagnosis and individual understandings of alcoholism. As such, I contend that this culturally blunt approach to comprehending a highly individual process has not only come to dominate recovery efforts, but that the outcomes of such an approach to recovery become quickly and consequentially felt by Japanese alcoholics.

Chapter 2, "Divine Drink," gives historical background on alcohol in Japan by first looking at sake's (rice wine) early links to Shintōism, religious practice, and the sacred. Following this the chapter looks at post–World War II depictions of alcohol in advertisements, contrasted with first the work of Japan's temperance unions and more recently NGO and NPO groups trying to strengthen Japanese laws pertaining to beverage alcohol. The chapter concludes by looking at the positive framing of alcohol and its consumption through numerous media forms and the gendering of alcohol consumption. I am particularly interested in articulating Japan's linking of alcohol consumption to fun and revelry, and the use and manipulation of history to maintain such connections. Others have made reference to the culturally constructed importance given alcohol and socialization in Japan, but as an auxiliary within other areas of focus (Allison 1994, Edwards 1989, and Ohnuki-Tierney 1994). Here I emphasize the consequences of these connections for alcoholics, particularly the ways in which it can limit employment options, curtail friendships, impede shifts in notions of self, and maintain established gender norms of socialization.

Chapter 3, "Sobriety and Disease," considers in greater detail how understandings and concepts of addiction have undergone substantial historical change, and remain today the subject of much disagreement and debate.

Addiction is often viewed as a biomedical certainty, yet it is also rife with cultural and contextual considerations shaping the struggles, setbacks, and attitudes towards recovery for individual addicts. One outcome of wrapping addiction and treatment methodology in biomedical authority is frequent neglect for how these approaches are then viewed and accepted or rejected across a diversity of cultural and religious views. Making this process gravely consequential is the dominant position atop the recovery hierarchy forged by AA and the not yet mentioned Danshūkai (Sobriety Association), which together form Japan's two major sobriety support groups, leaving little room to consider alternative forms of treatment or how the major philosophical underpinnings of both groups are met and interpreted by Japanese alcoholics.

Chapter 4, "Sobriety Groupings," looks at alcoholism and recovery in Japan. It begins with a more comprehensive description of AA and Danshūkai. This is followed by a detailed account of the specific meeting groups I worked with, including important features of the location and interpersonal dynamics of the group members. I am concerned with articulating in this chapter how admissions of alcoholism among Japanese men are culturally problematic. Following this is a look at Japan's prevailing recovery methodology for alcoholism. Finally, the performance of an alcoholic identity both in and out of sobriety group meetings, including how group member sobriety constitutes "living in recovery," concludes the chapter. The path towards recovery as presented in meetings and AA or Danshūkai publications is often individually experienced in a markedly different manner from the one outlined in group literature. I emphasize these differences as they often distinguish how Japanese men understand, experience, and disclose or hide their alcoholism.

Chapter 5, "Moral Failures," examines alcoholism and the self, starting first by looking in greater detail at the structure and content of sobriety group meetings. Also addressed are the rules of conduct during meetings, how individual members talk about their alcoholism and the methodological distinctions between AA and Danshūkai. Additionally, in looking at the difference between meeting dialogue and the lived experiences of group members, particularly the frequent use of disparaging language and phrases when speaking about their alcoholism, the struggles with living sober become clear. Language use by members, especially men, that mentions the "moral failings" they feel as a result of identifying as alcoholics is particularly prevalent during meetings. The consequences of this language use, made all the more significant in a setting many feel is the only route to recovery and lasting sobriety, are explored in detail. Finally the chapter looks at national and institutionalized victimization in an attempt to clarify "why me?" questions—"why must my family suffer?"—that individual members frequently and often rhetorically pose during group meetings.

Chapter 6, "Ten Yen Coins," looks at healing the self and the possible resumption of a place and role in larger society. The chapter examines the socialization of individuals into AA or Danshūkai members through their use of appropriate terminology, group slogans, and acceptance of a self-ascribed identity as an alcoholic. In particular, the role given spirituality in both organizations, evident in the prominence of God, "*as you understand Him*" at AA and the family in Danshūkai is explored (Alcoholics Anonymous 2001, italics in original). Finally the chapter calls attention to individual frustrations, shame, and challenges to the established sobriety group methodology, including a brief look at the growing use of the Internet as a possible recovery tool and alternative to AA and Danshūkai.

Chapter 7, "*Futsū* or *Fushigi*: Normally Drunk and Oddly Sober," examines how collective conceptions of "futsū" (normal) and "fushigi" (unusual) help shape drinking and drunkenness in Japan as expected and normalized conduct, while marking refusals to drink and sobriety as abnormal outliers. The chapter first looks at how a pervasive acceptance and comfort with addiction as a potential aspect of identity in the United States, due in large part to AA's popular visibility, is largely absent in Japan and as such, not something Japanese sobriety group members can rely on when revealing their alcoholism to those unfamiliar with the organizations. Not only does this absence of popular visibility contribute to secrecy and reluctance among many group members to widely disclose their alcoholism, it feeds popular imaginings of alcoholics as degenerates beset by a morally weak individual character. The irony of such views, raised often by group members during meetings, is Japan's ongoing comfort with drunkenness, including public and sometimes messy intoxication, as expected, anticipated, and normalized behavior.

The concluding chapter, "The Imperial Drunkard," highlights Japan's importance, particularly the wide ranging insights it offers, to the study of alcoholism, addiction, and other forms of substance use. The admission of alcoholism by the now deceased Prince Tomohito of Mikasa, a cousin of Emperor Akihito, is raised for the cautious optimism it engendered among sobriety group members that a change in the popular perception of the alcoholic was on the horizon, as well as their subsequent frustrations when such change failed to transpire. Specifically, the struggles of men in Japan to find a public alcoholic persona widely accepted as socially appropriate are revisited through the admissions, struggles, and frustrations of the men filling sobriety group meetings in Tokyo and throughout Japan. For these men, their sense of both masculinity and place in Japanese society has been gradually pulled apart through first struggles with alcohol consumption and then their efforts at maintaining sobriety. As such, the focus of the final chapter is the process of trying to repair this sense of masculinity and place within Japan, including expressed frustrations and thwarted attempts at re-masculinization and re-emergence by group members. The chapter ends by broadly considering how anthropology can make meaningful contributions to better understanding addiction and recovery, both in Japan and globally, in part through a methodology that is adept at revealing discontinuity between prescribed and sanctioned systems of recovery and the culturally influenced realities facing individual alcoholics.

NOTES

1. "Street of disrespectful children" is an accurate translation; however, many call Oyafukō-dori "piss off your parents street," a rendering that better captures the area's overall mood and typical clientele.

2. I have written of this aspect of my fieldwork elsewhere; see Christensen 2012 and Christensen 2014.

3. In keeping with standard anthropological practice, and the desire of many alcoholics to remain anonymous, all names are pseudonyms and when necessary location names are altered or withheld. A single name, either an individual's first or family depending on how they identified themselves at meetings, is also widely used as it is in keeping with AA and Danshūkai's emphasis on informality.

4. 『アル中』(*aru chū*)

5. 『アルコール依存症』(*arukōru izonshō*)

6. In conversation with others familiar with AA in the United States, it was noted that this format had been popular but is largely not followed today as the American AA membership is often familiar with the Big Book's content. In Japan, however, this meeting style remains popular.

Chapter One

Drying Out

The Painful Liver

Toshi, a short, strong man in his late fifties with a gruff-looking exterior hiding a talkative disposition, was one of the first alcoholics I met in Japan. Now retired, he volunteers with AA's Japan Service Office (JSO) doing administrative work, answering the phone, organizing mailings, and helping out with other tasks as needed. On my first visit to the office he sat at a table along the wall folding fliers while I spoke with Aki, an AA member, employee, and my initial contact with the organization. Later Aki introduced us and said I should come back again next week to interview Toshi, to which he agreed but wondered aloud what possible interest I could have in talking to him. A week later I returned to the JSO and we began a conversation that continued throughout my fourteen months in Tokyo.

Toshi started drinking relatively late in life, at around the age of 23 or 24, and initially did not like alcohol. However, this quickly changed with his first job. Toshi worked for Japan's patent office, a bureaucratic position within the government that afforded him the luxury of a workplace largely devoid of stress and brimming with a constant stream of invitations to go drinking. Readily accepting these invitations, and then gradually becoming the one organizing others for an evening in the bars, Toshi spent the bulk of his employed life with a hangover. He added that "attendance" ensured a satisfactory job performance, meaning as long as he arrived to work on time in the morning, his hangovers and sluggish productivity were of little concern or consequence to co-workers and superiors.

Twenty years later Toshi was well into his forties and of failing health. Pain radiated constantly from his liver, his hands shook, and myriad other health concerns racked his body. He found that pressing the side of his body hard against his desk dulled some of the liver pain, and spent over a year sitting like this while co-workers went about their duties around him without comment. Other aspects of his life also languished in gradual collapse. His wife left, but did not divorce him, out of frustration with his refusal to acknowledge the physical and interpersonal damage brought on by his drinking. Toshi's two adult children also gradually distanced themselves and eventually wanted nothing to do with him.

Family splintering brought bank account balances to zero and Toshi's health continued to deteriorate, yet his drinking persisted without colleague critique or criticism. More than anything else, the refusal from co-workers to acknowledge or confront him about the increasingly visible evidence of bodily destruction caused by drinking continues to hurt Toshi, even after years of sobriety have restored his health. When he could no longer tolerate the liver pain he finally decided to meet with his doctor and "honestly" discuss his level of alcohol consumption. The doctor said that Toshi was an alcoholic and would soon die if he continued to drink. While this was not the first time Toshi's physician had told him this, he said during our first interview, "I had refused to hear him before." With newfound but reluctant acceptance, Toshi entered first a three month hospital program designed to flush his body of alcohol followed by initially reluctant but regular AA meeting attendance.

When we met in the summer of 2007 Toshi was more than five years sober. His anger from the early weeks and months after he joined AA had faded, now replaced by frustration with himself for being an alcoholic, with those he once worked with for doing nothing while he slowly drank himself to the brink of death, and with Japan for the manner in which alcohol is consumed, sold, and enjoyed by so many. Toshi is, in short, a living amalgamation of the topics broached in the pages to follow: a Japanese man who drank heavily because he felt it culturally requisite and sanctioned to do so, and who now struggles under the sometimes self-imposed burden of sobriety group membership and a desire to find a place of recognized existence without alcohol.

SCOPE AND FOCUS

The central focus of this book is to describe and theorize the ways in which alcoholism is understood, accepted, and taken on as an influential and lived identity among Japanese men. At the most general level, I explore how a subjective idea comes to be regarded as an objective and unassailable fact (Tiger 2013: 36). Here such a process concerns how the culturally and temporally specific treatment methodology of AA, upon which much of Danshūkai's recovery philosophy is also based, has come to be *the* approach in Japan to diagnosing, treating, and structuring alcoholism as an aspect of individual identity. In particular, the gendered consequences, how this process transpires among Japanese men, are considered, as it offers substantial insight into how diagnostic categories of illness and disease are created, particularly the ramifications of dominant forms of such categorizations across progressively porous cultural borders. Consequences that become starkly obvious when the persistent connection between notions of masculinity and alcohol consumption in Japan are considered from the perspective of the alcoholic and sobriety group member. Depictions of an alcohol saturated Japan populated by intoxicated salarymen, beer dispensing vending machines, and a generally tolerant approach to public drunkenness typify domestic and international perceptions of Japanese drinking. Even the very definitions of Japanese masculinity are interwoven with narratives on personal alcohol consumption in public settings: gender norms that exclude and marginalize the alcoholic. And yet the alcoholic exists in Japan, and exists in an often contradictory manner revealing of the dominant processes by which alcoholism and addiction are globally influenced, understood, and classified.

At its core then, this is a story about alcoholic Japanese men. More specifically, it looks at how admissions of alcoholism and sobriety group membership challenge Japan's prevailing masculine gender norms. My contention is that Japanese men who identify as alcoholics are placed in a struggle between recovery ideology and societal assumptions of appropriate gender norms. They engage a recovery and sobriety ideology borrowed largely from Alcoholics Anonymous in the United States. As such, to be an alcoholic is to negotiate an ideology reflective of several idiosyncratic positions, notably an underlying influence of Christianity and a specific understanding of the condition as a disease, from which one cannot be fully cured, that has persisted in American recovery communities with meager contestation or controversy since the 1930s. What emerges is a paradoxical existence for alcoholic men in Japan, a struggle between being appropriately sober, appropriately Japanese, and appropriately masculine, while also aware that personally destructive drinking patterns brought them to such a place. Thus, Japan's alcoholics cluster in tangible and metaphoric apprehension along the societal margins, caught between cultural inclinations implying that "unless a man is successful in terms of power, authority, and possession, he cannot be considered to be a 'real man,'" and the constitution of "being a real man" through alcohol consumption (Roberson and Suzuki 2003: 8).

More generally, what follows is an account of Japan's "nots," those who cannot and do not consume alcohol when so many around them frequently imbibe. In order to articulate the struggles undertaken by Japan's "nots," I seek to create a space in which various theories and methodologies pertaining to alcoholism, addiction, and masculinity can be challenged to articulate new understandings of these sociocultural processes. The individuals who provide the content contained here do not drink because through sobriety group membership they have come to believe that consuming alcohol will lead to their death. It is not an immediate, or likely even a quick, death. But as sober and recovering alcoholics actively participating in a sobriety support group, any alcoholic beverage is regarded as a "deadly poison."[1] If they begin drinking again, death is organizationally understood as the only and eventual outcome. "Nots" are thus the alcoholics who fill the membership ranks of AA and Danshūkai, Japan's two major sobriety groups that at the most generous membership estimate comprise less than 25,000 individuals among Japan's more than 128 million citizens.[2] Yet they are also a collection of individuals assuming a self-identity as alcoholics that is unrecognized, or more accurately unrecognizable, to many they encounter in their daily lives, and for this reason the negotiations and even subterfuge involved in being a "not" are significant.

While sobriety group meetings are held in all of Japan's forty-seven prefectures, albeit sporadically in more rural locales, the members of AA and Danshūkai concentrate disproportionately in Japan's urban centers. In Tokyo, the primary setting of the pages to follow, there are multiple meetings of both organizations every day of the week in a variety of locations, from the spare rooms of Christian churches to community centers, unused school warehouses, and government owned buildings. However, even something as prosaic as obtaining regular meeting space can sometimes be problematic, a process reflective of the persistent challenges faced by Japan's alcoholics and returned to in later chapters.

Tokyo's sobriety group members are a community both insular and welcoming. I was readily invited into meetings, yet listened to numerous speeches by group members about the difficulties and lengths taken to hide their alcoholism from co-workers, friends, and family. Owing to this, it is at least initially productive to think of the sobriety group meeting as an inversion of the oft-noted *soto*, "outer context where one relates with restraint and deference," and *uchi*, "inner context where one unharnesses spontaneous expression," duality in Japan (Rosenberger 1994: 8). It is in the *soto*, the outside, among a collection of AA "fellows," some the speaker might know well and others they are seeing for the first time, where the requirement for active participation is revealing and spontaneous expressions of deep emotion.[3] Inversely, among one's *uchi*, the intimate group of friends, family, and close co-workers, alcoholics often carry themselves with constraint or even secrecy, unable or unwilling to openly disclose and discuss their alcoholism.

SOBER GROUPINGS

Self-identifying as an alcoholic in Japan, or elsewhere, is typically constituted through membership in a sobriety organization. AA is dominant among such groups in the United States, as well as other national settings, as evidenced in recent works from Australia (Chenhall 2007), Honduras (Pine 2005), and Mexico (Brandes 2002). Unusually, Japan has two major sobriety organizations, as AA shares space and membership with the larger and indigenously derived Danshūkai. The groups diverge at several major points, most notably Danshūkai's allowance for the participation of non-alcoholic family members in meetings.[4] Other smaller differences include group financials—Danshūkai requires membership dues (typically about ¥100 per meeting)—while AA is strictly donation-based, and the production of literature (AA's canon is extensive and growing while Danshūkai's publications are by comparison minimal).[5] Most importantly, Danshūkai is based on AA, and early group members in the late 1950s and early 1960s believed they were establishing "Japanese AA" when they altered American AA's rules to, in their view, better suit a Japanese membership. This transformation is returned to later as it marks not only an important division within Japan's recovery community, but also highlights individual struggles with fully incorporating group tenets into a context that lacks the popular pervasiveness AA garners elsewhere in the world.

In practical terms, becoming a member of either group is simple. An individual must have a stated desire to maintain sobriety by refraining completely from alcohol and participating in meetings through regular attendance, generally understood as several meetings per week. However, the straightforwardness of such a process conceals the difficulties, negotiations, and shifts undertaken by individuals as they become group members. More than joining a support organization, new members must learn to present and think of themselves as alcoholics, a definitional category heavy with the baggage of addiction, illness, and the need to constantly live "in recovery." This final point is particularly important, as living in recovery involves adherence to the established self-help group framework of admission, acceptance, and surrender to a "Higher Power" as necessary in acknowledging an inability to control one's drinking. This process also demands recognition that one will never fully recover and must live each subsequent day as an alcoholic, the basis for AA's popular slogan "one day at a time," which is often the first conceptual notion imparted to new members in Japan. Consequently, an inquiry in to how Japanese men negotiate institutional norms and individual experiences with alcohol raises several significant issues. Collective institutional certainties regarding alcoholism and more broadly addiction are predicated and developed on an individual's acceptance of membership in AA or Danshūkai and their sustained engagement with group ideology. To be an alcoholic is to accept the group's institutional definitions and then live within the outlined parameters. Further, understanding contemporary definitions of alcoholism is the process of revealing how those same parameters are presented as serving and helping the alcoholic in their recovery, how institutional forces, from doctors to other group members to individuals, shape afflictions through the lens of group teachings. In short, sobriety groups have built a tight logical circle around which members are asked to interpret their memories of past drunkenness, as long as conformity to established conventions are maintained and filtered through the mandated norms of conduct.

Relevant to the above, sobriety group teaching dictates that a "spiritual awakening" is a crucial aspect of an individual's transition from destructive drinker to an alcoholic capable of living in recovery. Initial confessions of powerlessness over alcohol enables one to "constitute oneself. In the act of speaking, through the obligation to produce words that are true to an inner reality, through the self-examination that precedes and accompanies speech, one becomes a subject for oneself" (Rose 1999: 244). By placing a spiritual transformation at the center of the recovery process, sobriety groups also shift responsibility for success or failure entirely to the individual. As Michel Foucault notes, without subjectification one cannot live as an ethical subject, and this is accomplished through "monitoring, testing, and improving of the self" (*ibid*: 245). Adoption in AA and Danshūkai of such a framework ensures that Japan is part of an internationally consistent approach to the care and treatment of alcoholism. Yet it also neglects any processes of cultural assimilation. Individual alcoholics must instead attempt to forge culturally recognized spaces within which a now sober sense of self can exist, while also following a recovery model that makes limited concession for such efforts or actions.

Finally, AA's success in crafting, and sometimes bending, expert opinion to fit their approach to recovery has contributed greatly to the organization's expansion and international relevance (Brandes 2002, Carr 2011). The usurping of medical authority that transfers power back to the "powerless" alcoholic is a deliberate organizational construct indicative of collective efforts to, above all else, work at healing the souls of group members and repair their often shattered lives. As Mariana Valverde notes, "whether or not it works to cure alcoholism, AA has certainly succeeded in developing a whole array of non-professionalized, low-cultural capital techniques for acting on oneself that have profoundly shaped our present" (1998: 19). Here I am interested in divergence from this approach, as Japanese physicians typically act as the diagnostic gatekeepers and brokers of this "expert knowledge," wielding substantial authority and influence over the membership of Japan's sobriety groups and the recovery process, all within a system established to usurp such authority.

PSYCHOACTIVE ETHNOGRAPHY AND THE DISEASE MODEL OF ALCOHOLISM

Anthropology, both in and out of Japan, often frames alcohol as an ethnographic aid, loosening tongues and allowing bits of knowledge to slip forth that might otherwise remain unsaid. Being drunk, or at least a little tipsy, lowers the metaphorical *uchi/soto* barriers between individuals more commonly called social convention. As such, drunkenness provides a viable and accepted route to shared vulnerability and solidarity between drinkers, a sanctioned setting for sharing information that otherwise remains unspoken and concealed. This is also the reason why drinking, particularly in the context of Japan, is often mentioned as a potential tool in revealing sought-after insights veiled behind cultural mechanisms (Johnson 2003: 151). So common are passing references to drinking in many written accounts of Japan—the presence of beer bottles on the table during an insightful conversation—that they often pass throughout the ethnographic frame without further examination, or are cited in lauding terms as aiding the anthropological process.

However, returning again to Valverde, "alcohol has been a problematic substance . . . because questions of addiction have been and continue to be important sites upon which the complex dialectic of personal freedom and control/self-control has worked itself out historically" (1998: 5). The "problematic" nature of alcohol is particularly evident in the context of Japan, as I am interested in the transnational movement of a methodology for confronting alcoholism, itself a culturally constituted category that has contributed to how the affliction is currently defined. Alcoholism, as popularly understood in the United States today, arose out of the formation of AA and the social, historical, and religious context of 1930s America. Currently it is the dominant method of defining and disseminating information on alcoholism, as well as addiction and illness as lived categories of identity, in North America and other areas of the world with an active AA presence. In Japan, the impact of AA and Danshūkai in shaping popular understandings of alcoholism outside the sobriety group membership has been minimal. As such, my goal here is to examine how individual decisions to abstain from alcohol have been made to fit, or not fit, within Japan's popular understandings of masculinity. Many of Japan's sobriety group members discuss the shame and embarrassment that accompanies admissions of alcoholism during meetings, prompting here the need to examine the larger socio-historical processes stigmatizing AA and Danshūkai membership. As I hope to demonstrate, the situation is not as simple as alcohol being favorably regarded in Japan and therefore a decision to not consume is unfavorably viewed by the majority of Japanese. The negotiation is not only more nuanced, but has much to say about constructions of gender norms and the processes shaping how addiction and disease circulate between Japan and the global as culturally meaningful categories of identity and designation.

My interest in alcoholism and psychoactive substance use stems from a perceived need for greater anthropological work on the liminal spaces created around the ingesting of addicting substances, including alcohol (Hunt and Barker 2001). Early anthropological accounts of alcohol consumption emphasized the cultural construction of drunken comportment, the behavior allowed, encouraged, and tolerated in a specific setting when alcohol was consumed, instead of the consequences of consumption or the changing nature of addiction and recovery as culturally meaningful categories. Recognizing that drunken comportment differs markedly between locations and cultural groups, early scholarship allowed prevailing contemporary views of intoxicated behavior to emerge, particularly why certain punishable behaviors when sober are tolerated during moments of drunkenness (Douglas 1987, Heath 1958, MacAndrew and Edgerton 1969, Marshall 1978).

AA's ceaseless advocacy of the disease model of alcoholism in the United States, has also imparted widespread societal awareness and acceptance of this definitional framework. The disease model frames addiction, to alcohol or any other habit-forming substance, as an illness marked by an individual inability to control consumption. However, as an illness, alcoholism occupies a problematic definitional category. It takes on many of the characteristics typically assigned to disease—recognizable symptoms that follow a consistent pattern of onset and progression—yet these symptoms also result from an individual's consumption of alcohol. Thus, while the disease model is practically useful, particularly for newly sober individuals working to reestablish a degree of stability in their life, it also creates a host of new questions concerning the possible consequences that can result from the ubiquity of this approach. Questions that are explored in the chapters to follow.

Japan's long tenured sobriety group members have embraced the disease model, yet also speak candidly during meetings about the frustrations they feel in maintaining such a position. Further complicating matters is the disease model's lack of recognition and acceptance within the Japanese public, making it a difficult position to articulate outside meetings. An example of this skepticism was raised succinctly at an AA meeting in late February, 2008 when a vocal middle-aged male with several years of sobriety recounted an angry exchange with a superior at work. He recalled how, after several minutes of increasingly heated exchange between the two he shouted in exasperation "I'm sick!," as explanation for his sobriety and inability to go drinking. Yet this outburst of frustration was met with a skeptical and deriding "really?" from his boss, that once recounted in the meeting drew sympathetic nods of the head and frustrated smirks from the other members—responses that also reflect the exasperation felt by many at Tokyo's AA and Danshūkai meetings when recounting the lack of acceptance that typically greets their disclosures of sobriety. This lack of popular support for the central pillar of sobriety group recovery ideology, a deficiency that many members note with a touch of envy is typically not confronted by American AA members, also persists as an impediment to wider acceptance in Japan of alcoholism and sobriety group membership.

Knowledge of the disease model among AA and Danshūkai members comes from two sources. AA's extensive literature, including most notably *The Big Book*, advocates and outlines in great detail the disease model approach to alcoholism. Similarly, Danshūkai's approach to treatment, the "three pillars of sobriety," medicalizes alcoholism as an illness requiring extensive inpatient hospital care and constant monitoring. Danshūkai's three pillars, hospitalization, anti-alcohol medication, and self-help group meeting participation, mandate regular meeting attendance following a diagnosis as alcohol dependent and extensive hospital treatment designed to rebuild the individual from a broken drunk into an ill, yet also sober and recovering, alcoholic.[6] It is a recovery methodology that buttresses a medicalizing process directly linked to hospitalization, and the physician's diagnostic authoritative is firmly fixed upon the alcoholic (Foucault 1994). Yet, as Pertti Alasuutari notes, alcoholism, as currently understood, "portrays heavy drinking as a long-standing problem which can be managed and handled, *but not cured*" (1992: 2, italics added). Further, alcoholism "distinguishes between normal and abnormal (or pathological) drinking," conceptualizations that profoundly influence the lived experience of Tokyo's alcoholics (*ibid*). Framed against the frustrations many sobriety group members express during meetings, the disease model becomes a problematic and confining approach, mandating conformity to international standards with limited concern for the role of the individual and thwarting discussion on how alcoholism and addiction are approached in Japan as lived categories of identities.

This is not to suggest that Japan simply borrowed treatment and recovery methodology on alcoholism from the United States. Quite the contrary. The compelling piece of this puzzle lies in the prominent influence AA-rooted notions of alcoholism and recovery continue to assert alongside major changes to recovery methodology, particularly within Danshūkai, undertaken to make the organization "more Japanese" but also struggling to engage those outside the ranks of sobriety group members. Danshūkai's largely male leadership incorporated significant elements of AA ideology into their recovery program, including an emphasis on alcoholism as a "very normal illness" with the potential to afflict anyone.[7] Danshūkai's national website adds that alcoholism should not be borne as a source of shame, and afflicted individuals are far more numerous than many in Japan acknowledge or comprehend.[8] Where such assertions become problematic, as demonstrated in my accounts of meetings to follow, is in the lack of widely held popular acceptance for alcoholism and the disease model as valid forms of recovery and individual identity.

LIMINAL SELVES

In theorizing the production of an alcoholic self among Japanese men, I am interested in persistent expression of feelings of social marginalization by Tokyo sobriety group members. This point is particularly salient when the emphasis in sobriety groups on the "profound" and "spiritual" transformation, self-attributed in group literature to getting and staying sober by working the organizational program, is considered (AA 2001). Tokyo's predominantly male sobriety group membership exists "in liminality . . . structurally if not physically invisible in terms of his culture's standard definitions and classifications" (Turner 1974: 232–233). The result is a marginal existence for group members that, as Turner adds, has "no cultural assurance of a final stable resolution" to their ambiguity, resulting in a struggle to create spaces where alcoholism can exist for Japanese men as an acceptable aspect of masculine identity (*ibid*). Consequently, sobriety and AA or Danshūkai membership for many in Japan is a negotiation of the ambiguity surrounding their identity, personhood, and masculinity. With their existence framed through marginality, the alcoholics at Tokyo meetings enter a process of organizationally structured self-governance designed to remake the individual, yet that is also largely unrecognized by those outside the meeting.

Self-governance, Michel Foucault's "conduct of conduct," the managing of self in a manner appropriate to agreed upon societal norms, becomes a significant analytical pillar around which Japan's engagement with alcoholism as awkwardly positioned social construct can be understood (Gordon 1991: 5). The governing of public settings and behavior, as taken from Nikolas Rose, has seeped into the private sphere in order to "constrain the external manifestations of morality in 'visible' conduct" (1999: 229). Yet intoxication's external manifestations of visible conduct in Japan typically take on a tolerated and indulgent character. The creation of Japanese men as "self-responsible subjects," particularly throughout Japan's postwar rise to economic prominence, demanded shared alcohol consumption and drunkenness with other men (Song 2009: 12). Furthermore, this logic "defends society," here understood as moments of shared homosocial intimacy over consumption, a process that also renders Japan's alcoholic as culturally challenging and problematic figures (*ibid*). What results are refusals to drink and efforts at maintaining sobriety being viewed as challenging Japan's view of what is appropriately masculine, while reinforcing ideas of the alcoholic as disruptive to the normative practice of shared consumption and drunkenness among men.

AA's established recovery methodologies for treating alcoholism mandate the reshaping of individual behavior through rigorous introspection and meaningful interpersonal engagement with group teachings. Importantly, the success of such an arrangement is dependent on shifting the forces of public opinion towards acceptance of such an approach to treatment as the standard form for confronting alcoholism. As such, it is an approach that not only allows alcoholics to "have their behavior managed back to normality through an expertly designed programme employing the systematic use of sanctions and rewards," but one that is also resistant to challenge or criticism of the treatment methodology (Rose 1999: 239).

AA's advocacy work has also done much to shift popular understandings of alcoholism in the United States to a view that mirrors the disease model approach. Such a view mandates total abstinence from alcohol and submission of a higher spiritual authority, while marginalizing treatment methodologies that fall outside these categories. Within this framework the individual is "remodeled so that it can succeed in emitting the signs of a skilled performance" of a new person happy in their sobriety (*ibid*: 243). "The self-understanding of the individuals joining AA must come to reflect and incorporate the knowledge organized by the AA system of beliefs; cultural knowledge must become self-knowledge" (Cain 1991: 211). Here I examine the intersection of this self-transformation as dictated in sobriety group teachings with Japanese understandings of alcohol consumption and appropriately male conduct, as they are often rooted in dissent and disagreement. It is a process of highlighting persistent gaps and inconsistencies as now sober Japanese men attempt to incorporate cultural understandings of manhood into treatment conflicting treatment methodologies.

OF MEN AND LIQUOR

Drawing upon recent scholarship pertaining to masculinities, I am concerned with how Japanese men negotiate their understandings of manhood once they stop drinking. My contention is that admissions of alcoholism challenge prevailing masculine gender norms of drinking and homosociality. Becoming an alcoholic creates a struggle for Japanese men between medicalized conceptions of sobriety and an appropriately lived recovery, set against societal expectations indulgent of alcohol consumption. What results is Tokyo's sobriety group members caught in a cluttered mix of conflicting views on masculinity, addiction, and recovery that here demand disassembling established definitions of alcoholism to demonstrate the ways in which they contribute to this confusion.

Such an approach can also minimize Japanese women's struggles with alcoholism and sobriety group membership. Aki, a major voice in the pages that follow, is a women in her late thirties as well as an AA member employed at the JSO. While her accounts and insights are given prominence here, they are largely not contextualized in gendered terms. Yet alcoholism and addiction among Japanese women is an area of growing concern, evidenced in numerous recent papers looking at rising alcohol consumption rates, particularly among young women (Higuchi et al. 2007, Higuchi et al. 2006). Unfortunately, I must neglect these topics here as a necessary concession in order to focus sufficient attention on the ways in which masculinity and alcoholism intertwine in Japan.

Alcohol and its consumption has received substantial attention and commentary in the major anthropological works on Japan. In the 1940s Ruth Benedict wrote that "Japanese men enjoy being tipsy and there is no rule which bids a man carry his liquor well" (1946: 285). Several decades later Chie Nakane added that "it is Japanese tradition that whatever is said in drink is excused and should be forgotten" (1970: 125). Building upon this idea, Takie Lebra emphasized the importance of bars in Japan, noting that "on a daily basis, workers spend their evening hours after work at bars enjoying intimate interaction with co-workers while drinking" (1976: 118). More recent work has added new layers of nuance, reexamining drinking to note the individual and small group diversity evident alongside the prominent and propagated images of Japan's tolerance for alcohol consumption and public drunkenness (Borovoy 2005, Gill 2001, LeBlanc 2010, Roberson 1998). Building upon this scholarship, I seek to draw attention to Japanese men now unable or unwilling to drink alcohol, as the ways in which such a decision is regarded reveal much about the forces structuring life for Japan's addicts.

My contention is that societal constructions dictate that in order to assert a masculine presence in Japan, men must drink and get drunk with other men. But the sobriety group members introduced in the chapters to follow cannot do this, and in AA or Danshūkai they work renegotiating what it means to be a man in Japan without alcohol and while shouldering the burden of alcoholism. I concentrate on Japan's interpretations of addiction, particularly the influential role given physicians and how alcoholism is set aside from other illicit drugs and addictive substances. By approaching alcoholism, as well as addiction generally, through inquiry into what happens to an individual's sense of self and gendered identity when they can no longer participate in the drinking activities that once helped define them, I illustrate the wider power behind such forms of identity creation and maintenance.

As is also the case elsewhere, masculinity in Japan is often framed as in the midst of crisis. Recent mass media infatuation with "herbivorous" men, the increasing number of Japanese males rejecting alcohol consumption and labeled as uninterested in sex and adverse to competition, reflects this pattern of crisis creation (Bardsley 2011: 133). In short, "in Japan there have been changes in media images of men . . . explicit critiques (by men as well as women) of traditional Japanese ideals of masculinity" (Connell 2000: 4)—critiques that are ongoing and reflective of changing attitudes towards alcohol consumption that must increasingly be made to factor into understanding of Japan's drinking patterns and practices (LeBlanc 2010: 81). However, these critiques of masculinity overlook the alcoholic, giving prominence instead to the shared drinking among men and the cultural importance of alcohol consumption and intoxication. This is due in part to Japan's widespread tolerance for alcohol consumption, rooted in its perceived contribution to the nations "postwar development" (Moeran 2005: 25). Ideas on consumption and drunkenness that are here explored to better understand the ways in which they work to marginalize Japan's alcoholics.

A pervasive metaphor of masculinity in Japan is the *daikokubashira*, the "great central pillar that supports a house," understood in the contemporary as primarily financial contribution (Gill 2003: 144). Such a view works to exacerbate the marginalized masculinity of alcoholics as it paradoxically makes explicit their inability to provide such support. Japanese men are typically insulated from a problematic view of their alcohol consumption as long as the roof protecting one's family, both metaphoric and physical, is supported. And like the homeless and day laborer populations in Tom Gill's account of life on Japan's economic margins, the men introduced below "constitute only a small minority of the Japanese male population" that are socially significant because of their antithetical position to the pervasive cultural norms used to express masculinity (*ibid*: 146). However, unlike Gill's impoverished day laborers, the men at Tokyo sobriety group meetings struggle to find "alternative narratives of Japanese masculinity . . . when constructing their own identity" (*ibid*: 152). Instead, alcoholic men are subject to a physician's diagnosis of alcoholism, extended hospitalization, and then encouraged or sometimes required to attend meetings, all done while nostalgic feelings for a return to a time when drinking was unproblematic persist for many. Many member speeches at AA and Danshūkai are filled with expressions of longing for what are now denied claims to alcohol consumption and normalcy—claims that also confound the formation of counter-narratives to Japanese masculinity within sobriety group meetings and run counter to the stated treatment methodology of forthright confession and eventual transformation into a new person happy in their sobriety.

As such, a major area of focus here is how Japanese men who no longer consume alcohol try to renegotiate and reinterpret their understandings of masculinity. This position presupposes alcohol consumption as a fundamental component to Japanese masculinity, operating across a range of occupational, social, and regional differences. The male white collar workforce of "salarymen," either in actuality or as caricature, remains a dominant, as well as problematic and mocked, motif of Japanese masculinity (Dasgupta 2000, Leheny 2006, Roberson and Suzuki 2003: 12). Furthermore, drinking among this group was long perceived as prevalent, required, and without significant cause for concern (Allison 1994)—a view that while increasingly challenged remains pervasive and persuasive today (LeBlanc 2010).

Additionally, James Roberson's work among Tokyo factory workers has broadened the ethnographic scope on the cultural significance of alcohol consumption to include smaller companies lacking the lifetime employment security "corporate Japan" once promised, and deftly conveys the pervasive importance of homosocial relationships, solidified over drinking, between men. "At the conclusion of most, although not necessarily all, larger after-hours gatherings, many of the participants will have already made plans to go together somewhere else for a 'second-party' (*nijikai*). Others may make more spontaneous arrangements with friends, typically to go to either an *izakaya* restaurant or to a snack bar . . . such simultaneous acts of parting and keeping company with others from the factory draw attention to one of the socially most significant, if at once natural and oddly overlooked, aspects of working for companies in Japan; friendships are formed with fellow employees" (Roberson 1998: 155).[9] Specifically, relationships are formed with fellow employees through alcohol consumption and the intimacy that develops between men who work and drink together. In turn, the absence of these relationships among sobriety group members is a source of emasculating frustration, vocalized by many during meetings and explored in detail throughout the chapters to follow.

This is not to say that Japanese men are bound to a particular and immutable relationship with alcohol. I have elsewhere noted the emergent means by which Japanese men can resist or decline invitations to drink (Christensen 2012). Instead, it must be emphasized that Japan's prevailing constructions of masculinity create subjectivities that make it difficult for men to refuse alcohol and in its absence find a voice recognized as masculine. At its core then this book seeks to highlight the consequences for Japanese members of AA's focus on "either total abstinence or total relapse" that result from the early organizational influence of Protestantism and puritan dominated values (Hobsbawm 1996: 235)—a point that emphasizes the importance of remembering that AA "was not effectively designed as a movement to abolish, still less to limit, mass alcoholism, but to define and set apart the class of those who had demonstrated by their personal force of character that they were distinct from the un-respectable poor" (*ibid*: 235–236). Japan's divergent historical trajectory and comparative absence of Protestant-derived puritanism over understandings of gender and character have made the importing of such an ideology on alcoholism, addiction, and recovery challenging, contributing to the individual struggles voiced by many Tokyo sobriety group members.

Sherry Ortner notes how masculine gender norms are "made by 'structure,' and at the same time always makes and potentially unmakes it" (1996:

2). My position is that while gender norms may appear rigid, they possess a fluidity that allows the men at Tokyo AA and Danshūkai meetings to adjust how they perceive themselves as men. By looking at the discourse within meetings, as well as the normative-inducing images and advertisements used to sell alcoholic drinks throughout Japan, I demonstrate how male members try to move from being individuals that previously consumed alcohol in ways that were physically and personally destructive to sober and recovering alcoholics. Drawing upon Joan W. Scott, my goal is then to highlight "conflict . . . between the subject's need for the appearance of wholeness and the imprecision of terminology" (1986: 1064). Crucial to such an approach is calling attention to the "structural inequalit[ies]" of masculinity, and thereby allowing for exploration of how even in a "patriarchal or male-dominated society," these same structures work against some, often marginal, men (Holter 2005: 19). As Ty Tengan advocates, "we need to see gendered social actors as complexly situated, located, and positioned in multiple settings and historical contexts," disrupting the dominant views of appropriate Japanese masculinity (2008: 15).

Finally, to write of alcoholism and masculinity is to write of and about the male body. The body is both the inescapable vehicle from which masculinity takes its defining components, and what is ravaged by alcohol until the effects of heavy consumption can no longer be ignored. R. W. Connell writes that the "constitution of masculinity through bodily performance means that gender is vulnerable when performance cannot be sustained," and the emergence of this vulnerability through prolonged and heavy alcohol consumption not only weakens masculine bodies but also their ability to conform to the forces of normalcy (1995: 54). She continues, noting that the "body is virtually assaulted in the name of masculinity and achievement" (*ibid*: 58). Both in and out of Japan, the systematic destruction of the body through alcohol consumption, the symbolically defining component of masculinity, is a pervasively and persuasively masculine pursuit. Drinking is an act that simultaneously serves to perform, solidify, and maintain masculinity. Yet by asserting their masculinity through drinking with other men, Japanese men also destroy that same masculinity with their alcohol consumption. The strong body that typifies a dominant masculinity, bodies frequently and ironically displayed in the use of professional athletes, famous actors, or other masculine icons selling alcoholic beverages through various media forms, become for Tokyo sobriety group members the damaged and weakened reminders of alcoholic emasculation.

ALCOHOLIC TOKYO

To study alcoholism in Japan is to study something confounding for its pervasiveness that also remains somehow hidden in plain sight. While alcohol is available everywhere, from convenience store shelves to train station kiosks, and nearly every other step in between, alcoholism among Japan's AA and Danshūkai members is a new "lifelong social identity" that can also act as a stigmatizing force, especially for men (Valverde 1998: 122). As such, the world of Japan's alcoholics is hidden from most, with meetings tucked into small rooms far from the pulsing neon and inescapable advertising of Tokyo's urban centers, yet also has much to say about how alcoholism and addiction are structured and understood. I attended more than two hundred AA or Danshūkai meetings, growing comfortable with the meeting format and content, yet listened to an abundance of speeches that rarely overlapped. I left evening meetings to weave my way through crowds of intoxicated individuals while navigating my trains home across Tokyo's urban congestion, all while sharing the occasional knowing glance with other meeting attendees as we waited on station platforms. I discussed this research and my time in sobriety group meetings over beers with colleagues and sometimes typed field notes with a glass of wine. The permeating presence alcohol has etched into the social landscape of Japan, evident in the prodigious visibility of alcohol advertisements or the tolerance afforded the publicly intoxicated, particularly men, has left the small and typically hidden, but also culturally significant, group of alcoholics laboring at the margins of social acceptance.

In Tokyo, three weekly meetings were my consistent sites for data collection between April 2007 and August 2008. Mondays were reserved for a beginners AA meeting held in a hospital on Tokyo's western border with Saitama prefecture. Participants were required to attend as part of their ongoing recovery program, a dynamic that altered the meeting's content and tone in significant ways, a topic discussed in later chapters. This overlapping of hospitalization with what is for many individuals their first exposure to a sobriety group meeting is also a trait that distinguishes Japan from other national contexts and is a point later explored in detail. Wednesday evenings brought me to the "Central Group" AA meeting, a pseudonym given for the meeting's location in the geographic heart of Tokyo. The Central Group is a long running "theme meeting," where a concept or phrase is chosen at the onset to help focus everyone's speeches, and characterized by a core constituency of "home group" members who rarely miss a meeting and take on the various duties involved in keeping the proceedings running smoothly, as well as numerous "guests" who attend sporadically. Finally, Friday nights were spent at Ohashi Danshūkai meetings, so named for the *ohashi*, or "big bridge," that served as a major landmark for this suburb not far by train from

Tokyo's Shinjuku Station. Ohashi Danshūkai is an independent Danshūkai group, meaning they are not aligned with the *Zendanren* (the national Danshūkai organization), and draw many of their members from the immediate area around the meeting site. However, the group is well known among Tokyo's Danshūkai community, in large part because of their charismatic and colorful leader Nakamura, and "guests" from Zendanren-affiliated Danshūkai groups are not only present at every meeting but welcomed without question or reservation.

Beyond these regular meetings I also visited other AA and Danshūkai groups at a variety of locations throughout Tokyo. My approach was to solicit invitations when appropriate from regular Central Group and Ohashi Danshūkai meeting attendees. This approached allowed me to observe a wide range of meetings, as individual members often wanted to show me another meeting they regularly attended because it differed in some substantial way from the format at the Central Group and Ohashi Danshūkai. As such, accounts of attended meetings are at the center of my work, supplemented by individual interviews with group members and informal conversations before or after meetings. I feel this approach presents the alcoholics in their own words, highlighting how they describe their experiences and understandings surrounding alcoholism as a lived affliction, while also making explicit their engagement and struggles with group ideology.

Turning more towards the significance of geography, to say Tokyo is a busy place grossly understates the crackle of human energy and purpose that runs throughout the city. While this makes the city a fascinating place, it also challenges the fieldwork process by removing much that resembles a well-delineated and defined research site. As Patricia Steinhoff notes, herself critiquing an anthropological romanticization of a clearly bounded field site, "a fieldworker normally begins by finding a site . . . and then settling down to observe and interview people in their natural setting" (2003: 36). Following from Steinhoff, alcoholic Tokyo demands significant methodological flexibility in order to "find the trails that lead to my invisible subjects and then work out ways to talk to them and observe their activities intermittently, in scattered locations" (*ibid*). My initial challenge was integrating into a group marked by a fluid and changing membership. This was followed by the need to weave together the disparate experiences of individual sobriety and recovery around AA and Danshūkai's standardized recovery ideology, in order to produce a meaningful narrative on the lives of Japan's alcoholics.

I began by contacting the JSO and introducing myself and the research topic. My initial contact was Aki, the already mentioned JSO employee and AA member, who later laughed and told me of her early bewilderment as to why I was interested in this topic. Theodore Bestor writes that "networks choose me (or choose to accept me) much more that I can possible select them," a position I felt deeply as initial contact with the JSO led to interviews with the AA staff, that then precipitated invitations to meetings, more interviews, introductions to Danshūkai members, and more interviews and invitations to Danshūkai meetings (2003: 315). My presence at sobriety group meetings was also welcomed, as long as I respected and protected the privacy of individual members. In all, one email spun itself into a vast network of individuals spread across two large organizations, each working for the same goal of helping members maintain their sobriety, within which I could not only place myself but negotiate a meaningful and contributory presence.

Additionally, alcoholic Tokyo, and Japan, does not cluster around any readily discernible or delineated centers. Instead, it exists as a shifting network of meetings sites and relationships, some acutely meaningful and others tenuous or even confrontational, between members, doctors, social programs, blogs, and group ideology, as well as the innumerable non-alcoholic individuals encountered each day. Fixed meeting sites introduce a degree of manageability to this web of shifting positions, identities and motivations laid out across and beyond a crowded urban landscape. These stable "spots on the map" served as my primary sources of data around which impromptu moments of ethnographic relevance flourish (Gupta and Ferguson 1992: 10). Thus, these three sites, the meeting locations of the beginners AA meeting, the Central Group, and Ohashi Danshūkai, served not only as locations rich in ethnographic significance, but also as the impetus for numerous interviews and other meaningful exchanges, conducted typically before or sometimes after meetings at nearby cafés, restaurants, parks, and even train station platforms.

Finally, AA's JSO office near Ikebukuro Station in western Tokyo was a fourth site of sustained fieldwork. The JSO office, occupying one floor of an unremarkable five-story building set just off a major thoroughfare, serves as organizational hub, storehouse of AA literature, bookstore, crisis call center, and periodic social space for members needing to talk with the staff or other alcoholics. The floor plan is open, like most Japanese offices, and one enters first a reception area with a large table always laden with snacks and other *omiyage* (souvenirs, usually individually wrapped foods specific to a region or country) brought by employees and visitors. I visited the office whenever possible to observe daily activities and talk with employees, interactions that proved especially fruitful in conveying a greater sense of the ties and gaps between AA in Japan and its "father" organization in the United States. The JSO also differs in character and purpose from Danshūkai's Zendanren office near the Akihabara neighborhood in central Tokyo. Largely empty of employees on my two visits, the Zendanren office seemingly acts as a storehouse for group mailings and other printed material, with much of the organizational activities occurring either informally between members or at group conferences and the long-established sites of prominent meetings.

When relevant, this book also includes my observations and interactions with drunkenness among encountered Tokyoites as I moved throughout the city. Such observations are important, because they are too often overlooked when a collective scholarly, or even popular, focus is turned upon contemporary Japan. Put differently, the social banality of Japan's publicly intoxicated has also muted inquiry into how this tolerance emerged, why it persists, and what consequences it enacts upon the alcoholic. Thus, I note here the presence of alcohol advertisements, how groups of intoxicated revelers were treated by bartenders or other service providers, and the disposition and behavior of wait staff, station workers, taxi drivers, and others when faced with a passenger incapacitated by alcohol or a mess of vomit that they must now clean. My position is that ethnography's importance is found not only in overt moments of participant observation, but also in unexpected and sometimes mundane everyday occurrences. As such, moments of observed drunkenness across Tokyo, and the insights they offer on Japan's prevailing attitudes towards alcohol consumption and intoxication, form a portion of the analysis to follow.

Finally, Tokyo's role as both ethnographic character and cosmopolitan mega-city must be emphasized. "Other Japans" persist across a range of geographic, socioeconomic, racial, and gender lines that give the nation an impressive diversity often not immediately evident (Ivy 1995, Lie 2001, Robertson 1994). This book briefly mentions some of these "other Japans," understood most prominently as rural Japan, and the different set of considerations that surround admissions of alcoholism outside Tokyo or other urban centers. The most prominent and practical of these is the reduced density of a public transportation network, making the by comparison relative absence of concern for drunk driving in Tokyo problematic when attention shifts to more car dependent areas of the country. However, my focus and emphasis here is for the most part firmly rooted in the capital city, as a detailed account of alcoholism elsewhere in Japan, especially as it pertains to the nation's rural urban divide, merits its own and dedicated attention.

SOBERING LITERATURE

Japanese literature on alcoholism and recovery has a longer history than most initially imagine. Starting in the 1920s Japan, like the United States, had an active temperance movement. Japanese temperance unions were sponsored by the Salvation Army and other Christian organizations operating in Japan. And like their American counterparts, Japan's temperance movement advocated and lobbied for government-imposed restrictions and ultimately a prohibition on alcohol. Unlike in the United States, prohibition was never realized and the upheaval of World War II and subsequent rebuilding in the postwar period largely reversed or abolished any legislative gains won by the Japan Temperance Union (JTU). Despite a dwindling membership the JTU still operates today from a small home in Tokyo's western suburbs. Yet while the organization survives largely as a historic afterthought, the bigger legacy of Japan's temperance movement persists in written records, including newspapers and widely circulated pamphlets that provided first Danshūkai and then AA a source of historical precedent from which to draw inspiration and legitimacy.

While well-organized, the JTU was unable to assert a pervasive and moralizing voice that could demand limiting one's alcohol consumption, and Japan's temperance movement withered in the immediate postwar years (Kasai 2008). This absence of popular moralizing around drunkenness, punctuated by the JTU's struggles in gaining a widespread following, left an expertise vacuum that later helped cement physicians as diagnostic gatekeepers invested in hospital-affiliated AA and Danshūkai programs. Today these groups advocate a view of successful recovery that mirrors those put forth in sobriety group ideology and attempts to shepherd patients from hospitalization to AA or Danshūkai membership. Such a structuring of alcoholism also limits the possibility of challenging AA and Danshūkai's conceptions of successful recovery, despite frustrations among group members concerning how alcoholism is put forth as a category of identity. Central to this explored paradox is the struggle between a recovery model, rooted in a Protestant worldview and used to define alcoholism, abutting Japan's entrenched popular understandings of the alcoholic as social and mentally deviant, leaving sobriety group members with limited recourse to dictate the course of their recovery (Hunt and Barker 2001).

Interestingly, despite the prominent influence of Christianity within Japan's temperance movement, being a Christian was not a requirement or even an actively advocated position for membership (Katō 1995). American Women's Christian Temperance Union representatives were brought to Japan on speaking tours in the late 1800s, giving rousing accounts that framed temperance and a curtailing of alcohol consumption as a component of larger moral reforms requisite for national modernization. "While these speakers were Christian, their approach was largely non-secular, and they emphasized the health effects of abstinence and the importance for moral reform and good health generally rather than religion" (Chenhall and Oka 2006–2007: 117). Reducing consumption and increasing awareness of alcoholism were presented as moral imperatives, necessary for a nation eagerly working to emulate the Western models of modernization Japan's leaders saw as essential to growth and global prominence. The divorcing of temperance from Christianity and appeals to moral reform allowed Danshūkai to emerge from the historical ashes of these same temperance unions in the postwar as a culturally sanctioned model of recovery. It also positioned contemporary

Danshūkai as the "more Japanese," according to some members, of Japan's two major sobriety groups, despite drawing that validity in part from a historical precedence of interaction with American religious organizations and significant borrowing from AA's recovery model.

Today, AA and Danshūkai's literary requirements are satiated internally, primarily through two influential texts, AA's widely circulated "Big Book," known officially as *Alcoholics Anonymous*, and the biography of Danshūkai's founder, Harushige Matsumura (Matsumura Harushige: Danshūkai Shodai Kaicho: 1990). While each text is strongly linked to its respective organization, many in Danshūkai have read the Big Book, just as many AA members are well-versed in Harushige Matsumura's biography. Combined these books shape how alcoholism should be understood and approached as a component of identity and an affliction requiring constant vigilance to the outlined recovery steps. They also offer a roadmap to sobriety and living in recovery for Japanese members that largely avoids mention of the many auxiliary factors contributing to the burdens and struggles Tokyo sobriety group members frequently mention during meetings. The Big Book is put forth as "a design for living" and required reading for anyone joining AA, the words by which members are to dictate and live their now sober life (Alcoholics Anonymous 2001: 28). And for this reason it is worth quoting at length:

> If you are as seriously alcoholic as we were, we believe there is no middle-of-the-road solution. We were in a position where life was becoming impossible, and if we had passed into the region from which there is no return through human aid, we had but two alternatives: One was to go on to the bitter end, blotting out the consciousness of our intolerable situation as best we could; and the other, to accept spiritual help. This we did because we honestly wanted to, and were willing to make the effort (Alcoholics Anonymous 2001: 25–26).

Herein is AA's framing of an alcoholic and the requisite steps necessary for one to live "in recovery." The individual must be at a pivotal and monumental split in their life, one path leading to continued drinking followed closely and inevitably by death, the other to a spiritual salvation only possible due to the depth of their personal despair. Additionally, the emphasis AA places on "spiritual transformation," despite a deliberate distancing from overt ties to Christianity in Japan, demonstrates the importance of Western religious practices on how sobriety and "living in recovery" are presented to and understood by Japanese sobriety group members. To find success in AA demands at least acceptance of several philosophical positions central to a Christian worldview, notably the presence of a single supernatural begin, "God, *as you understand Him,*" and your ability to surrender control through confession to this spiritual entity. As such, while AA emphasizes inclusions of all who want to stop drinking, it is an approach to recovery that necessitates acceptance of a specific worldview.

Instead of a religiously rooted philosophy on recovery, the biography of Danshūkai's Harushige Matsumura emphasizes his life and accomplishments, highlighting his thoughts on how a "sober life" is possible. Danshūkai's website provides further information on their founder, including a list of fifty popular quotations, the *Matsumura Goroku*, he is credited with creating and propagating, many resembling similar phrases and concepts in AA.[10] Additionally, Danshūkai sets forth principles for members to follow that include the importance of "spiritual relationships" in maintaining successful and sustained abstinence from alcohol (Oka 2011: 32). Danshūkai groups have also created a methodological basis around which definitions of successful sobriety and recovery can be constructed and passed between group members. This methodological apparatus, known as the "three pillars of sobriety: hospitalization, anti-alcohol medicine, and self-help group" meeting attendance, is a framework for maintaining sobriety often mentioned in Danshūkai meetings.[11] It is also distinguishable from AA's literature in that the three pillars approach makes hospitalization and medicalization immutable components of an alcoholic self-identity. Yet despite these differences, AA and Danshūkai both emphasize the importance of "spirituality," however defined by individual practitioners, in getting and staying sober. And making spirituality a core component of group ideology necessary to living a successful recovery will also prove consequential and sometimes divisive, as attested by individual members introduced in the chapters to follow.

Consistent with other ethnographic accounts of AA and Danshūkai, my position is that alcoholism, sobriety, and the path taken into group membership varies widely between individuals and defies attempts at generalization.[12] However, large-scale patterns are evident in Japan that highlight distinct aspects of alcoholism as an aspect of one's lived identity. Specifically, the central role of hospitalization as the gateway through which group members are introduced to AA and Danshūkai, and then often encouraged to join one group based on the attending physicians' assessments of their background, place of residence, marital status, and occupation, heavily medicalizes alcoholism in Japan. This aspect of Japan's alcoholic community is discussed in detail later; it is raised now to illustrate the complexity and variety inherent in alcoholism among individual group members. Despite a singular pattern funneling individuals into sobriety group membership, the process by which one comes to question their consumption and seek out care in hospital remains varied and nuanced. Additionally, Japan's persistent hospitalization, and the resulting medicalization of alcoholism, is the major area of divergence from sobriety group practices elsewhere in the world, as well as the muddling stick turbidly swirling around how interactions between ill individuals, notions of medical expertise and competence, and prevailing cultural norms of consumption are understood.

SHARED EXPERIENCE

Being in AA or Danshūkai means speaking aloud about one's alcoholism and the often graphic, humiliating, and debilitating memories each member carries from their years spent drinking. Speaking about their alcoholism, either in meetings or interviews, is also a therapeutic exercise for AA and Danshūkai members, fostering an eagerness to talk as well as a sadness at reviving and remembering painful memories. These semi-public and personally revealing disclosures at meetings are also the defining and unifying trait of AA and Danshūkai members, the language that becomes a defining aspect to demonstrating a changed identity and a powerful tool in the recovery process. Yet, as I aim to demonstrate, these disclosures have yet to assert a societally and culturally pervasive power in Japan that then eases frustrations, particularly acute for men, at the limitations inherent in a life lived soberly.

Looking at violence and alcohol consumption in Honduras, Adrienne Pine writes that "despite high rates of abstinence, alcohol is central to most definitions of masculinity . . . an important tool for differentiating men from women" (2008: 97). In a similar fashion, Stanley Brandes, notes that among Mexico City's alcoholics:

> Manhood and drinking are closely enough linked in ideology and observable behavior that men—at least, most men in the Mexican laboring classes—come to associate imbibing and inebriation with male identity. Male ritual roles and norms regulating friendship are too deeply ingrained for them to reject or ignore this feature of life. Similarly, the roles and norms guiding female comportment offer such a striking contrast that it would be easy for a man in such circumstances to question his manhood should he decide to abstain (2002: 111–112).

In Japan, men have often found their descriptive home in accounts of alcohol-mitigated exchanges between co-workers and clients in the male dominated setting of bars, hostess clubs, and *izakaya* that rejuvenate tired minds and bodies after the rigors of the workday. Alcohol consumption is regarded as pivotally important to the social life of Japanese men, allowing exchanges to transpire that are viewed as impossible while sober. Male bonding is predicated on the presence of alcohol, just as the masculine fortitude needed to confront the challenges of daily life can also be drawn from the solitary glass of whiskey or sake. Alcohol consumption and intoxication also allow necessary and measured transgressions from the social norms that many regard as holding the ingredients for communal harmony, as well as individual success, reanimation, and personal solace (Schnell 1997). I am concerned with how Japanese men who have elected to stop drinking because of the destruction it brought to their lives, either voluntarily or as a result of their doctor's orders, fill the void left when alcohol and all its validation as a substance of cultural significance is removed. The next chapter looks at Japan's connections, rooted in religion and notions of the divine, between alcohol, drunkenness, and happiness. Later chapters return to how these links impact and restrict the lives of alcoholics.

NOTES

1. 『猛毒』(*mōdoku*)
2. http://www.stat.go.jp/english/data/kokusei/2010/basic1/pdf/summary.pdf
3. 『仲間』*Nakama*—literally "fellow," it is the term used by AA members to refer to others in the meeting they do not know.
4. In the United States Al-Anon acts as a support group for the family members of alcoholics, and maintains the same standards of anonymity found in AA. Al-Anon has a nascent presence in Japan, with a single group initiated in Tokyo in 2006.
5. At the time of writing (July 2013) the exchange rate was approximately 99 yen to the dollar, making ¥100 nearly equivalent to a dollar.
6. 1) 通院 (*tsuin*) 2) 抗酒剤 (*koushuzai*) 3) 自助グループ (*jijō gurūpu*)
7. アルコール依存症は酒を飲む人なら男女を問わず誰でもかかる可能性のあるごく普通の病気なのです (bold in original). See http://www.dansyu-renmei.or.jp/susume/index.html for more information.
8. 推定患者数は全国で８２万人です。恥ずかしがるような特別な病気ではありません(bold in original). Again, see http://www.dansyu-renmei.or.jp/susume/index.html for more information pertaining to Danshūkai's definition of alcoholism. It must also be noted that this number far exceeds other estimates of the number of alcoholics in Japan and was not referenced in any Danshūkai meeting I attended.
9. In a Western context an *izakaya* most resembles a pub, a place where drinking while typically sharing and eating many small plates of food is common. A snack bar is a small establishment where individual patrons typically buy and keep a bottle of liquor at the bar to drink from when visiting.
10. See http://www.dansyu-renmei.or.jp/zendanren/goroku.html for the list of phrases attributed to Harushige Matsumura.
11. Hospitalization 通院 (*tsuinn*), anti-alcohol medicine 抗酒剤 (*kousakezai*), and self-help groups 自助グループ (*jijyo gurūpu*) form Danshūkai's three pillars of sobriety.
12. A sampling of recent anthropology publications on alcoholism and recovery include the following: Borovoy 2005, Brandes 2002, Carr 2011, Chenhall 2007, Mitchell 2004, Pine 2008, and Smith 1988.

Chapter Two

Divine Drink

HISTORICIZING DRINK

The prominence of beer and alcohol across Japan sets the nation apart from other areas of the imbibing world. Alcoholic beverages are not only available from vending machines and age of sale restrictions typically ignored by shopkeepers, but public intoxication and its aftereffects—vomit and semi-conscious consumers sprawled on sidewalks and park benches—are commonly seen across Tokyo and occurrences of Japan.[1] What I argue in this chapter, by charting Japan's historical intertwining of alcohol and socialization, is that the degree to which alcohol consumption is culturally embedded, the expectation, particularly heavy for Japanese men but increasingly applied with equal vigor to women, that when called to do so one will drink beer, wine, sake, or whatever else is on offer, also renders much of Japan *kiken* (dangerous) to the nation's alcoholics trying to live sober. The result is areas once regarded as fun and desirable—parks, cafes, and sports stadiums—are made dangerous for the alcoholic through the presence of alcohol, and as such not only the temptation to consume but also the need to engage with or at the very least observe those who are already intoxicated. Thus, these spaces become areas into which many alcoholics feel they can no longer venture—a feeling that transforms large swaths of public space across Japan, spaces set aside for all to access and designated for recreation and rejuvenation, into areas now understood and experienced by the alcoholic as dangerously inaccessible. Further complicating this reinterpretation of public space is the assumption of safety typically given to Japan's urban landscape. In essence, what is safe for the imbibing masses has come to be understood as dangerous, even deadly, for the alcoholic, a process that works to marginalize individuals identifying as alcoholic while also marking alcoholism as a questionable category of identity and affliction.

To chart such a process this chapter examines how drinking, drunkenness, and alcohol came to occupy positions of social prominence throughout Japan. In following these connections, I link discourses pertaining to the spiritual, notably the historical links between sake, rice, and Shintō religious practices, to tolerant contemporary attitudes on drinking and drunkenness (Schnell 1997: 2). These connections, as well as postwar efforts on the part of advertisers to maintain an unproblematic and enthusiastic view of alcohol consumption, are significant because they thwart efforts to popularize critical views of drunkenness and spread awareness of alcoholism. And as such, Japan and Tokyo have an abundance of options and outlets for all manner of drinker, yet limited, restrictive room for those wanting to abstain. This absence is the result of a dominant historical narrative surrounding alcohol as sanctified consumable, as well as contemporary efforts to appropriate interpretations of the sacred into commodified forms for popular consumption, all hindering the growth of alternative or critical views capable of challenging the consumption-indulgent status quo.

However, it is not just Japan's heightened opportunities and temptations to drink that makes admissions of alcoholism personally and socially problematic. Instead, the sober alcoholic is an unrecognizable figure to many, an anomaly so counter to the purpose and practices behind so much of socialization in Japan that their very presence would tear at the social fabric. The result for AA and Danshūkai members is their alcoholism, instead of signifying an identity transformed through a profound spiritual transformation and ensuing happiness in sobriety (the outcome set forward in group ideology if one diligently works the organizational program), is a burden endured at great personal and social cost that excludes group members from large portions of Japan's public geography. In short, as drinking and drunkenness feature prominently and expectantly in social gatherings, bars and izakayas, as well as parks, stadiums, cafes, and any number of public spaces are made inaccessible to alcoholics, particularly during Japan's numerous festivals throughout the year. Yet before these feelings of alcoholic alienation can be explored, a better sense of the prevalence and purpose for drinking and drunkenness in Japan is required.

FROM MOUTH CHEWED TO GLOBAL ICON

Alcoholic drink begins in Japan with sake, a beverage derived from fermenting rice that in its earliest versions was likely quite potent in its intoxicating properties and widely varying in taste and flavor. The *Kojiki*, one of Japan's oldest historical texts, locates sake's origins in the "age of the gods," immediately linking its consumption to communion with the supernatural (Kondo 1996: 14). More concrete dating put early varieties of sake as emergent during the Nara period (AD 710–794) with people no doubt experimenting with distilling for much longer. This embryonic sake made unsavory yet effective use of early fermentation techniques found elsewhere in the ancient world. Mouthfuls of half-chewed rice were spit into clay pots and left to ferment in cool, dark rooms. The result, *kuchikami no sake* (mouth chewed sake), was the by-product of the enzymes in human saliva causing a reaction that allows the starches in rice to convert to sugar and become alcohol. The end product was an alcoholic mash typically shoveled with chopsticks from a bowl into one's mouth.

It is also out of these half chewed mouthfuls that the linking of sake to Shintō religious ritual emanates. "In some areas, the head of the village would lead all the members of the village in performing the ceremony of chewing the rice and spitting it into a vessel" (Kondo 1996: 15). These early religious rites established sake as a conduit between humans and the divine. "By partaking of this marvelous beverage, human beings could assume god-like qualities" (*ibid*: 18). As Harumi Befu notes, drinking sake allowed mortals a moment of "communion with the gods" (1974: 199). To be drunk, and to share that feeling with fellow drinkers, was to transcend temporal life and commune with the gods. These divine connections continue in Japan today, as sake is not only an essential drink of ritual at weddings, shrine festivals, building dedications, and nearly any celebration marking the beginning or end of a major endeavor, but also requisite to the marking of transition through life stages and other moments of meaningful change (Edwards 1989). More importantly, drinking and drunkenness as a process of purification cement bonds between human ritual participants and supernatural deities (Schnell 1999: 131). Under such an arrangement it is exceedingly difficult, if not impossible, to participate in festivals without imbibing, thereby excluding alcoholics from joining in these community-making and maintaining events (Schnell 1997: 1). Furthermore, as nonparticipants in such communal rites, alcoholics are also unable to symbolically cleanse or purify themselves through the ritualistic ingesting of sake, exacerbating feelings of exclusion and marginalization.

Rice, as sake's primary ingredient, plays a pivotal role in creating and sustaining ties of cultural significance between alcoholic drink and the divine. Emiko Ohnuki-Tierney notes that "rice and rice products such as rice cakes and rice wine have been the food for commensality between humans and deities, on the one hand, and among humans, on the other" (1993: 58). She adds that, "wine (sake) is the most important item of commensality in social settings, especially among men" (*ibid*: 97). The *Nihonshoki*, also among the oldest surviving Japanese texts, gives rice, and the other consumable items created from rice, including sake, a place of prominence over other grains and marks these as sacred items (*ibid*: 51). Today sake, along with beer, shōchū, wine, whiskey, and other contemporary alcoholic beverages, constitute the material items of cultural significance around which bonds of intimacy, particularly homosocial intimacy, are forged in Japan. This deep connection between drunkenness and understandings of the divine also exacerbates the difficulties Japan's sobriety group members feel in making known their alcoholism, as it is a declaration directly challenging to established norms of sociality.

Sake's place of divinely ordained cultural importance in Japan contributes substantially to the relative absence of condemnation and moralization directed toward drunkenness. While the scope of such a statement obscures some small but vocal dissension, Japan's prevailing outlook has been indulgent of drink as an item of connoisseurship and social lubricant, a libation that creates and strengthens social bonds, particularly between men. Examples of these cultural connections abound across Japan, the ceremonial breaking open of a sake barrel at large events, the ritualized sipping from small cups in a Shintō wedding ceremony, even the importance of *kanpai* (cheers) and toasting fellow drinkers, all of which strengthen unproblematic views of drinking and drunkenness. Whether the motivation is steeped in ritual importance, or in simply wanting to get drunk and enjoy oneself, drinking alcohol is constructed as imperative to bringing individuals together and allowing for exchanges understood as impossible when sober. What results is alcohol consumption, especially for Japanese men, embraced as culturally significant and individually requisite in forging intimate bonds of friendship with other men.

Consequently, this structuring of alcohol consumption also makes admissions of sobriety disruptive, socially problematic, and frequently perplexing to others. Japan's popular construction of sake and alcohol as divinely inspired make consumption the unproblematic norm, done today primarily through advertisements that continue to anchor Japan's alcoholics at the cultural margins. This marginalization stems not only from the alcoholic's presence challenging conventions of socialization and male bonding, but also the ways in which they undermine long held and culturally powerful views on the sanctity of drink. Refusal to drink from Japan's alcoholics, rooted in a recovery philosophy heavily influenced by a Protestant and middle class American worldview that shaped the emergence of AA, becomes an affront to this sanctity, allowing challenge and derision to flourish around the explanations offered by group members for why they believe they can no longer consume alcohol.

Additionally, the importance of generational shifts on drinking practices and prevailing attitudes towards consumption underlies any look at Japanese attitudes towards alcoholism and sobriety. A 1987 pamphlet titled "Alcohol Eras: A Visible History" published by the Japan Specified Nonprofit Corporation to Prevent Alcohol and Drug Problems, referred to as ASK from the abbreviation of the organization's Japanese title, gives an account of how major postwar generational shifts are remembered and reflect popular attitudes toward alcohol. ASK labels the mid-1950s through the mid-1960s as "the era of male drinking," where the hard work of rebuilding the nation after the destruction of World War II was rewarded in the evening over drinks.[2] Japan's immediate postwar years saw the linking of alcohol consumption to physical recovery and masculine revitalization, whether from a hard day of work or the devastation of World War II. As Jeffrey Alexander highlights, Japan's major beer producers were, by 1954, "already cultivating the social acceptability of drinking to excess, which was clearly equated with power and masculinity" (2013a: 175). Such connections served to indelibly bind alcohol consumption in the Japanese psyche with the male identity. Japan's return to global prominence through economic growth, beginning in the 1950s, is a process remembered through the camaraderie of shared drinks between men that helped the nation not only cope with memories of loss, but also reassert a sense of masculine pride after military defeat (Ivy 1995: 14).

The mid-1960s through the mid-1970s, presented to pamphlet readers as "the era of buying roadside alcohol," saw the introduction of alcohol dispensing vending machines and the rise of private car ownership that accompanied growing income levels. The next decade, from the mid-1970s to the mid-1980s, is titled "the era when women and young people began drinking," marking shifting cultural norms of work as well as high levels of national affluence. The pamphlet's final era describes the waning years of the 1980s as "the era when everyone drinks anywhere at anytime." While these broad generalizations muffle voices of dissension, they are indicative of perceived changes concerning how drinking was and is broadly understood in postwar Japan. Finally, a likely moniker for the years following the bursting of Japan's economic bubble in the early 1990s would likely read "the era of stagnation and questioning." Such a broad framing remains evident today in the uptick of alcohol consumption levels among young Japanese as well as the resurgence of "hoppy" and other nostalgia inducing alcoholic drinks from the immediate postwar years, developments easily linked to changing economic and cultural realities (Christensen 2014).[3] Without room for inclusion, Japan's alcoholics have watched these postwar shifts from the margins, aware of the change as well as the omnipresent cries of advertisers trying to maintain consumption levels in the face of increasingly sluggish amounts of actual drinking, yet divorced from making any contribution to the direction of change (Higuchi et al. 2007). For many at AA and Danshūkai then, these shifts are evidence of alcohol's ongoing and powerful influence throughout Japan, as well as testament to their exclusion and invisibility.

MODERNITY AND DRUNKENNESS

Uncle Tory got drunk the first time he met the Japanese public. The introduction takes place in an animated black and white television commercial from the late 1950s, a moment coinciding with the proliferation of televisions sets to a Japan emerging from war and optimistic about a peaceful future. Dressed in a Western business suit and walking alone on dark city streets, Uncle Tory initially appears tired and dejected. He enters a bar, sits at the counter and thinks for a few seconds, all the while gradually beginning to smile and relax. He then proceeds to rapidly drink nine glasses of whiskey before leaving the bar with a broad smile, a spring in his step, and a fresh cigarette between his fingers. While drinking Uncle Tory also recovers the color and complexion to his face; he is transformed before the viewer's eyes from sullen and ashen to flushed and healthy through his ample whiskey consumption. Alcohol, and in this instance quite a lot of it, is rejuvenatory instead of impairing, helping reanimate Uncle Tory while also shedding the stresses of the work day.

While one television commercial does not shape an entire nation's attitudes toward alcohol, Uncle Tory is indicative of a deliberate process to frame drink and drunkenness as important, requisite components of a rich and fulfilling cultural life for Japanese adults. Looked at from a broader level, these advertisements "constructs idealized images of people, depicts their patterns of interacting with others, and positions them in a social hierarchy" (O'Barr 1994: 3). Further, they are visual images "sponsored by and supportive of capitalism" and sustained consumption, acting as a guide on how to be happy, social, successful and appropriately male or female (*ibid*: 2). In this regard, Uncle Tory becomes part of an advertising process that Wakao Fujioka, the executive responsible for the iconic *Discover Japan* campaign of the 1970s, outlines as needing to ask "what society or the masses are searching for" (Ivy 1995: 45). Japan, stable and economically prosperous after a generation of war, is searching for comfort and camaraderie, and the nation's advertisings are equally eager to forge historical ties that connect these feelings to alcohol consumption—a practice keenly evident in beer campaigns eager to link their product to feelings of home and nostalgia, all while continuing to gender consumption norms and strengthen associations between masculinity and shared drinks (Alexander 2013: 176).

Japan's transitions from postwar economic recovery to global prominence was accompanied by rising levels of national alcohol consumption and a growing range of beer, whiskey, and other advertisements. Several years after Uncle Tory walked into his favorite Tokyo bar he was headed to Hawai'i, in a widely popular national advertising campaign. The "let's go to Hawai'i" promotion launched in the early 1960s, several years before the ban on Japanese nationals traveling abroad was lifted in 1964, and offered 100 vouchers for a trip to Hawai'i, or the cash equivalent which the majority of winners opted to take. In the iconic commercial, Uncle Tory has exchanged his suit and tie for an Aloha shirt and flower lei, smiling broadly as he eats pineapple, drinks whiskey, and invites others to participate in an international cosmopolitanism just becoming visible on Japan's horizon. It is a message of optimism, a call to shed any remaining anguish from the war years and bask in Japan's reemergence on the global stage as a wealthy and welcomed nation.

As noted earlier, Japan's per capita alcohol consumption increased "steadily since the end of World War II" until only recently beginning to languish in the last several years (Higuchi et al. 2006: 359). The contributory factors, rising personal incomes, a proliferation of choice, and an extolling of the virtues and social importance linked to drinking, all helped sustain this upward trend. Recent years however, have brought stagnation, as the levels of pure ethanol consumed annually, the standard measure of national consumption rates, has remained steady at around seven liters per person.[4] This figure places Japan in the middle of global consumption levels, behind Russia and much of eastern and western Europe, indicating that a plateau, reflective of wider issues including an aging population and shrinking corporate expense accounts for nights out, has been reached (*ibid*).[5] The response from Asahi, Kirin, and other major brewers and distilleries is greater efforts at diversifying Japan's available drink options and increasing the number of regular drinkers, particularly through advertisements targeting young women, regarded as an until recently neglected portion of the available market. As discussed in detail below, beer in particular has experienced a recent explosion of possible options including "healthy," "low calorie," and a growing array of "zero" or non-alcoholic varieties that encourage Japanese drinkers to insert (non-alcoholic) beer consumption into moments of their lives where it was previously impossible, illogical, or illegal.

GENDERED CONSUMPTION

Despite the recent flood of attempts to attract new drinkers from among Japanese women and young adults, drinking, especially with other men, remains a distinctly masculine pursuit. The popular Tokyo Broadcasting System (TBS) program *Soko ga Shirita!* (Let's Find Out!) from the 1990s fondly emphasized this gendering of drinking in many of its episodes. In one particularly obvious example the host follows several middle-aged men out drinking for the night at their favorite bars across Tokyo. The importance given drinking with other men, and the tolerance for such outings the show's subjects are afforded by their wives, is made immediately apparent. One customer even regularly sleeps in his favorite bar after closing, showing the amazed host the blanket and sleeping pad he keeps in a closet and getting the bartender to confirm the arrangement. He said his wife prefers this as she knows where he is and that he is safe, and does not need to care for him as she would if he arrived home drunk. The show ends with the host's voiceover offering commentary on how men are "most manly" (*otokorashi*) when they are out drinking with other men. Such a presentation of drinking outings in popular media as unproblematic and requisite in the assertion of a healthy, normal masculinity also renders the admissions of alcoholism by Japanese men culturally problematic and potentially emasculating when widely disclosed (Befu 1974: 201, Smith 1998).

The bursting of Japan's economic bubble in the early 1990s and the subsequent decades of economic stagnation have restricted the frequency of expensive drinking sessions, as well as the purported requisite nature of such outings. While Tokyo still abounds with bars and customers similar to those Anne Allison described from her work at a posh hostess bar in the mid-1980s, economic challenge has significantly altered the contemporary imbibing landscape (1994). However, this extended period of national economic malaise has not widely impacted the meaningful cultural connections between gender norms and alcohol consumption. Instead, alcohol, and the diversity of interpretive frameworks its consumption inspires, persist as a significant marker of gender while also expanding to envelope an array of paradoxically applied associations. Connoisseurship of alcohol, wine, shōchū, and sake in particular, allow some Japanese drinkers to engage in *jibun sagashi*, or the "search for self," where individual pursuits are satiated through consumption and cultivation of knowledge around a particular varietal (Christensen 2014, Sterling 2010: 197). Yet, despite tremendous change in large-scale consumption patterns since the bursting of the economic bubble, links to masculinity and the strength of ideas surrounding the perception of Japanese men as "most manly" when drinking remain a powerful force shaping cultural attitudes on consumption and comportment.

Powerful forces are also ever assertive of their cultural importance in the face of contemporary challenge. Drink and drunkenness create spaces where men are told they can be men, assert a masculinity elsewhere undermined by the now more than twenty years of dour economic and employment forecasts. Drinking is still cast in Japan as a rejuvenatory pursuit healing men from their everyday stresses and making it easier to confront life's challenges. Suntory Old Whiskey's popular series of commercials depicting the relationship between an aging salaryman father and his young adult daughter neatly reify this practice. One commercial in particular relies heavily on emphasizing the necessity of alcohol in strengthening interpersonal relationships and mitigating potentially awkward social encounters, in this instance the daughter bringing her very nervous boyfriend home to meet her father. With the three of them seated around a table, the young man is barely able to summon the nerve to stammer a few words, presumably wanting to say that they intend to get married, before the father gets up from the table and storms out of the room. The daughter finds him in the kitchen getting glasses, ice, and his finest bottle of Suntory Old Whiskey, which has clearly been saved for just such an occasion, to be shared by the three of them to mark this occasion. Before she can protest his departure from the table he turns to her and says, "it's too bad, I really wanted to dislike him," before they rejoin the thoroughly perplexed boyfriend for a drink.[6] The message is clear, while women can now share in the drink alongside their father and future husband, it is still the medium through which meaningful bonding and communication between men is made possible—a point made all the more evident in the commercial when alcohol makes it possible to transgress spoken communication and allow meaningful moments of change in individual lives to remain unspoken.

NEW TERRITORY

Holding a baseball tightly in one hand, Yu Darvish, the well-known Japanese pitcher who left the Nippon Ham Fighters in 2012 to play in the United States for the Texas Rangers, scowls down at Tokyo from large billboards advertising Asahi Black Beer. Darvish, a readily recognized celebrity in Japan, is also following a now well-worn path of prominent Japanese baseball players peddling beer, an endorsement that has also typically followed quickly on the heels of signing a lucrative and widely discussed contract with a Major League Baseball (MLB) team in America. An immediate significance of this endorsement when considering alcoholism is the illegality of such contracts outside Japan. Because of Darvish's popularity in Japan, baseball offers an ideal lens through which to document the larger dissimilarities underscored in popular understandings of consumption, as MLB prohibits its players from endorsing alcohol, tobacco, and any other product deemed objectionable or age sensitive in America. As such, Japan's untroubled link between strong, famous, and athletic men selling alcohol is also indicative of tolerant outlooks on consumption, that through prominent display across the country not only reinforce such views but thwart efforts to bring a nuanced look at alcoholism into popular conversation. To drink is to be masculine, and embodied in these powerful male bodies is the tacit message that baseball players like Darvish, Ichiro Suzuki, Daisuke Matsuzaka, Hideki Matsui, and other prominent Japanese athletes endorse and even advocate for the need and importance of drinking beer with other men.

Finally, as ideological conveyors, alcohol advertisements cement specific gendered interpretations for the purpose and necessity behind consumption. They "provide a clear and consistent image of the masculine role; in a sense they constitute a guide for becoming a man, a rulebook for appropriate male behavior, in short, a manual on masculinity" (Strate 1992: 78). And Japan's postwar history has confirmed such a connection. The introduction of canned beer to Japan in the late 1950s and early 1960s witnessed Sapporo emphasizing the "manly" aspects of this new packaging in its advertisements, and being rewarded with a ten percent increase in monthly sales (Alexander 2013a: 180). While Japan uses professional athletes to sell beer and other alcoholic drinks, individuals who typify a strong and vibrant masculinity and rely on heteronormatively "manly" behavior to convey the message that alcohol is necessary in order to create and affirm masculine bonds, it is also not the only route through which such gender-coded messages are conveyed. Despite ongoing economic struggle, product advertisements for alcohol "through their military references to battle, victory, defeat, and death in relation to the white-collar employee's total devotion to his company . . . fashion the white-collar worker as a peacetime incarnation of the warrior" (Frühstück 2007: 56). A television spot for Asahi's Sparx, a canned shōchū based cocktail noteworthy for its high alcohol content, relies on exactly such a format in linking masculinity and employment to consumption.[7] In the short commercial an army of young, fit salarymen negotiate an obstacle course reminiscent of basic training requirements for military draftees. The obstacles are a straightforward metaphor for the hard work they undertake each day, and Sparx is their reward at the end of the day when they all collapse in happy exhaustion. Thus, alcohol consumption is incessantly presented to Japanese men as requisite for adherence to a narrowly defined set of gender norms, limiting attempts at challenge to such convictions while maintaining an internal elasticity that allows for expansion and diversification of the targeted audience.

Not surprisingly then, Japan's rules and regulations governing the advertising and selling of alcohol have typically been advantageous for the purveyors of drink. Beyond the lack of legal regulations concerning who can endorse a particular product, restrictions on the age of sale—twenty in Japan for both alcohol and tobacco—are typically ignored by cashiers or shopkeepers. These restrictions are also wholly circumventable, as Japan is to the best of my knowledge the world's only nation where alcohol is widely available from vending machines, many of which do not require any kind of age verification. Additionally, in a further break with many other industrialized nations, there are no restrictions on the time of day that beer and other alcohol commercials can be shown on television. And while restrictions on advertising alongside children's television programs or during the morning are "voluntarily" imposed by Kirin, Asahi, Suntory, and the other major beverage corporations, Japan remains a pervasively tolerant nation for the buying and selling of alcohol (ASK, personal communication 7/8/2012). In short, Japan offers what ASK's chairwoman described as "heavenly" conditions for marketing and selling alcohol—conditions resulting from appropriations of a history remembered as lauding of alcohol consumption, as well as an emphasis on consumption driven socialization that rewards imbibing and endorses drunkenness. Combined, the impact of these converging cultural conditions on Japan's alcoholics is inescapable, as it structures their existence in a society tolerant of drunkenness and skeptical of a refusal to consume.

HEALTHY BEER

Beer is the most widely consumed alcoholic drink in Japan, accounting for more than half of all alcohol sold, and dominated by the three major breweries of Asahi, Kirin, and Sapporo (Higuchi et al. 2006: 363). However, the amount of beer consumed has also dipped since the early 1990s, a decline attributable to a persistently sluggish economy and an aging population, as well as the diversification of available drink choices and shifting demographic patterns of consumption (Higuchi et al. 2007). Faced with this unstable landscape, the major breweries have searched for new outlets for their products, as well as new ways, moments, and opportunities to entice the Japanese public to drink. These include "healthy," "low-calorie," "free," and non-alcoholic, as well as paradoxically higher alcohol content drinks, all vying for space on already crowded store shelves and coolers in an attempt to attract new consumers.

Recently introduced health conscious beers claim to cut the calories in each can, dispense vitamin supplements and other previous absent nutrients, and, most gallingly, imply ever so gently that they offer hydration during Japan's hot and humid summer. Related to such claims is the connection, never directly stated in advertisements but subtly implied, between drinking these new variants of beer and living an active, athletic life of leisure. Drinkers are depicted playing volleyball, swimming, and even SCUBA diving in moments of alcohol-fueled summer revelry on Japan's picturesque beaches. These advertised links caused Goto, a Danshūkai member and avid SCUBA diver, to dryly note during our interview how potentially dangerous it is to even hint at the possibility of drinking and then diving. To Japan's alcoholics this is all a reminder of the persuasive strength supporting the untroubled links between alcohol consumption and revelry. While many AA and Danshūkai members are dismissive of these constant and capitalistically manipulative images, saying that while they do not drink it is also not their place to judge the conduct of others, the underlying theme emphasizing the necessity of consumption is a significant barrier to changing popular attitudes on drinking, addiction, and alcoholism. These are changes that are further confounded by the creep of beer and other alcoholic and nonalcoholic drinks into new areas and activities of everyday life.

Indicative of such creep is a tolerance for consumption and a manufactured frustration with daily moments that previously forbade or limited drinking, evident in a recent proliferation of non-alcoholic beer on Japan's supermarket shelves. Pregnant women, drivers, golfers, yoga enthusiasts, and young fashionable families playing with their children can all now drink Kirin Free and other non-alcoholic beers during those few portions of the day when it was previously impossible, or at least inappropriate, to do so.[8] Alcoholics are again excluded from all this fun now made possible through the technological circumvention of moments and activities still strong with societal deterrents to drunkenness. For them, non-alcoholic beer creates a greater onus instead of a solution, as its presence does not solve any of the symptomatic individual struggles embedded in understandings of alcoholism, addiction, and illness that each individual carries as a sobriety group member. Instead of a solution to their sobriety, as many outside the groups regard non-alcoholic beer, it exacerbates the alcoholic's feelings of marginalization. By appearing to resolve any mandates for total sobriety, non-alcoholic beers make acknowledgment of addiction, particularly as it is set forth in AA and Danshūkai, all the more easily dismissed.

Further, in the scant moments when alcoholism does appears in Japanese popular culture, it is typically presented in deliberately gendered and disruptive circumstances. Prominent among such examples is the feature film *Mainichi Kaasan* (2011), that first garnered popularity as an animated television drama and *manga* (comic) series. The film tells the story of an alcoholic manga artist mother, her alcoholic war photographer husband and their two young children. While alcoholism is directly discussed in the film, it is shown as symptomatic of deeper interpersonal issues stemming from the extraordinary stresses of the husband's work. In confronting the worst aspects of humanity through travel in war zones, the husband has found himself unable to drink "normally," and it then becomes the wife's duty to support him through such troubles. While this also conflicts with her equally gender-normative charge to care for their children, a tension the film explores, it is ultimately a story rooted in the need to maintain conservative gender roles, even in the face of great challenge. The husband's alcoholism is treated as a means to emphasize the need for *gaman* (perseverance), particularly for wives and mothers, with little attention given to inquiry into addiction, treatment, or recovery.

NGOS AND THE MORALIZING OF CONSUMPTION

Despite Japan's pervasive tolerance for drunkenness, oppositional voices are not entirely absent. Instead, a range of NGO and NPO groups, many based in Tokyo, are working for legislative as well as societal change to the prevailing indulgence of consumption. These organizations, of which the already mentioned ASK is among the largest and most vocal, draw legitimacy from Japan's temperance movement discussed earlier. This history is largely rooted in the Women's Christian Temperance Union founded in Japan in 1886 with a broad agenda of reform targeting prostitution and drunkenness while encouraging Imperial loyalty and patriotic service (Lublin 2010). In 1889 they helped launch the more general and less overtly religious Tokyo Temperance Union and ten years later the organization expanded into the already introduced JTU. The onset of World War II disbanded both organizations until 1949, when the JTU was reestablished in Tokyo, where it continues to operate today with severely limited resources and membership.

The establishing of Danshūkai in the late 1950s signaled both the emergence of sobriety organizations in Japan and attempts by "members of the Japan Temperance Union and a number of doctors . . . to look for humane and effective ways to treat alcoholics" (Smith 1998: 291). The next chapter looks at the formation of Danshūkai, as well as AA's 1975 arrival in Japan, in greater detail. Of importance here is the simultaneous postwar rise of AA and Danshūkai as distinct sobriety groups alongside non-sobriety focused groups like ASK, invested in working to strengthen, change, or implement new legislative precepts pertaining to alcohol. These efforts, largely a reaction to frustration with Japan's widespread tolerance of consumption among founding members, have been unevenly successful in enacting meaningful change.

ASK's advocacy work today includes anonymous telephone consultation with individuals questioning their substance use, publishing sobriety and addiction related titles, maintaining a library and website, annual "no alcohol" campaigns designed to help university undergraduates resist *aruhara* or "alcohol harassment," and lobbying efforts calling for greater enforcement of legal regulations and restrictions on alcohol sales. Their work, and willingness to court controversy as discussed in the sections to follow, has made ASK the primary advocacy group working to humanize alcoholism and addiction throughout Japan. As AA and Danshūkai lack the national prominence AA commands in North America, and both organizations severely restrict institutionally supported legislative and political work, ASK is Japan's de facto force for institutional change regarding alcoholism and addiction. ASK's advocacy work has been largely regarded as positive, inspiring meaningful collaboration between the organization and both sobriety groups. However, concerns with ASK as an advocacy and activist organization being among the most prominent of voices discussing alcoholism and addiction in Japan have also caused some at AA and Danshūkai to wonder if they would be better served through stronger efforts to widely assert their views on living in recovery.

Relevant to such efforts, ASK has endeavored to reduce drunk driving in Japan through various campaigns that rely primarily on a moralizing discourse. Their efforts, motivated by several tragic and widely reported accidents, most notably a 2006 incident in Fukuoka where a city employee ran a minivan off a bridge killing three children, have helped sustain media attention on the topic and swayed popular perceptions decidedly against drinking and driving. This and other accidents, as well as sometimes sensationalistic media reports of a persistent culture of heavy drinking among highway bus and semi-truck drivers, has enabled ASK to help pass in Japan some of the world's most stringent drunk driving laws (Arno 2011). The result is a blood alcohol content level above just .03 constituting "driving while impaired," and any level in excess of .08 is the more severely judged "driving under the influence." Minimum penalties for such infractions include up to three years in jail and substantial fines.[9] Additionally, a recently enacted law makes Japanese passengers legally culpable for riding in the car with a driver they know has been drinking. These legal changes have not only created a new category of criminal, they also speak to the pervasive and seemingly successful moralizing that has come to surround popular views of drunk driving across Japan. However, despite these efforts and their localized successes with drunk driving, ASK's moralistic language and influence has not extended as forcefully to other areas of legislative focus, notably underage consumption, public intoxication, and excessive drunkenness among Japan's undergraduates.

The waning influence of ASK beyond efforts to reduce drunk driving is also reflective of limited national concern regarding popular attitudes on consumption. Despite producing an abundance of literature and propaganda designed to educate and sway national opinion away from widespread tolerance and endorsement of drunkenness, and raise awareness of alcoholism, little tangible impact is evident. ASK's publishing and assertiveness training seminars are designed to empower individuals, particularly Japan's college students and young adults, to refuse orders to drink from their peers in positions of seniority. Their work includes the distribution on university campuses throughout Tokyo of posters, fliers, cardboard coasters, and other accessories that can be used to convey to others that the drinker has had enough. This printed material is intended to help students resist aruhara from upperclassmen and social group leaders. Produced annually, the 2007 version of ASK's anti-alcohol harassment coasters were shaped like a hand telling someone to stop. Below the hand was a brief message stating that the drinker will not *iki-iki* (chug-a-lug) drink their beer, will not drink because they are driving later, or will not drink because their body cannot take any more alcohol.

Despite these efforts, many at ASK are resigned to the limited impact they have so far had in changing Japan's alcohol consumption practices.

ASK cannot track the use levels of their printed material, and even casual observation at festivals and other events on university campuses across Tokyo reveal the prominent role given alcohol consumption and drunkenness—a prominence made particularly ironic when considering that many Japanese college students are not yet twenty, and thus legally not allowed to consume alcohol, a reality few if any forces of authority attempt to enforce. And it is because of dangerous consumption practices among college students that ASK began these education campaigns, as the beginning of Japan's university calendar in April has been consistently followed by a steady stream of seemingly annual tragedies, marked most distressingly by numerous incidents of students drinking themselves to death. These stories have settled into a predictable pattern where typically an underclassman joining a campus club or social group is either ordered by a senior member of the group, or decides himself in order to impress everyone, to quickly drink a large amount of alcohol. The subsequent shock to the body of rapidly finishing an entire bottle of vodka or shōchū can result in acute alcohol poisoning and death. With a heavy sigh ASK's director returned again to age when recounting the tragic regularity of such events, and how almost no newspaper articles, editorials, or other discussions of this topic highlight how these students are typically not yet twenty years old.

VENDING MACHINES

Japan's abundance of vending machines is a characteristic of the national landscape frequently noted in travel guides and other popular accounts of the nation. Japan is the world's only country that allows alcoholic drink to be sold from vending machines in public spaces with at best minimal checks or restrictions on the purchaser. While less frequently seen around Tokyo today than in years past, these machines still sit prominently outside liquor shops and along many side streets, often next to their ubiquitous soft drink or cigarette vending cousins. Older model alcohol vending machines are programmed to turn off automatically between 11:00 pm and 5:00 am, and newer models require the purchaser to scan their identification card and prove they are of legal purchasing age. Yet older machines still abound and technological change does little to limit Japan's ease of access to beer or other drinks and, in the view of ASK, the accompanying tolerance of consumption.

To alcoholics these machines are also periodic tormentor and shame inducing physical reminder of past drunken behavior. During an Ohashi Danshūkai meeting in late February 2008, one member spoke at length about the vending machine he walks past every day on his route between home and the train station. Before getting sober he would visit this machine numerous times throughout the day, only buying one or two cans of beer and sake at a time so as not to appear out of the ordinary, and using it instead of the adjacent shop for the anonymity it provided him. As his excessive drinking began to cause incontinence, these short trips—often his only venture outside the home for days at a time—became an increasing "gamble" with his bodily capabilities. Finally, he said, "I lost" and urinated on myself while hurrying home with several cans of beer. Not only are such moments of abject bodily breakdown characteristic of alcoholism in Japan, often serving as the final and indisputable impetus for individuals to seek medical help, they also linger on in sobriety group member speeches as evidence of unresolved embarrassment and anger with themselves and those around them. While his sobriety has brought stability, that same machine still sits along his walk to the station as a mechanical mnemonic of his interpersonal struggles, as well as the financial cost and bodily damage inflicted by his drinking. Thus, while the widespread visibility of alcohol and tolerance for consumption is certainly not restricted to Japan, the presence of vending machines and negligible enforcement of age restrictions helps cultivate societal tolerance of public intoxication. This tolerance, while embraced by many as indicative of developed and necessary outlets for fun and leisure, also fortifies the marginalization of alcoholics and their struggles for wider recognition and acceptance.

TELEVISED DRUNKENNESS

The final point this chapter explores is the abundance of alcohol on Japanese television. Alcohol, including its active consumption, commands a prominent piece of Japan's television landscape. A standard format for beer commercials is to have an actor quickly drink a large mug of cold beer before exclaiming *oishii!* (delicious!) in a loud voice. Advertisements for whiskey, chū-hai, and other alcoholic drinks also make frequent use of the absence of legal restrictions on showing actors actively drinking, a practice denied advertisers in many other parts of the world. Yet while these commercials are significant, a recent controversy over a segment on Fuji TV's popular and long running variety show *Mecha-Mecha Iketeru* is illustrative of the acceptability drunkenness enjoys on Japanese television. Known as *Mecha-Ike* to many, this popular weekly show brings together a troupe of well-known comedians in a series of challenges and often humiliating surprise tasks. A recent segment put the show's comedians and *tarento* (celebrity) in a large room designed to look like an izakaya. Once assembled everyone can order drinks and food, just as they would in a standard izakaya, yet they must each continue drinking until only one "champion" remains. Each participant can drink whatever they want—and numerous "strategies" are offered on the best drinks to sustain oneself over the course of the competition—and at their own pace, but they are not allowed to stop drinking for an extended period of time. When a participant is determined to have stopped drinking, or elects to quit because they are too drunk to continue, they retire to a darkened room filled with futons adjacent to the festivities where they can sleep. Not surprisingly the rules for this contest quickly become haphazard and inconsistently applied, yet the result is a room full of unmistakably drunk celebrities broadcasting their antics to the nation.

Editing moves the viewer quickly through several hours of revelry and the effects of drunkenness become overtly obvious within minutes. Slurred speech and impaired coordination abound, while impassioned conversation and strong opinions are freely voiced. In the summer of 2012 ASK complained to Fuji TV about this segment and launched a publicity campaign calling for its removal. Their efforts met with significant resistance and backlash from Japan's viewing public, as angry emails and phone calls inundated the ASK office for weeks. Supporters and fans of the segment, and there were many, argued that it was comedy and did not encourage over consumption or glorify drunkenness. These events came to a head on the day I reunited with ASK's director in July 2012, and we had to promptly end our conversation after an hour as representatives from Fuji TV arrived to discuss the disagreement further.

ASK's frustration with the segment stemmed from its portrayal of drunkenness as funny and requisite for intimate and candid conversation. ASK views such broadcasts as sustaining Japanese perceptions of extreme drunkenness as necessary for meaningful and enjoyable interpersonal interaction. Further, for alcoholics the onscreen images render claims to illness and sobriety group membership antithetical to prevail norms of socialization. As "dark" and "sullen" individuals, borrowing from many AA and Danshūkai members' descriptions of how others see alcoholics, group members are the opposite of the laughing and witty or assertive yet sincere drunks broadcast by *Mecha Ike* across Japan. Above all else, ASK regards the case of *Mecha Ike* as continuing to make alcoholism abnormal and sustaining popular interpretations of the Japanese alcoholic as a person deficient in character and slovenly in disposition. As ASK's director was quick to note, their opposition was not to comedy, but to the perpetuation of a Japan demanding of drunkenness from its adult population.

Above all, there is limited prominent and popular conversation or critique in Japan on the potential consequences of heavy alcohol consumption and drunkenness. A history of tolerance and indulgence of consumption has helped an assertive contemporary voice, typically disseminated through advertising and television, link fun and revelry to drinking while marginalizing the alcoholic. As the chapters to follow highlight, the deficiency of achieved prominence for AA and Danshūkai has helped maintain limited acceptance of sobriety, especially among men, and caused many to be aggressively secretive about their group membership. More broadly, it has sustained popular views of alcoholism as a deficiency of character, views that run counter to sobriety group advocacy for recovery as a struggle against a disease. The result is a persistent tension between AA and Danshūkai's interpretation of alcoholism as an illness, from which one cannot ever fully recover, and the demands for individual, group, and societal vigilance, alongside popular understandings of alcoholics as degenerates.

BEYOND PERSISTENT INDULGENCE

On a brisk fall afternoon I was walking to the JSO office with Toshi, an AA member at the time sober more than five years, and Ryota, an "ACA" or Adult Child of Alcoholics, who was also sober and periodically helped the office with computer issues. The three of us negotiated the ever-present crowds filling the underground shopping arcade at Ikebukuro Station, one of Tokyo's busiest transit hubs. We passed numerous bars and shops prominently displaying their available alcohol. Near the station's exit Ryota nudged Toshi and, pointing at a chalkboard being set up outside a British-themed pub, said "that's what's wrong with Japan" in a tone of obvious frustration. The board was advertising the evening's special, a *nomihodai* (all you can drink) from 5:00 pm to close for ¥3,000 (about $30.00). Turning to me he added, "everything [in Japan] tells you to get drunk." At that particular bar, for a nominal fee patrons could drink as much as they wanted over six hours. And our short walk revealed that such offers were far from unusual.

Living as an alcoholic in Japan is inherently paradoxical. Success for an alcoholic "living in recovery" is constituted through total sobriety, regular meeting attendance, and deep thoughtful engagement with group literature and ideology. The promised result of all this is a fundamental transformation of self into a new individual able to find happiness and fulfillment without alcohol. Yet for many Japanese members of AA or Danshūkai, such transformations and the expected happiness are elusive, and a successful period of sobriety makes them culturally transgressive figures. Yet, it is a transgression easily dismissed and popularly hidden by Japan's pervasive tolerance for consumption and drunkenness, a passive revolt against the status quo that makes success as a sobriety group member a marginalizing existence. Continuing to treat addiction through AA or Danshūkai's established treatment programs, the only approach available for those questioning their alcohol use in Japan, is asking the individual to fit their experiences into the dictates of the group. And as such it is an approach that strands many Japanese alcoholics, rendering much of their lived environment dangerous and forcing cautious, limited interactions that leave them unfulfilled and isolated.

This chapter argued that a history of tolerance and acceptance of drink and drunkenness in Japan today fuels indulgent attitudes on consumption. A broad consequence of this tendency is strengthening the marginalization felt by many of Japan's alcoholics and other addicts. While other factors also contribute to the contemporary structuring of sobriety group membership, factors explored in the chapters to follow, the easy accessibility of alcohol and Japan's largely tolerant views of drunkenness leave little room for alcoholism to assert itself as a lived category of identity. As the next chapter demonstrates, the consequences of this on sobriety group members are not only sometimes severe but also experienced and understood as permanent conditions.

NOTES

1. The age to purchase both alcohol and cigarettes in Japan is 20, placing it high on the scale of global thresholds for consumption restrictions.
2. While awkwardly rendered in English, the mentioned eras refer to the Showa 30s (1955–1964), Showa 40s (1965–1974), and Showa 50s (1975–1984)—decades during the reign of Emperor Hirohito that ended with his death in 1989.
3. Hoppy is a beer flavored drink containing almost no alcohol. It was introduced in Japan in 1948 and combined with shōchū as a substitute for beer, which was prohibitively expensive to most in Japan at the time. It has experienced a recent and heavily nostalgic revival in Tokyo.
4. See http://www.economist.com/blogs/dailychart/2011/02/global_alcohol_consumption for a chart of global alcohol consumption rates.
5. I have argued elsewhere that national data hides meaningful internal drinking trends, the rapid rise in consumption levels among young Japanese women being the best example (Christensen 2012). It is important to keep in mind that the stagnant level of nation consumption obscures meaningful localized practices that can be made visible through ethnographic work.
6. While the indexing of YouTube clips is unstable, the commercial could be viewed here http://www.youtube.com/watch?v=cfHxDZ5fP7s as of 7/24/2013.
7. The commercial can be viewed here: http://www.youtube.com/watch?v=rr-KFxhy3qI
8. Examples of these commercials can be viewed here: https://www.youtube.com/watch?v=EYty-0v63oo, https://www.youtube.com/watch?v=UAcdNB8dD6s, and https://www.youtube.com/watch?v=F21gKD_F9Co
9. In comparison, drunk driving laws in the United States differ by state. However, punishments for a first DUI offense are typically a very short jail sentence and a suspended license for a period of time.

Chapter Three

Sobriety and Disease

ADDICTION AS ENTERTAINMENT

AA is everywhere in the United States. Even when not overtly obvious or easily detected, its presence is rarely far away. "Easy does it" and "one day at a time," slogans pulled from AA's recovery ideology, are today used by many outside the organization, often without an awareness of their connection to sobriety and recovery. Popular culture, television and film especially, make frequent use of the AA meeting format for any number of dramatic or comedic purposes. This popularization of addiction is also evident in the distinctly American proliferation of "rehab" and televised interventions, practices that go far beyond their original meanings or purposes (Garcia 2010b). The result of this visibility, unintended or otherwise, is AA as the naturalized lens through which addiction is popularly interpreted, understood, and disseminated across North America. AA has made admissions of alcoholism mainstream and infused a familiarity with the meeting format—"Hi, I'm John and I'm an alcoholic." "Hi John!"—to many individuals who will never need to seek out a meeting or confront interpersonal demons related to addiction.

There are also distinct consequences to addiction's easy American visibility. Rehab and recovery reality television are major programming sub-genres that turn addictions, both deeply troubling in the case of A&E's long running program *Intervention* or potentially less so with TLC's *My Strange Addiction*, into a form of entertainment that offers tidy solutions at the end of a thirty minute episode to messy, chaotic, and potentially lifelong struggles (*ibid*). Such programing also popularizes the disease model of addiction and relies on viewer awareness of AA's central belief that total recovery is never possible. By doing so, this programming further infuses AA's approach to recovery from alcoholism as *the* approach to treating addiction. Additionally, while AA has always emphasized inclusiveness, rejecting attempts to label it a Christian organization and telling members to surrender to "God, *as you understand Him*," it is predicated on individual acceptance of a single and omnipotent God, and unable to recognize any worldview that does not conform to this outlook (italics in original). Thus, while AA and Danshūkai deserve praise for insisting on institutional openness and welcoming anyone seeking help into their meetings, they have structured understandings of addiction around several fundamentally important governing principles that for many Japanese members require not only substantial self-reflection, but are also potentially easily dismissed as culturally antithetical concepts or meaningful categories.

Additionally, it must be noted that AA constructs success in recovery as a return to financial productivity and stability. Within such a system the burden of authority and responsibility lies with the individual, while "chronicity" which "likens addiction to lifelong disease such as diabetes, asthma, or hypertension," put the cause of addiction beyond the control of individual addicts (Garcia 2010a: 13). Finally, even addiction itself remains a still unfolding area of scientific and neurological attention, and as such I echo here Angela Garcia's approach rooted in inquiry regarding "how the scientific understanding of addiction shapes—or to be more precise, does not shape—local understandings and experiences of addiction" (*ibid*: 14). As such, I am interested in how local understandings of the alcoholic in Tokyo and across Japan, particularly when coupled with the efforts of sobriety group members, are shaping or not shaping popular perceptions of alcoholism and addiction.

This chapter begins with a look at the historical evolution of alcoholism and addiction as categories of medical knowledge as well as targets of legislative and punitive intervention. This is done by looking at early work on addiction, primarily in the United States, before moving on to consider the importance of prevailing societal discourse and major influential forces structuring popular views of alcoholism. This process, often reflective of larger cultural perceptions and understandings, says much about how alcoholics are regarded and treated in differing national contexts. Finally, the chapter turns back to Japan, noting AA and Danshūkai's relative absence of popular visibility and highlighting how this lack of established awareness for alcoholics is felt and discussed by sobriety group members.

FROM MORAL FAILING TO DISEASE

As a conceptual and medical category, addiction is relatively young. Alcoholism, and addiction generally, emerged as widely recognized medical categories within only the last 150 years. Prior to this, prevailing understandings of the habitual "drunkard" in the Western world were that they afflicted individuals of weak character, marking them as those within a community prone to behavior that failed to meet societal standards of morality and decorum. Not surprisingly, such categorizations were also disproportionately disbursed upon poor and marginalized populations, leaving wealthy male drinkers largely unaffected by such associations. Yet as addiction began to attract greater attention within the American medical establishment of the late 1700s, alcohol consumption and intoxication came under heightened scrutiny. Benjamin Rush (1746–1813), a Scottish-educated physician, signer of the American Constitution, and eventually a professor of chemistry at the University of Pennsylvania, was among the first prominent medical voices to speak of alcoholism as an addiction and equate such a diagnosis with disease. He identified alcoholism as a disease in which "alcohol is the causal agent, loss of control over drinking behavior . . . the characteristic symptom, and total abstinence the only effective cure" (Meyer 1996: 162). Rush, a man unafraid of taking controversial positions, was also an early and initially contrary voice in larger medical discussions across western Europe and the United States on addiction as a new and legitimate category of medical inquiry, all at a time when cocaine, heroin, and morphine were standard pharmaceuticals in the doctor's dispensary, and would remain so for several decades (Markel 2011). As the first prominent figure to frame alcoholism as a "loss of control," Rush's influence, and thus his enduring relevance, over contemporary approaches to alcoholism and recovery is not only pervasive but also stubbornly resistant to challenge despite more than a century of ongoing inquiry (Durrant and Thakker 2003, Levine 1978).

By the late 1800s and early 1900s prevailing views on alcoholism and addiction, particularly in the United States, had shifted away from innate individual genetic inferiority to disease, with new theories and approaches to treatment emerging alongside. America's period of national prohibition (1920–1933) is indicative of such shifts as popular opinion on drinking swung first in favor of illegality, and then away from this extreme towards a more moderate recognition that many could consume alcohol without falling victim to habitual drunkenness and violence. Of importance here is the challenge to what had once been the Prohibition movement's primary claim to moral authority, that comprehensive and total abstinence from alcohol was the only effective cure to the ills of drinking. Unmoored from the Prohibition movement, this position evolved in the United States throughout the 1930s and 1940s, a historical moment coinciding with the emergence of AA in 1935, into a politically charged outlook revealing wider societal acceptance, at least to certain substances, for addiction as a legitimate and not necessarily inherent affliction.

A pivotal moment in this societal shift came out of E. M. Jellinek's influential writings in the 1940s and 1950s which "proposed a scientific understanding of alcoholism" (Fingarette 1988: 19). Jellinek's widely circulated publications advocating for the disease model of alcoholism, an approach to addiction that "goes back to a cultural emphasis on abstinence and temperance that emerged as early as the 1780s," were actively taken up by AA as an endorsement from the medical establishment of their approach to framing treatment and living in recovery (Campbell 2007: 13). As Jellinek notes, "one of the greatest roles in bringing the illness [disease] concept to the widest reaches of public opinion was played by the fellowship of Alcoholics Anonymous" (1960: 10). The disease model approach casts alcoholism as an illness, albeit one from which total recovery is impossible, and maintains that the "primary treatment goal" is lifelong abstinence from alcohol (Bride and Mackerud 2002: 125). While it is a frequently criticized approach, in part because it "hinders *exploration of alternative, politically more challenging understandings of destructive drinking*," the disease model benefits from a strong, vocal, and powerful ally in the ideological underpinnings of AA and Danshūkai (Singer and Baer 1995: 305, italics in original). The significance of this is crucial, because as alcoholism's definitional mechanism of pervasive influence in the United States, Japan, and numerous other nations throughout the world, the disease model shapes the lived experiences of alcoholics around a restrictive range of recovery options that give little if any credence to cultural or religious variety.[1]

Further, by continuing to define alcoholism as a disease and resisting challenge to this position, dominant contemporary views of treatment in the United States confirm "major elements of the AA view" (Fingarette 1988: 19). Thus, individual diagnosis as an alcoholic is confirmed through encouraged sobriety group participation that then thwarts inquiry into alternative forms of treatment and recovery. Within this framework individual alcoholics are tasked with coming to see themselves as suffering from an incurable illness that mandates lifelong sobriety and ongoing participation in sobriety group meetings. The significance of such an approach lies in how it entrenches a single and specific definitional framing of alcoholism, disease, and addiction, while casting alternative views as antithetical to recovery. As Jellinek himself noted, "*a disease is what the medical profession recognizes as such*" (1960: 12, italics in original). The result is the locally felt consequences to such interpretations of alcoholism made explicit, as AA's definitional premises originally emerged from a largely white, strongly Protestant and upper-middle class American orientation that in Japan confronts ongoing popular disjuncture and antagonism. Addiction and alcoholism are global issues, rife with locally specific concerns crucial to understanding how treatment should be approached and undertaken, that in Japan increasingly struggle for recognition in the face of AA and Danshūkai's pervasive influence.

SOBERING STRUCTURES

Bill Wilson and Bob Smith established Alcoholics Anonymous in Akron, Ohio in 1935. Bill Wilson was a World War I veteran and worked as a stock speculator in New York City during the late 1920s and early 1930s. He also drank heavily and constantly, despite mounting evidence it was leading to professional and personal ruin, until his life became in his words "unmanageable." In 1934 "Bill W.," as he is affectionately known in AA, was introduced to the Oxford Group, an evangelical Christian organization invested in helping individuals who want to stop drinking. However, in May 1935, he was in Akron and felt a strong temptation to drink after a short period of sustained sobriety. He called Bob Smith, a physician, local Oxford Group member, and alcoholic he had never met, and together the two of them helped Bill maintain his sobriety. About a month later, on June 10, Bill in turn helped "Dr. Bob" achieve a sobriety that would last the rest of his life and establish Alcoholics Anonymous as an organizational force across North America. This encounter also serves as the building block for AA's ideological framework, rooting organizational legitimacy in an account of homosocial friendship between two men wanting but initially unsure of how to find sustained sobriety.

Much of AA's approach to recovery requires acceptance of several religiously rooted and decidedly Christian principles. New members must make individual admissions of powerlessness over alcohol, surrender themselves to a "Higher Power," and take a "searching and fearless moral inventory" by working the Twelve Steps, the result of which is sobriety as well as a spiritual awakening and transformation to a new and happy individual (Alcoholics Anonymous 2001).[2] "There is an intentional effort made to disassociate AA from any conventional religious frame of reference" in order to ensure inclusiveness, yet these religious elements also form a significant part of living sober and in recovery (Matthiasson 1987: 22). As such, this recovery framework emphasizes how membership in a sobriety group is about much more than no longer consuming alcohol. AA and Danshūkai put forward a promise and possibility for resurrection from the pain wrought upon individuals and those close to them by addiction's destructive power. A chance for new members to remake themselves as long as they are ready to "hear the message" and fully commit to the recovery program. Group membership offers the possibility of transforming ruinous drunks into recovering and sober alcoholics who can lead productive and happy lives—albeit a productivity conceived and understood by AA as a return, through spiritual transformation, to individual economic independence and sustained employment, a reinvigoration of wage labor efficiency designated as the source of self-worth and individual fulfillment.

Yet what a language of inclusion from AA hides is the powerful centrality of a specific view on religion's purpose, however broadly defined, in an individual's life. Surrender to a Higher Power denotes a monotheistic worldview, a strict hierarchy of the supernatural, with a single and unquestioned deity at the apex. AA's inability, or unwillingness, to recognize that this is a culturally specific position that, absent individual recognition of its relevance, makes the recovery program difficult to accept and integrate into one's daily life also makes it deeply consequential. Such a situation is particularly evident in Japan, where, as Steven Heine notes, religion functions less as an abstract spiritual guide to notions of appropriate moral conduct, and more as "an integral part of daily life" (2012: 56). Such an approach to religion and notions of the spiritual allows for the plurality of religious practices easily observed in Japan, the integration of Buddhism, Shintō, indigenous animism, and even elements of Christianity, into everyday life.[3] It does not, however, allow religion to serve as a strong central motivator for fundamental transformations of self—a singular force to which an individual declaration of powerlessness and surrender carries significant meaning and validity. Thus, as AA demands that individual members cede absolute authority to God, *as you understand Him*, as the only way to live in recovery and achieve the promised transformation of self, it neglects individual reservations at making such a declaration.

Additionally, the strength of the disease model brings larger issues of relevance concerning diagnostic authority, cultural borrowing, and gendered understandings of masculine ideals into focus. "Given that the medical profession has fully embraced the disease concept of alcoholism, physicians have provided expert validation of worldwide AA ideology" (Brandes 2002: 159). At Tokyo AA and Danshūkai meetings this point is emphasized with a distinct twist, as members often lament that despite having a doctor's diagnosis as alcohol-dependent to bolster the legitimacy of their claims, they frequently clash with others around alcoholism's lack of popular acceptance or mainstream recognition in Japan. It is this point, the collision between a position fully embraced by many of Japan's doctors encountering the entrenched popular resistance and failures to account for established concepts of manhood, that I explore in greater detail below.

Surrender and individual recognition of a loss of control over any ability to regulate and limit alcohol consumption is a linchpin of AA and Danshūkai's recovery ideology. Upon joining a group, individuals must begin making admissions of powerlessness and surrender, turning their sobriety over to the care of others and the fellowship of the organization, and "fearlessly" revisiting past drunken behavior through this new interpretive framework. Thus, regular and involved participation in group meetings, periodic session of "inventory taking" where transgressions, lapses, and other areas of concern are aired, and reliance on the support of others all become essential and requisite to maintaining sobriety. This is also where ideological differences begin to emerge in Japan between AA and Danshūkai concerning understandings of spirituality and constructions of recovery, a point revisited in later chapters.

The importance of understanding alcoholism as a disease is also immediately evident as it shifts the burden of maintaining sobriety to the individual, yet also absolves any past transgressions stemming from drunkenness as the behavior of a sick and suffering soul. Within such a framework individuals must not only want to stop drinking but also come to see themselves as alcoholics. In short, an individual must fundamentally transform their understanding of themselves into something congruent with sobriety group ideology. As should now be clear, the disease model is a cultural construction, firmly rooted in a distinct historical moment and set of cultural values that, through ongoing advocacy from AA and other similarly aligned groups, dominates the ways in which alcoholism and addiction are individually experienced. What such a structuring leaves is a recovery process largely unconcerned with localized norms of culture, gender, and history, and instead requires individual members to find ways of adjusting their lives to fit the organizational apparatus (Brandes 2002). The result is a narrowly specific but widely followed understanding of alcoholism and the manner in which it should be treated that gives some in Japan deep and meaningful solace, yet leaves a larger numbers of individuals skeptical and wanting for an alternative approach to their struggles with addiction.

ADDICTION, RECOVERY, AND JAPAN

The strong cultural presence of alcohol and drinking across Japan sweep sobriety group members and their individual struggles with addiction to the societal margins. As Amy Borovoy notes, “many physicians who treat alcoholism in non-specialized hospitals still treat patients’ liver problems and, after a brief detoxification period, dismiss them with the advice that ‘a little’ alcohol should not be a problem” (2005: 52). Such responses reflect not only limited awareness and recognition of addiction, even among some in Japan’s medical establishment, but also emphasize the depth of skepticism Tokyo’s alcoholics can face when discussing their sobriety outside the context of meetings. Interestingly, addiction as a metaphorical concept is prominent across Japan’s popular and medical landscape, frequently invoked in discussion of work, education, and family issues of national prominence. Conservative political movements and advocates of *Nihonjinron* (theories of Japaneseness) have sometimes co-opted “workaholism” and other similar afflictions as tolerable, even praiseworthy examples of quintessentially “Japanese” addictions (Befu 2001). Such renderings of the addict in the abstract, as a descriptive tool for supposedly desirable characteristics, coupled with discourses that emphasize alcohol's rejuvenatory powers, a popular piece of folk wisdom stating that there is no better medicine than alcohol, have in Japan divorced addiction from its potentially debilitating impact on the individual.[4]

The result is Japan's alcoholics most often regarded as incurable drunkards, the homeless and the dysfunctional living at the margins of culturally appropriate conduct. Such associations are sustained in popular imaginings of geographic areas that link alcoholism to day laboring and the large numbers of mostly middle-aged men eking out an existence in these ignored corners on the edge of Japan's affluence (Fowler 1996, Gill 2001, Stevens 1997)—areas, like San'ya in Tokyo and Kamagasaki in Ōsaka, that are not only popularly viewed as the places where one finds alcoholics, but also perpetuate the popular linking in Japan of alcoholism and addiction to failure, dirtiness, and homelessness. And while alcohol and alcoholism are certainly prevalent in San'ya and other areas similarly marked by abject poverty, they are equally present yet socially insulated along the moneyed streets of Tokyo's posher neighborhoods.[5] Thus, a consequence of the embrace of drinking and normalization of drunkenness is Japanese alcoholics as an easily dismissed, mocked, and sometimes denigrated caricature through processes that demonize Tokyo's poor and homeless while also impeding recognition of alcoholism among those able to maintain employment, a marriage, or some degree of interpersonal stability.

It is not however, simply that sympathy is withheld from the alcoholic. Instead his presence, even his existence, falls outside the range of awareness or comprehension for many in Japan. The evidence of this was starkly apparent during a free public lecture on alcoholism, given by a prominent doctor specializing in alcohol treatment, at a suburban Tokyo community center in the spring of 2007. During the question and answer session that followed the lecture an elderly women first thanked everyone involved and then said, "I never thought my son was an alcoholic, I just thought he liked to drink," before trailing off and then sitting back down. Despite not posing a question, the doctor sympathetically responded by noting that this was not uncommon, and that the families of most patients he treats know little or nothing of alcoholism when first receiving his diagnosis. And, he added, this is why he makes sure to devote substantial time to countering any concerns and associated stigma they feel when getting this news. The older woman then spoke again, saying she now feels complicit in her son's addiction, as she had helped him get undressed and into bed on the many nights he arrived home drunk. She was also the one who got him out of bed in the morning, fed and hydrated with "energy drinks," and then out the door for work the next morning, regardless of the severity of his hangover (Roberson 2005).[6] She had regarded such conduct as good and her "*gimu*" (duty) to help ensure her son's corporate advancement, just as she treated his drinking and constant hangovers as normal aspects of his career. Behavior that was now, as she spoke, becoming a series of monstrous acts contributing to her son's alcoholism, firing, and ongoing struggles to find new employment. The doctor tried to convey reassurances, saying fault lies not with her but Japan's overall reluctance to seriously consider alcoholism and addiction as important medical categories that can potentially befall anyone. While she appeared to take some comfort in his words, the lecture had also given her a new and disruptively challenging interpretation of her son's drinking, and the role she played as a dutiful mother in facilitating its continuation.

Such moments of cathartic exchange and education are also unusual, and Japanese alcoholics continue to be viewed by many not as an addict requiring care or an individual capable of "living in recovery," but as someone abnormal, even immoral, for their inability to drink "like everyone else." The normalization of drinking and drunkenness becomes in Japan a tyrannical force at odds with sobriety group tenets demanding openness, honesty, and transformation of the self into a happy and sober new person through rigorous self-reflection and supportive group membership. AA and Danshūkai meetings typify the marginalization that surrounds alcoholism and sobriety group membership, as they work to create a space where a male alcoholic identity is possible, yet find little success in challenging Japan's popular assumptions of the alcoholic. Sobriety group meetings, and an alcoholic identity generally, persist as something contested and unstable, reflective of a lingering popular discord between organizational ideology and the lived reality of many members that structures group membership.

In essence, addiction and alcoholism have sat stubbornly at an impasse with popular notions of illness and recovery throughout much of Japan's postwar history. Methods of treatment and recovery advocated first by specialists and more recently by a growing number of Japan's general medical practitioners rely heavily on a methodology borrowed from AA in the United States. This AA influenced approach also mandates spiritual transformation, self-control, and rejection of expert medical opinion or diagnosis as the only path to sustained sobriety and a life lived happily in recovery. Yet Japanese group members are typically told by the attending physician how the recovery process will unfold, as well as the sobriety group they should join, with married men directed towards Danshūkai while women and unmarried men are encouraged to first try AA. Such conventions are at odds with AA's insistence on transferring authority over recovery from the physician to the individual alcoholic, a process of making the individual accountable for past drunken behavior and vigilant in maintaining their sobriety. As others have accurately noted, "coerced involvement is contrary to the precepts of AA, which advocates noncompulsory participation" (Brandes 2002: 193, Miller and Kurtz 1994). Additionally, such a framework is rooted in a worldview that privileges a narrative of maximizing individual productivity through wage labor and self-responsibility, positioning it awkwardly in the context of Japan between a medical apparatus advocating for such a recovery format and a population of sobriety group members seen as at odds with prevailing conventions of socialization and normalcy. This impasse between sobriety group members and the Japanese public becomes unmistakably consequential when Japan's dearth of alternative treatment options for those struggling with their drinking is considered, a topic addressed in the next section.

FROM ACQUIESCENCE TO ACCEPTANCE

A major issue many of Japan's alcoholics face every day is trying to live within sobriety group ideology, itself designed as a guide for living one's new and sober life that is unrecognizable to those around them. AA and Danshūkai are presented to new members as being about much more than helping an individual stop drinking and stay sober. Both programs are offered as comprehensive blueprints for a new life devoid of alcohol and the destruction it brought to the individual and others around them—a new life that AA and Danshūkai present as happy, fulfilling, and free from the misery and eventual death they say will result from an alcoholic's continued alcohol consumption. Yet as an ideology that is supposed to come divorced from the authoritative knowledge of the physician's diagnosis, but in Japan is conferred to individuals through exactly such a process, it is a paradoxically mandated transition of self that few outside the sobriety group context recognize. As such, Tokyo's alcoholics must not only stop drinking, they must also fundamentally change how they understand themselves and then assert this transition to a skeptical and sometimes dismissive public outside the comforts of group meetings. Such a process not only leaves many group members frustrated, it also fails to resonate with a large number of those who are hospitalized in Japan for alcohol-related complications.

Many AA and Danshūkai members actively work to confront this awkward conceptual disjuncture, volunteering at hospitals around Tokyo to educate patients on the ideological framework of recovery as well as the necessary steps to becoming an active group member. However, the encounters between patients hospitalized for alcohol-related issues and the AA or Danshūkai volunteers leading these "beginners meetings" are inconsistent with fundamental components of group ideology, as they are often a requisite part of the hospital program and occur at the request of and with approval from attending physicians. "Beginners meetings" create a hierarchy between the physician, the sobriety group volunteers leading the sessions, and the hospitalized patients, all while advocating an egalitarian organizational structure that empowers members to transcend such hierarchical structures by drawing upon shared experiences to heal and live in recovery. As such, beginners meetings also reveal the frustrations many Japanese men face when questioning their alcohol consumption and confronting the limited range of treatment options, particularly if they find AA or Danshūkai incompatible with their recovery needs or strongly held convictions.

I regularly attended a long-running beginners AA meeting at Nerima Hospital in the northwest of Tokyo, near the city's border with Saitama prefecture. The meeting was part of an addiction recovery program initiated by Dr. Mori, a petite woman in her fifties whose gentle disposition could easily give way to steely assertiveness when confronting those who challenged her methods or credentials. She had previously clashed with Danshūkai leaders who were unwilling to listen to a woman and dismissed her views and expertise on how best to educate patients seeking help for their drinking. As a result she now directs everyone she treats into AA and views Danshūkai as sexist, overly hierarchical, and conservative in its approach to recovery. Additionally, Dr. Mori is a strong advocate of an active therapeutic community as essential to maintaining long term sobriety, and requires all her patients to participate in weekly beginners meetings while hospitalized in her three month in-patient program.

Three volunteers from Tokyo AA and Al-Anon groups, Toru, Masa, and Hiroka, regularly lead Dr. Mori's beginners meeting, speaking to the patients about the governing principles of AA and their life as alcoholics in recovery. Toru, a tall, energetic man in his early fifties who works as a lawyer with one of Japan's major automobile companies, leads most of the meetings with a commanding presence. Masa, also in his fifties and slight in stature, takes over the occasional meetings that Toru cannot attend. He speaks in a soft and measured voice that give the meetings he chairs a far quieter tone. Hiroka, a bubbly woman always quick to smile despite years of interpersonal hardship, was the wife of a now deceased alcoholic and abusive husband. She typically speaks after the men and offers her perspective as a family member who suffered physical and emotional anguish for many years at the hands of an alcoholic spouse. She is also working to introduce and grow Al-Anon in Japan, AA's affiliated organization for the family members of alcoholics, yet is finding it difficult to attract a steady membership.

Patients attending the meeting assemble a few minutes before 7:00 pm in a room that was once an open courtyard inside the hospital complex until a roof was added later. The area is now used for storage and participants arrange folding chairs facing a whiteboard at the back of the room amidst the clutter of boxes and unused furniture stacked along the walls. Masa always brings a stack of informational fliers and notices for other AA meetings around Tokyo and Saitama, yet few patients ever leave with any. The experienced patients, some chronically hospitalized in this program, tend to have an area of the room where they always sit and wave over late-arriving friends to a chair they saved for them. For many of these men the meeting is a standard weekly exercise, an event to get through before returning to the television or newspapers in the patient lounge down the hall. Each meeting was typically attended by about twenty patients, all of them men, the majority in their fifties and sixties, and many bearing the scars and ill health from years of heavy drinking. Chronicity marks their alcoholism and the success of treatment is measured in maintaining daily stability. This cyclical pattern is evident when these patients are discharged at the end of the three month program, as many quickly return first to drinking and then, after typically a few months, the hospital. Inversely, newer patients often paused awkwardly at the door, seemingly unsure of where they want to position themselves in the room. When asked to speak, their responses are typically short, polite, and emphasize a commitment to rapidly move on from this program and returning to their "normal" lives. What is notable about this beginners meeting, and others like it throughout Tokyo, is the split between the chronically institutionalized and those eager to find a speedy recovery and skeptical of the sobriety group message that alcoholism is a permanent condition from which total recovery is impossible and lifelong sobriety requisite.

Toru, Masa, and Hiroka follow a deliberately consistent format at each meeting. Toru or Masa first distribute the "AA textbook," which they and other volunteers created for this program, before calling the meeting to order promptly at the stroke of seven. The evening's leader, typically Toru, then welcomes everyone with a standard greeting—"I'm Toru and I'm an alcoholic"—before reminding those assembled that this is a beginners meeting where they will continue learning about sobriety, recovery, being an AA member, and individual renewal. Following this everyone recites aloud the Twelve Steps in unison before spending the next hour looking in detail at three thematically linked steps and the larger symbolic meaning they are meant to convey. This "step study" was typically done as a lecture, which often involved extensive use of the room's whiteboard, well-developed metaphors on the power of the Twelve Steps, and impassioned examples drawn from Japanese history as well as the speakers' experiences with living in recovery. Following step study the volunteers lead a truncated version of a "normal" AA meeting in the remaining thirty minutes. As they would at a typical meeting, each AA volunteer stands, says their name and states that they are an alcoholic, before speaking for several minutes on a topic relevant to the steps and examples discussed over the previous hour. Generally this is an exaggerated example of how they might speak at their regular AA meetings, with deliberate attention given to emphasizing how the Twelve Steps act as a guide to living without alcohol. When the AA volunteers finish the patients are given their chance to speak in the time remaining, typically about twenty minutes, which is usually more than enough for everyone to take a turn saying something. While a few carefully follow the format outlined by the AA volunteers and offer heartfelt speeches on their struggles with alcohol, others are unsure or reluctant and many simply stand, state their name without including alcoholic, and then add a trite set-phrase—"thank you for coming and speaking with us tonight"—before quickly sitting back down.

These curt responses from patients, typical I found for beginner meetings, also help illustrate the difficulties Toru, Masa, and other volunteer AA members face when trying to persuade those in hospital to join a sobriety group and incorporate its ideological underpinnings into their lives. During most of the beginners meetings I attended, the patients, who are required to attend but not evaluated on their level of participation, sit quietly in their chairs with arms folded across their chests or eyes cast down to the floor, waiting for the meeting to end so they could return to the communal television in the lounge area down the hall or the smoking area outside. For many of the patients, hospitalization and the accompanying meetings were but another required component of their stay, corresponding to a diagnosis as alcohol dependent that many of them regard with suspicion. What becomes clear is that the presence of interpersonally destructive drinking is not a sufficient motivator for many patients to seek out treatment and sobriety, as many remain skeptical of a diagnosis as alcohol dependent. And while Japan is not alone in this regard, this skepticism highlights the limitations of available treatment options and the difficulties facing AA and Danshūkai volunteers when trying to reach new potential members.

Yet, while sullen disinterest was often on display at beginners meetings, it was not the only reaction AA's material generated among the assembled patients. On a cold night in February this disinterest turned to active resistance, further highlighting the gap between sobriety group members and the Japanese public concerning the prevailing perception of alcoholism. The meeting was nearing its end as Toru and the other AA volunteers had finished their speeches and were now asking the patients to each take a turn briefly speaking. Several patients went formulaically through the motions of rising, stating their name, and thanking the volunteers for their time, with some adding "I'll do my best to not drink again" before sitting back down. A new patient was one of the last to speak that evening, an older man, likely in his early seventies, and noticeable healthier in appearance than many of the other patients. He stood, slowly looked at each of the AA volunteers and then confidently thanked them for their time but said that he could not accept their program and tonight's meeting had been a waste of his time. "It stinks of Christianity" he said in a derisive tone, dismissing in a single broad stroke AA's therapeutic model as religiously motivated, foreign, and incompatible with his Japanese disposition.[7]

Some background on Japanese polytheism is necessary here to put the power of this statement into an appropriate context. As Western observers of Japan are quick to note, many Japanese live comfortably with a fluidity of religious views and practices that disrupt the Abrahamic religions' outlook on the purpose and necessity of such systems. Put simply, religions, predominately Shintōism and Buddhism, fuse with innumerable aspects of Japanese life. It allows individuals to simultaneously take part in Shintō and Buddhist rites throughout the year, with a bit of Christianity and other folk practices included for good measure or out of individual interest, while at the same time likely expressing a degree of ambivalence on the profundity of such actions (Hendry 1996: 116). Importantly, AA's notion of a Higher Power rejects this blending and pluralism, as it is a starkly monotheistic view of spirituality without room for a diversity of viewpoints or religious practices. Organizationally it treats "the concept of surrender (akin to conversion), the confession and testimony of the saved, the personal relation to God, the individual's voluntary decision to seek help, the individual's responsibility for his or her own recovery, and AA's egalitarian structure that rejects authority," as culturally benign notions enjoying easy universal acceptance, when the reality is the opposite (Jarrad 1995: 213). Thus, for AA to "stink" of Christianity, while also proffered as one of only two viable and markedly similar treatment option for alcoholism, is to hoist an impossible choice onto many Japanese men between spiritual practices from which they derive little meaning or continued alcohol consumption, compromised health, and likely an early death.

In part because of such conflicting views on the role and purpose of religion, his statement enlivened the other patients, causing many to sit up in their chairs and murmur encouragement as he continued to criticize Toru's earlier lecture on Steps One, Two and Three that had emphasized the necessity of surrender, confession, and powerlessness for a successful recovery. Toru listened intently and then began to respond, saying AA emphasizes inclusion and "spirituality," switching back and forth between the somewhat arcane Japanese term *reiteki* and the English transliteration *supirichuaru*, not a specific religious doctrine.[8] He then tried to add that members are free to interpret "Higher Power" in a way they find individually meaningful, yet was stopped before he could say everything he wanted. "It's not for me," the older man said as he returned to his chair, effectively ending the discussion and the meeting, while sending the other patients back to the lounge and smoking area in a far more animated mood than I ever remembered seeing them.

Saying AA "stinks of Christianity" also neatly captures the ideological gap Japan's sobriety groups face when trying to reach potential members and the general public. The mechanisms and practices sanctioned as medically appropriate for treating addiction—acknowledgment of a lack of control, surrender to a Higher Power, and acceptance that one now hosts an incurable disease—are derived from a religiously rooted perspective some in Japan find antithetical to their understanding of a "Japanese" worldview. While such a position discounts the ever changing nature of any worldview and the problematic stance of invoking certain tendencies and practices as Japanese or non-Japanese, the power of such invocations is revealing. Sobriety group methodologies, particularly the spiritual and Protestant influenced language of AA, make it easy to broadly dismiss group membership, alcoholism, and addiction in Japan as something foreign and culturally incompatible with local sensibilities. As such, by working the steps and participating in meetings, men in AA and Danshūkai are not only challenging through their sobriety Japan's prevailing conventions of socialization, they can also be viewed as representing an embracing of a foreign outlook on the cosmology of life.

The absence of alternative recovery outlets or programs to AA and Danshūkai only increases the consequences surrounding individual dismissals of sobriety group methodology. AA's organizational structure makes it difficult to extract accurate measures of success and failure rates among members. A widely cited figure estimates that forty percent of American members drop out within the first year and that those who find success are the individuals most motivated to realize sustained sobriety (Arkowitz and Lilienfeld 2011, Kownacki and Shadish 1999). As others have noted when looking at AA in Mexico and Honduras, such statistics also fail to capture the ethnographically evident individual negotiations around membership and meeting participation (Brandes 2002, Pine 2008). At the JSO, Aki informally estimated that "eighty percent" of those who attend a meeting in Japan do not stay sober more than a year, highlighting Japanese sobriety group struggles in first attracting and then retaining members. More importantly, a large number of Japanese patients hospitalized for alcohol related problems reject the calls to join AA or Danshūkai during their stay in hospital and find no alternative treatment method or approach. Despite these shortcomings, the positive impact AA and Danshūkai have brought to untold individuals, who through the program were able to reverse destructive drinking patterns many feel would have eventually culminated in their death, must again be emphasized. And my aim here is not to dismiss or ignore such accomplishments, as they are impressive and worthy of attention. Instead, I want to call attention through ethnographic data, testimony, and participant observation to the consequences of the power extended and exercised by the sobriety group format, whether in the more spiritually inclined AA or family oriented Danshūkai, as it fails to resonate with a substantial number of patients passing through Japan's hospitals—a lack of resonance that becomes consequential when it also dictates the categories of success or failure surrounding a diagnosis of alcoholism, addiction, and the structuring of a life lived in recovery.

Finally, it is important to remember that it is the view among many AA members, particularly in the United States, that AA's *program* is perfect and any failures or shortcomings lie not with the organization but with the individual and their unwillingness or inability to "hear the message" and "work the steps." AA and Danshūkai members frequently emphasize that the program works for those who want to stop drinking, and does not work for those who do not. Thus, criticism of particularly AA and how it is integrated, or not, into Japan's cultural landscape becomes organizationally impossible, as fault is placed entirely with the individual who, for whatever reasons, did not find meaning and sustenance in the prescribed methods. While such a recovery framework has helped many with their sobriety, when placed alongside discourse that mandates a disease model approach as the only legitimate way of understanding alcoholism, it is also an impediment to expanding the reach and scope of treatment or changing how Japan popularly regards addiction. In short, the neat logical circularity stifles conversation on alternative methods for treating alcoholism, as AA and Danshūkai are cast as above reproach and any failure to find sobriety is not due to organizational dictates but the fault of the individual who did not yet "hear the message."

The conflation of so many factors—illness, chronicity, popular acceptance or rejection, gender norms, religion and spirituality—creates a muddled picture that exacerbates the difficulty felt by Japanese men in making admissions of alcoholism. More importantly, the reliance on and power of sobriety group ideology shapes current understandings of alcoholism and addiction in ways that thwart the growth of alternative options for men in Tokyo who are questioning their drinking. Scientific and neurological work continues to sharpen human understandings of alcoholism and addiction and how they impact various systems of the body. However, cultural interpretations of addiction continue to be neglected and are equally important to consider, as they can dictate how an individual will respond to a diagnosis as alcohol dependent, interpret available treatment options, and embrace or reject the foundational components of sobriety group membership. The next chapter turns to these issues in greater detail as it explores how Central Group and Ohashi Danshūkai members experience, discuss, and integrate sobriety group ideology into their daily lives.

NOTES

1. While Danshūkai's sphere of influence does not extend beyond Japan, AA has an established and likely growing international presence including, but not limited to, active groups in Brazil (1995), Mexico (Brandes 2002), Finland and Poland (Mäkelä 1996), and Honduras (Pine 2008).

2. See the appendix for a full list of the Twelve Steps, as well as the Twelve Traditions of AA and the Danshūkai Oath.

3. Some marriages in Japan occur in churches and cathedrals made to appear Christian, including the prominent display of a large cross and a "foreign," typically white American or European "pastor" presiding over the ceremony. However, the churches and pastors are not ordained or sanctioned in any way by a recognized Christian organization. Instead they are

spaces available for a fee that give the appearance of a cosmopolitan internationalism during ceremonial moments.

4. お酒は百薬の著 (*Osake ha hyakuyaku no ch ō*) A popular idiom that read "alcohol is the best of all medicines."

5. San'ya, officially Minami Senjyu, is an interesting example as the area is undergoing gradual but immediately visible change. Once the location for executing criminals in the Edo (1603–1868) and Meiji (1868–1912) eras, its ties to the undesirable and socially marginal are long and deep (Fowler 1996: 17). Yet as one of the few contemporary pockets of Tokyo with affordable real estate close to the city center, there has been a recent proliferation of student and backpacker hostels catering to budget minded foreign travelers. The result is an intermingling of frugal or cash-strapped foreign visitors to Japan alongside the day laboring and homeless population, as well as the constant and abundant presence of alcohol.

6. Roberson's article looks at the marketing of Japan's numerous vitamin and energy drinks to salarymen as an urging to work harder and longer that is linked explicitly through advertising to masculine virility—a link so strongly forged that the distinct small brown bottles for most drinks is also a standard item in the "oyaji pose," a condescending depiction of the overworked salaryman standing dejectedly on the station platform while he awaits another gruelingly long commute (http://www.japantimes.co.jp/community/2005/12/06/issues/genki-drinks-riding-high/#.UffXDeDPXao). Many alcoholics also spoke about these "genki" (energy) drinks during meetings as necessary tools when facing a work day while suffering from a hangover.

7. His exact words were『キリスト教臭い』(*kirisuto-kyō kusai*).

8. The terms *reiki* (霊的) and spiritual (スピリチュアル) were interchanged deliberately by Toru and other members, as they feel it emphasizes AA's inclusiveness and the possibility for interpreting spirituality in ways that potential members find meaningful.

Chapter Four

Sober Groupings

AA's foundational story, Bill Wilson and Bob Smith meeting in the spring of 1935 discussed in the previous chapter, is a redemptive tale of friendship between two men awash in personal struggle and despair. As such, it is an account meant to signal to men considering AA the possibility of finding, without alcohol, continued comfort and support in meaningful male friendships. AA's legitimacy as a recovery organization is drawn from this initial meeting and the depth of emotional ties that subsequently developed between the two men, as it establishes a framework for confronting the staggering power addiction can wield over the individual. Thus, the message made deliberately explicit in AA's founding mythology is that men are not alone in their struggle, and with sobriety they will not lose the intimacy and camaraderie once found in drinking together. In doing so, AA and Danshūkai frame finding solace and success in sobriety as a redemptive process that also allows strong bonds between men to persist and grow without alcohol and drinking. However, as this chapter examines, such an outcome is often elusive for many of the men at Tokyo sobriety group meetings.

This chapter looks first at AA and Danshūkai in greater detail, particularly the history of both organizations in Japan. This is followed by a detailed look at the Central Group and Ohashi Danshūkai, the meetings where I did the majority of fieldwork. Attention is given to highlighting how both meetings strive to create an environment conducive to recovery and mindful of AA or Danshūkai dictates concerning how members can best live in recovery, while also encountering resistance or dismissal of these efforts from many in Japan outside the organizational structures. The chapter ends by looking more at how many men at AA and Danshūkai find admissions of alcoholism personally problematic and as a result go to great lengths to hide their group membership from others. The result is a delicate balance many sober Japanese men negotiate between guarded and cautious conduct outside meetings and encouraged openness and blunt honesty at group proceedings.

AA AND DANSHŪKAI

AA grew slowly after its founding in the United States, spreading around the American northeast largely through word-of-mouth conversations by those who met Bill W. or Dr. Bob. Yet steady growth over several years also necessitated some formalization of the organization's principles and practices. The result was the publication of the Big Book (officially titled *Alcoholics Anonymous*) in 1939, which for the first time clearly outlined the Twelve Steps and other organizational principles. AA's continued growth in the decades to follow lead to publication of the Twelve Traditions in 1946 and, in 1955, AA entered the American mainstream with a well-attended conference in St. Louis that drew extensive national newspaper coverage, followed by greater international expansion in the following years and decades. By 2012, AA estimated its total membership at slightly more than two million individuals worldwide, including more than 1.2 million members in the United States, and notable recent growth in Brazil, Mexico, and throughout Native American communities (Jarrad 1995, Mitchell 2004, Prussing 2011).[1]

As chapter 2 discussed, the chaos and destruction of World War II largely obliterated Japan's temperance movement and its strong ties to the YWCA and other groups with ties to organizations in the United States advocating for prohibition, as well as Danshūkai's early efforts to help individuals concerned about their drinking. Yet despite the interruption of war, Japanese concern and attention to alcoholism was not absent. Geshi Hospital in Kōchi, Shikoku, a significant city in Danshūkai's postwar reemergence, maintained facilities for treating alcoholism throughout the war and helped to quickly resurrect the organization after 1945. The hospital's founder, Dr. Takamaro Geshi, quietly opposed the war, going so far as to sign his medical school yearbook at the peak of Japan's militarism with the inscription "liberty and equality," written in French so as to minimize suspicion, and saw it as his moral duty to immediately resume alcohol-specific treatment at the end of the war. Renewed concern for those questioning their alcohol use brought the remaining Japan Temperance Union members and early Danshūkai supporters, many of them concentrated in Tokyo and Kōchi, to American AA literature and group methodology in the 1940s and early 1950s (Smith 1998). As nationwide stability returned to Japan, an array of sobriety organizations were established, starting with Danshūtomonokai (Sobriety Friendship Association) in Kōchi in September 1953. This was followed by Danshūshinseikai (Sobriety New Life Association) in Tokyo in December 1957 (Chenhall and

Oka 2006–2007). National lecture tours in the fall of 1958 by Danshūshinseikai members brought the Tokyo-based organization to Kōchi, an area well known for heavy alcohol consumption among local men as well as a growing and vocal sobriety movement.

It was during this lecture tour that Harushige Matsumura, a Kōchi resident who would become Danshūkai's national founding figure, was introduced to the Danshūshinseikai leaders. Under Harushige Matsumura's leadership Tokyo and Kōchi Danshūkai groups, along with the JTU, continued to study AA's methods and found what they determined to be significant differences in the thought, culture, and religious positions put forward by AA that were thwarting the organization's success in Japan. In their view, American AA's lack of an organizational hierarchy, as well as its strict adherence to anonymity and reliance on a donation system for financial stability were, in the context of Japan, "fatal flaws." In order to create a "more Japanese" sobriety association these components of AA were dropped and the process of forming a national Danshūkai structure accelerated. On November 10, 1963, Harushige Matsumura helped convene a large "formation conference" in Kōchi where a resolution on the "national relief for victims of alcohol" was passed, launching the Zendanren (National Association) and beginning Danshūkai's push to form a nationwide sobriety organization. Following this conference the Zendanren expanded across Japan, establishing new Danshūkai groups or working to integrate existing meetings into the national structure.[2]

AA officially began in Japan roughly a decade after Danshūkai's formation as a national organization, in March 1975 at Kamata Catholic Church near Tokyo's Haneda Airport. This location is significant, as Kamata Church has a long history of support and endorsement for groups and work advocating social justice, particularly among the city's underrepresented and impoverished, a history that made it amenable to hosting a foreign organization devoted to helping those in Japan perceived as outside the margins of social acceptability. This was further confirmed by AA's roots in a Christian edict of assisting the poor, evident in early organizational attention to helping Japan's homeless and socially marginal. From Kamata Church AA next expanded to San'ya, the area of Tokyo around Minami Senju Station east of Ueno long associated with poverty, day laboring, and homelessness. While these laudable efforts are rooted in AA's mission of inclusive ministry to those in need, it also deepened perceptions of the organization as foreign, Christian, and operating at the edges of societal appropriateness (Fowler 1996, Gill 2001, Oyama 2005).

AA's expansion in Japan since 1975 has been gradual, with a recent member survey putting total membership at between 5,000–7,000 individuals nationally (2011). The majority of members are also concentrated in urban areas, particularly around Tokyo and Ōsaka.[3] While AA's membership is more gender balanced than Danshūkai, a point returned to later, approximately seventy percent of survey responders were male and the content of meeting speeches is influenced by this disparity. AA meetings are available in all of Japan's forty-seven prefectures but rural areas often have only one weekly meeting. In contrast, multiple meetings are held every day in Tokyo, most scheduled for the evening hours immediately after work when the temptation to drink is highest. Finally, AA relies entirely on donations for financial support, collected by passing a hat during meetings, as well as any revenue generated from the sale of printed material.[4] Reliance on member donations is also an unassailable position for AA, as taking funds from government agencies or other philanthropic groups is understood as an unacceptable compromise of organizational autonomy.

At nearly 10,000 Zendanren-affiliated members across Japan, as well as numerous independent meetings that further increase this number, Danshūkai is the significantly larger of the two major sobriety groups (Oka and Hayashi 2010). However, this number demands explanation as the family members of alcoholics also frequently participate in meetings, and while haphazardly included in official tallies, their presence swells Danshūkai's membership rolls in ways impossible at AA.[5] Additionally, while Danshūkai advocates for family member meeting participation in terms that are gender neutral, in practice it is almost always male alcoholics accompanied to meetings by their non-alcoholic wives or mothers. Like AA, Danshūkai meetings occur in all of Japan's prefectures, with again a far greater concentration in urban areas. While meetings of both organizations are open to anyone, Danshūkai meeting participants are typically more predictable than AA, with a core group of members dutifully attending their regular weekly meeting. While AA meetings also has a core group of consistently present members, fluctuations in new or one-off individuals joining the meeting is far greater than I observed at Danshūkai. Finally, Danshūkai collects member dues in the form of a nominal fee from all attendees, generally ¥100 per meeting, as well as some government funding to sustain itself financially.

The last major point to consider is the influential role doctors and hospitalization play in shaping the general structure of Japanese AA and Danshūkai membership. Nearly all of Japan's sobriety group members join either AA or Danshūkai following hospitalization in a typical three month inpatient recovery program, often at a hospital that specializes in treating alcohol-related problems. The attending physicians at these programs also play a major role in determining which organization a patient will potentially join. As noted earlier, several physicians said they direct married men into Danshūkai while single or divorced men and women were typically steered towards AA. This is done because of Danshūkai's position that family member meeting participation is essential to maintaining sobriety, a practice that, in the view of numerous female Japanese AA members, fails to adequately welcome women and unmarried or divorced alcoholics into Danshūkai. As Aki remarked one afternoon at the JSO, "they [Danshūkai] are old-fashioned, and I always felt uncomfortable at their meetings." She, and many other women at AA, feel Danshūkai is stubbornly conservative in its treatment of women and Japan's changing attitude towards gender roles, a potentially detrimental tendency they link to the organization's declining membership numbers (Oka and Hayashi 2010). The result is AA as the de facto group for Japanese women and any men who are unmarried or had their marriage destroyed due to their alcoholism. The persistent rigidity of this arrangement, and its assumptions of middle class normalcy are returned to later as they constitute a major point of division between AA and Danshūkai.

CENTRAL GROUP

As noted in chapter 1, I worked with three weekly meetings, the Central Group—an AA meeting that gathered in the heart of Tokyo, Ohashi Danshūkai—named for the *ohashi*, or "big bridge" near the meeting site in the city's western suburbs, and the beginners AA meeting at Nerima Hospital, part of a specialized program for treating alcohol-related issues discussed in earlier chapters. The Central Group meets every Wednesday evening in a room attached to a Catholic church near the convergence of several train and subway stations in the middle of Tokyo. The rectangular meeting room comfortably holds the thirty adults who typically attend the meeting each week. Arranged before each meeting on tables against one of the room's shorter walls are AA pamphlets, announcements and informational fliers, and a hot water pot with instant coffee, cups, spoons, and other accessories. In the center of the room several long tables are arranged end-to-end with enough stools to accommodate about half the attendees. More stools line the walls and regular meeting goers often have an area of the room they favor and flock to each week. Finally, on the wall above the coffee and fliers is a large whiteboard where each week the group's name, the meeting's theme, and the words "welcome home!" (*okaerinasai!*) are written.

Attendees are divided into two groups, the core members who designate this meeting as their "home group," and the "guests," AA members who do not regularly come to this particular meeting, although some might attend nearly every week. Attendance is typically split nearly evenly between home group and guest members, and during meetings the distinction is impossible to discern. Yoshi, Gen, and Yuka, all in their forties and fifties and sober several years, are some of the Central Group home group members who also voluntarily take on the administrative duties necessary for maintaining a smoothly functioning meeting. Gen is middle aged, slight in stature, and prone to cleaning his glasses while speaking. He is employed as an accountant and as such handles the group's finances, collecting, tallying, and then depositing the weekly donations into the organization's account at a nearby bank after each meeting. Yoshi, a tall, skinny man in his fifties, is well-known in AA throughout Tokyo for his volunteer work with MAC, a San'ya based organization dedicated to helping impoverished alcoholic men after they are released from hospital. He also helped start the Central Group meeting and frequently acts as a meeting moderator when a volunteer is not forthcoming. Yuka, a woman in her early forties and always immaculately dressed in designer clothes, a holdover from her past office employment with a major Japanese corporation, has been a Central Group member for several years and like Yoshi often serves as meeting moderator on weeks when a volunteer is not forthcoming. Years of chronic drunkenness caused Yuka to lose her job and she now lives austerely on savings and monthly welfare payments linked to her being diagnosed as alcohol dependent. She rarely misses a meeting and often speaks forthrightly about her ongoing struggles with the temptations of addiction.

Most attendees, whether they are home group members or guests, know each other to one degree or another, having typically spent many hours together in meetings across Tokyo. Central Group meetings are also bookended by conversations, often just outside the door along the covered walkway where smoking is allowed, between acquaintances and friends catching up on the events of each other's lives. Beyond simple pleasantries, these exchanges are important indicators of how extended sobriety shifts Japanese social networks, as those at the Central Group draw heavily upon other AA members for friendship, or even just a dose of human contact. Finally, as a conveniently located meeting held in a large room, the Central Group also frequently plays host to "birthday meetings" for its own members as well as those from other AA groups. These usually occur about once a month and a cake is brought to these meetings, candles lit, the lights turned off, and happy birthday sung in accented English to those marking various sobriety milestones, measured either in weeks and months for new members or years for "old timers." In the weeks prior to these meetings, birthday cards circulate for each recognized individual across numerous meetings, often until the card is filled with inspirational messages from dozens of other alcoholics.

Central Group meetings are structured around a theme, with "one day at a time" (a popular AA slogan), thanks/gratitude (*kansha*), acceptance (*shinju*), companions (*nakama*), and perseverance (*gambaru*) being popular choices. The evening's volunteer moderator is also the first speaker and generally addresses why they selected that particular theme before weaving a personal narrative around it for several minutes. Once finished they ask for a volunteer to speak next and if one is not immediately forthcoming typically ask the person seated to either their left or right to speak. Everyone is given an opportunity to talk during the hour and a half meeting, with the option to pass should they not feel like saying anything. Time is expertly managed by everyone, with individuals adjusting how much or little they say to ensure each attendee has at least a minute or two to speak. The depth of shared information also varies markedly between members and even individually across the weeks. Some attendees will say little more than a few set phrases for several weeks—"with everyone's help I will do my best to continue to not drink"—before then speaking for several minutes on a deeply moving memory if a particular theme or set of events so inspires them.

The popularity of "one day at a time" as a meeting theme—nearly half of the Central Group meetings I attended used this theme—derives from the flexibility it affords speakers to talk about any aspect of their alcoholism. The flexibility of "one day at a time" derives from how it allows speakers to talk about everything from the mundane steps taken that day to avoid drinking prior to the meeting, to ongoing inner turmoil surrounding their acceptance of being labeled an alcoholic. Yet any of the themes are also loosely interpreted or ignored altogether if a particular speaker has a pressing issue they want to talk about that does not fit the posted theme. The "theme meeting" format is used to lend minimal organizational structure without infringing on the purpose of the proceedings, which are always to help others maintain their sobriety and remind them that they are not alone and there are others who share in their struggles—a purpose reflected in the efforts of group members to create a space where alcoholism, addiction, and the myriad auxiliary concerns and struggles facing group members can be aired without fear of judgment or criticism. Put simply, "talk therapy" allows group members to vocalize their own struggles and hear how others have faced similar difficulties. Meetings are thus an attempt to find meaning in the chaos that characterized their years of alcohol consumption, helping them maintain individually crafted distinctions between members' former drunk selves and their current sobriety. In anthropological terms the meeting is ritualistic and ceremonial, a space bounded by prescribed rules of conduct and comportment, allowing members to reinterpret their memories and past experiences in meaningful and productive ways conducive to a life now lived in recovery.

Central Group meetings are consistently organized and well-run by the evening's selected moderator, a reputation Yoshi and the other home group members are reticently proud of. Such organizational competence is due in part to AA's Twelve Traditions, a set of guidelines to meeting and organizational procedures all members are introduced to soon after joining AA. Yet this organizational proficiency also makes transgressions of the expertly managed space all the more evident, while mechanisms for challenging or correcting such breaches of etiquette are often poorly defined and themselves a violation of AA Traditions. Meetings are set up as a space free from the judgment and derision that can come from non-alcoholics. As such, open and direct critique of what is said during meetings is prohibited, under the assumption that all members should and will allow for equal participation from everyone assembled at a given meeting.

A guest attendee made the challenge of such an organizational structure clear during a well-attended meeting in early spring. Seemingly unknown to everyone else, he sat at the far end of the table and fidgeted constantly, checking his phone, muttering under his breath, and shifting in his chair, during the minutes leading up to the meeting's start. He quickly volunteered to speak after Yuka, the evening's first speaker and moderator, had finished. He then proceeded to speak for more than thirty unbroken minutes, leaving far too little time for everyone else to have a turn speaking that evening. His speech veered from initially his alcoholism to frustrations and lingering anger with his now ex-wife, disgust for the fashion and mannerisms of Japan's youth, and finally his views on the existence of extraterrestrial life. As everyone else at the meeting became increasingly frustrated with his monopolization of time, he remained oblivious to their nonverbal and increasingly overt hints. At one point nearly half of the meeting attendees had left the room to smoke and many glared angrily at him through the windows from the walkway outside. Finally, Yuka interjected with a stern *nakama!* (companion!) that stopped his speech. She quickly reprimanded him, saying everyone needed an opportunity to speak, and he had left them with very little time. He muttered an apology but sat fuming with anger for the remainder of the meeting, continuing to grumble under his breath after nearly every speaker. When the meeting ended he jumped from his seat and stormed onto the walkway outside, only to then stop, rapidly smoke several cigarettes, and insert himself into any nearby conversation. After speaking for several minutes he abruptly turned and left, breaking off what he was saying in mid-sentence to walk away, and never returned to a Central Group meeting during my time with the group.

The importance of his maddening monologue lies in everyone else's frustration and Yuka's eventual interruption. AA prohibits "crosstalk," offering commentary or judgment on what someone says in a meeting or challenging their opportunity to speak, and while this attendee showed no interest in allowing others to participate in the meeting, Yuka's actions were in a strictly technical sense a violation of the Twelve Traditions. More importantly, the incident is reflective of the marginal space Japan's sobriety group members occupy. Outside the meeting structure, group members have limited networks of support or consultation they can turn to when confronted with a member unable or unwilling to follow the rules of decorum. Dr. Mori's beginners meeting discussed in the previous chapter is innovative in part because it welcomes patients dually diagnosed with alcoholism and mental illness, including depression, anxiety, and schizophrenia. Yet her program is one of only a few that exists in Japan, and instead the burden for care concerning mental illness, or even a simple absence of attention and care to comportment norms, is often shifted to sobriety groups ill-equipped and trained to meet such demands. The consequences of this situation are two-fold, a perpetuation of stigma that surrounds Japan's popular conflation of alcoholism and addiction with various mental illnesses, alongside the marginality and perceptions of abnormality felt by many sobriety group members, limited their ability to assert a robust and prominent recovery community.

Related to such feelings of exclusion is discussion in Japan of the "meeting after the meeting," particularly how it is a major component of AA membership in the United States. The meeting after the meeting refers to gatherings, typically immediately after the formal meeting, when formality gives way to friendly exchange, likely at a nearby coffee shop or restaurant. Members can share advice and companionship with other alcoholics facing similar struggles, as well as more practical insights, how to live on a budget or get an apartment that many find difficult. As Eric, an American AA member living in Tokyo noted, such gatherings are when and where members learn the practical aspects of living life sober, often for the first time despite many being in their forties and fifties. While meeting attendance is understood as fundamentally important, learning to live outside the safe space of meetings without alcohol, being able to go into a restaurant and not order a drink, is something that many must also learn to do. Eric was also quick to point out how the meeting after the meeting remains underdeveloped among Japan's AA members. As Central Group meetings adjourned members would gather outside to smoke cigarettes and chat for several minutes. Yet once everything was in order and the room door locked, everyone began to quickly disperse to the numerous nearby stations or bus stops for their commute home. This pattern of departure from the meeting makes evident the demarcation between the sanctuary the meeting space affords members and the difficulties and uncertainties of life beyond its walls once everything is concluded for the week.

OHASHI DANSHŪKAI

Ohashi Danshūkai meets every Friday in a large, high-ceilinged, room on the second floor of a multipurpose building that is part of the city offices for one of western Tokyo's expansive suburbs. The Chūō train line, the nearest major link to the rail network, is a fifteen minute bus ride from the meeting site, making it an unusually isolated location despite the proximity to Shinjuku and several other busy urban centers. The room has been the group's home for many years, the same two hour block of time in the evening reserved for so long that their square on the whiteboard of events at the building's entrance still gleams like new while all those around it show the eraser marks of age. Arranged each week inside the room is an inner ring of folding tables and chairs, bounded on three sides by a second ring and finally a row of chairs along the walls of the room. In total there is ample room for the sixty to eighty attendees that typically fill each meeting. Members start to arrive about thirty minutes before the meeting begins and the group leaders, three or four long sober men, sit with their backs to the door, monitoring the sign-in sheet and taking everyone's ¥100 participation fee. Like Central Group meetings, fliers and other Danshūkai announcements are also available to take from the front table. The meeting is called to order promptly at 6:30 pm with a *mokosō* (meditation), thirty seconds of silent reflection as a group that clearly demarcates the sometimes somber tone of the meeting from the jovial conversations between friends that preceded it.

The meeting sign-in sheet also functions as a record of attendance, giving the evening's leader a reference log of names and group affiliation for all attendees, who he then calls on to speak. Most members are part of Ohashi Danshūkai, attending the meeting every week except in unusual circumstances, and a familiarity and intimacy achieved over the years spent together pervades the room. Guests from other Danshūkai groups are also welcome and several generally attend each week from various groups across Tokyo and sometimes farther afield. Unusually, Ohashi Danshūkai is independent, not affiliated with the Zendanren, Danshūkai's national organization. In practical terms this means Ohashi Danshūkai does not contribute financially to the larger organizational structure and makes little use of the paraphernalia that typically adorns the meeting rooms of Zendanren linked groups. These include cloth banners displaying Danshūkai's Oath, as well as flags with the Zendanren insignia and a large picture of Harushige Matsumura, common at other Danshūkai meetings but not displayed by Ohashi Danshūkai. While these visible differences are significant, and returned to in a moment, members from both sides move back and forth between Ohashi Danshūkai and Zendanren affiliated meetings without trouble or concern, ultimately viewing themselves as sharing an organizational allegiance.

Ohashi Danshūkai is led by Nakamura, a gruff yet caring man originally from Kyūshū and now in his late sixties. Nakamura is fond of wearing baseball caps and sunglasses to meetings regardless of the season, and as a young man was a *chinpira*, a low level gangster with aspirations to one day join the Yakuza. In Kyūshū he made *kasutori* (moonshine), drank heavily from the age of 15, worked as a "contractor" at Yakuza controlled construction sites, and was in his retrospective view on his way to an early death.[6] His family left Kyūshū for Tokyo in the 1960s and asked him to join them whenever they spoke. Unhappy with his drinking and life at the legal margins, and sensing that a complete break from his surroundings was the only way he could change, Nakamura finally moved to Tokyo in the late 1970s, quit drinking through nothing but force of will, and established Ohashi Danshūkai. Since then he has been the unquestioned patriarch and group leader, sitting commandingly at the first table during every meeting and always called upon to speak last. His meeting speeches are typically short and fatherly in tone, sometimes chastising everyone if he feels attendance has recently slacked, or lauding if he found the content of that evening's meeting impressive, but his is always the final word that brings each meeting to a close.

Unlike AA and the Central Group where the order of speakers varies each week and is of little consequence to the meeting proceedings, Ohashi Danshūkai inscribes hierarchy and procedure into the ordering of speakers. Older members, both in terms of age and length of time with the group, are called upon first as many of them no longer attend meetings with their spouse and typically offer only a set phrase or two when speaking—"I pledge to continue giving my best effort to stay sober!"—or diverge entirely from their alcoholism and briefly discuss the weather or how the Giants are playing.[7] Nearly half of attendees speak in this first round that rarely takes longer than thirty minutes. As this section of speakers concludes patients arrive at 7:00 pm from nearby Nakagawa Hospital, a major center for treating alcohol-related issues. The patients, typically around twenty individuals, file into the room and take their seats along one of the walls. The last patient gives a list of names to the meeting's moderator who, once they are settled, begins calling on them individually to speak. Most of the patients say very little; like those at AA beginners meetings they are required to attend the meeting as part of their stay in hospital and are often still struggling with accepting the recent physician's diagnosis of them as alcohol dependent. Many simply stand, thank everyone for allowing them to join the meeting, and pledge to *gambaru*, do their best, to not drink in the days ahead.[8]

Thus, in less than an hour two-thirds of the meeting attendees have taken their turn speaking. Those that remain, alcoholic men attending with their non-alcoholic wives and in a few cases mothers, also constitute the active core of Ohashi Danshūkai's membership as well as the speakers expected to deliver relevant, revealing, and powerful speeches on their struggles with alcoholism. The "family members," meaning nearly all of the women attending the meeting, speak first. As already noted, Danshūkai as an organization does not gender the roles available to members, yet in practice it is overwhelmingly non-alcoholic women who accompany their alcoholic husbands, fathers, and sons to meetings. Additionally, while individual speeches vary tremendously each week, a theme connecting the women at Ohashi Danshūkai is familial happiness, brought on by the removal of alcohol from their husband, father, or son's life, as well as the anxiety many continue to feel at the possibility his sobriety might falter at any moment. For the women of Ohashi Danshūkai then, their speeches typically oscillate between recounting particularly painful memories and expressing concern, sometimes even dread, when they feel the temptation to drink has been high for their alcoholic counterparts.

After the women have finished, the alcoholic men they accompanied to the meeting are called upon to speak in the remaining time, usually about thirty or forty minutes. While not as numerous as the other member blocs, typically around fifteen individuals each week, all of these men generally speak for several minutes each, much longer than the older members or hospital patients earlier in the meeting. Some challenge or respond to what their wife said a few moments earlier, others recall horrific, sometimes graphic, memories of their past drunkenness, citing such episodes as motivation and reason for continued meeting participation and evidence of their alcoholism. Their speeches are often moving, powerful, witty, and personally revealing. Some use humor while others are angry and aggressive. Unlike the non-alcoholic family members who often rhetorically asked why their family must suffer under the burden of alcoholism and addiction, these men rarely try to invoke pity, yet also continue to struggle with the integration of alcoholism, as an important aspect of their identity, into daily life.

Importantly, these men also frequently express longing and nostalgia for a time, likely one that never actually existed, when their drinking and drunkenness was not problematic. These feelings of nostalgia also deviate from the outlined path for living in recovery, as they reveal the absence of interpersonal transformation that should accompany sobriety. Instead of finding happiness without alcohol, many who form the core of Ohashi Danshūkai's male members' *gambaru* through their sobriety. Expression of such sentiment often coincides at Ohashi Danshūkai with the changing of the seasons and major holidays, moments of the year in Japan when drinking is etched into the social calendar, and are thus frequently raised by these men during meetings for the feelings of frustration and struggle they now invoke. *Hanami* (flower viewing parties) in early spring, New Year's, the start of baseball season, and *Obon* festivals in late summer are all now understood as *kiken* (dangerous) moments that overtake large swaths of Japan's public geography and constrict their alcoholic lives. These frustrations and feelings of danger are discussed in detail in the next chapter, as for sober Japanese men they constitute a major structuring element to how living in recovery is experienced.

A primary purpose of Ohashi Danshūkai meetings is maintaining a sense of community among the members. Many of the core members have known each other for years and going to the Friday evening meeting is fully incorporated into their weekly routine. This is also an aspect of the group that differentiates it from the Central Group and in some ways Danshūkai from AA generally in Japan. Many Ohashi Danshūkai members grew up and continue to live in the immediate area around the meeting site and are of similar occupational and socioeconomic standing. While many members regard these tendencies as strengths that have helped maintain the meeting during its now more than thirty year history, they acknowledge that it can also hinder bringing new members into the group. My introduction to the group is reflective of this situation. I came to Ohashi Danshūkai after meeting Alex, another American alcoholic and AA member living in Tokyo. Alex came to Japan in the early 1960s as a non-drinker and thirty years later woke up in a hospital he did not remember being admitted to, having nearly died from severe alcohol poisoning after several days of constant drinking. This moment motivated him to get sober and we first met at an AA meeting he attended. After the meeting we spoke about my research. He invited me to "his Danshūkai group." He first came to Ohashi Danshūkai because it met near his home and he liked its independence from the Zendanren. Other Tokyo alcoholics know of Ohashi Danshūkai through its relationship with Nakagawa Hospital, and while some patients later become group members, it is the exception. Thus, the concern Ohashi Danshūkai members share with many other meetings, both independent and Zendanren-affiliated, is that an aging membership without a sufficiently large next generation of members to fill organizational ranks will undermine the organization's effectiveness. Such a concern also begs the larger question of the sustainability behind an approach to living in recovery that is so strongly community-based.

The familiarity between members at Ohashi Danshūkai meetings also makes transgressions into the space dramatically evident. At a meeting in late January a middle aged man I did not recognize arrived late, bundled in a bulky jacket against the bracing winter cold. He walked unsteadily, pausing at the entrance to the room and looking around, incognizant of his disruptive effect on the meeting, before lurching forward to the sign-in sheet. Once finished writing his name he stood up so quickly he nearly knocked himself backwards before ambling to a nearby open seat. He had entered the meeting, it appeared, drunk, a transgression of protocol so galling it visibly upset everyone. Nakamura unwaveringly glared at the man as he struggled to find his seat with an intensity likely taken from his chinpira youth. The transgressor was quickly called upon and he spoke briefly and generally about how long it had been since he'd seen everyone and how good it was to be back at Ohashi Danshūkai. After a few more general statements he seemed to lose interest in speaking and slumped back into his chair, where he remained for the rest of the meeting, periodically drifting off to sleep and then snapping awake again. At the end of the meeting he left quickly and never returned to a meeting while I was in Tokyo. Like moments of transgression at the Central Group, the importance here is in revealing the fragility of the meeting space, and the agitated disruption an intrusion from the non-sober world can create. Meetings are spaces outside the typical in Japan where alcohol, and any of the conventions or comportment requirements that surround it, are absent and resisted. The presence of drunkenness is thus not only taboo, it is belittling to the assembling members, an intrusion and violation of one of the few areas Japanese alcoholics can wholly claim as their own.

Every Ohashi Danshūkai meeting ends promptly at 8:30 pm with Nakamura's closing words. Once concluded everyone applauds and then springs into action, folding the tables and chairs before returning them, in precise order, to the nearby storage closets. In minutes the once crowded room is empty of furniture, swept, and everyone begins making their way downstairs and outside. Many say goodbye at the front of the building as some make their way to the parking lot, others begin walking home, and the largest contingent heads to the two nearby bus stops. As one of the few who commuted to the meeting by train, I traveled in the opposite direction of most and often only shared the bus partway to the nearby station with patients from Nakagawa Hospital, before they disembarked after a few stops. Our conversations on these rides were friendly but brief and I was always struck by how frequently the patients changed yet how rarely one of them joined the group after being discharged. Within minutes each week all evidence of the meeting is gone until the next Friday, when the cycle is repeated again, as it has been for more than thirty years.

ADMISSION AS PROBLEMATIC

The crucial premise underlying AA or Danshūkai membership and mandating active meeting participation is a transformation of self into a new person happy in their sobriety, the promised outcome of diligently working the recovery program. It is not enough to simply stop consuming alcohol, members must also change how they perceive, identify, and present themselves to others. As Mariana Valverde notes, "the soul of the member . . . is the main object of AA's innovative approach to ethical governance, an approach relying primarily on *self*-governance rather than on advice or exhortation" (1998: 120, italics in original). AA and Danshūkai aim to create a membership of self-governing alcoholics, yet struggle when confronting Japan's established, and not easily dismissed, norms of drinking comportment and masculinity. AA's contention is that self-governing alcoholics result from a circumvention of the physician's diagnostic authority and a transfer of power to the alcoholic, who by weight of experience is the only one capable of understanding, appreciating, and confronting the strength of alcoholism's grip on his psyche—a position also echoed in Danshūkai's recovery principles. As Valverde again notes, "it was AA that came up with the notion that physicians should not have the monopoly on disease . . . it was AA that first succeeded in turning a disease into a full-fledged, lifelong social identity" (1998: 122). Yet in a practice distinguishing Japan from other areas under AA's influence and violating an essential component of group ideology, the authoritative gaze of the physician is not circumvented in Japan (Brandes 2002, Cain 1991, Mitchell 2004).

The result for many of the men in Japan's sobriety groups is alcoholism as both "lifelong social identity" and marginalizing force. Japanese alcoholic men inhabit, borrowing from Kathleen Stewart, a "doubly occupied space," where "culture becomes not a haven of ideas or a fixed state of experience but a social imaginary erupting out of a storied cultural real" (1996: 63–64). The physician, acting as a gatekeeper of alcoholism and guardian of the "social imaginary," diagnoses individuals as "alcohol dependent" and points them in the direction of the sobriety organization they believe most appropriate. Sobriety organizations in turn draw their members from those in hospital, perpetuating a membership that through prolonged treatment has come to accept a medically sanctioned diagnosis of alcoholism, yet often struggles with the concept's limited general acceptance throughout Japan and the inability of AA and Danshūkai to transcend prevailing societal opinion. In short, many group members feel caught in a "vicious circle" (*akujunkan*) where being a successful AA or Danshūkai member and incorporating sobriety ideology into their lives impedes any resumption of a place in "normal" Japanese society as a transformed individual happy in their recovery.

This struggle is captured in the difficulty many group members say they feel with openly identifying as an alcoholic. Gen, the Central Group's unofficial treasurer, spoke often of this anxiety as he said he lived in fear of being asked to go drinking with his boss and co-workers. In the early 2000s Gen lost a steady accounting job due to his chronic drunkenness and inability to perform his job with any semblance of competence. Following his firing, Gen struggled for several years, trying to find sustained sobriety and interpersonal stability while moving between periods of heavy drinking, hospitalization and then sporadic meeting attendance, before a return to drinking. Joining the Central Group finally brought stability and sobriety to Gen's life, and he was several years sober when I began attending meetings in late spring 2007. Around this time he also found a new accounting job that was increasingly becoming a source of anxiety. Gen had not told his new co-workers of his alcoholism or AA membership, and felt that he likely never could, resulting in the need to reject regular invitations to go drinking after work with lies and nonspecifics about being unavailable that night. Gen's persistent deception reached a breaking point later that year when his boss insisted he join everyone the next evening for drinks. Feeling unable to explain why he felt this was impossible, Gen instead never returned to work, eventually being fired for a second time and spending several months in self-imposed isolation at his parents' home outside Tokyo.

Gen returned to the Central Group in January 2008 and while he had maintained his sobriety from alcohol, he feared his growing use of pain medication was turning into another form of addiction. At his first meeting back Gen apologized to everyone for disappearing without warning for several months, adding that he had spent the time as a *hikikomori* (acute social withdrawal) in his parents' home, rarely leaving his childhood bedroom and sleeping most of the day. He only left their home after his fear of relapsing in front of them overwhelmed any reservations concerning a return to Tokyo. And while he had also been able to find another job at a fledgling and poorly regarded accounting firm, the same cycle of declining invitations to drink from his new co-workers had begun anew. His greater fear was that employment below this rung as an accountant, particularly with his now checkered job history, did not exist and should he once again walk away from this job in the future it would, in his view, make him unemployable. Of importance is the way in which Gen's situation illustrates the secrecy with which many men at sobriety groups across Japan carry themselves, a secrecy that derives primarily from concern for how others will interpret or respond to their disclosures of alcoholism. Thus, the label alcoholic makes, in these instances, the individual sobriety group member vulnerable to outside suspicion as someone abnormal, amoral, and deviant.

A December 2007 Central Group meeting neatly demonstrated the pervasive secrecy surrounding Japanese men's admissions of alcoholism. Shinji, a young man and recent AA member in his late twenties, brought Reizo, a friend and guest from another AA group, to that evening's meeting. Reizo had come from work and was well dressed in a stylish business suit. While he stated that he was separated from his wife, he continued to wear his wedding ring, adjusting and playing with it throughout the meeting. When his turn to speak came, Reizo immediately brought up his recent "coming out" to co-workers, friends, and family members after entering AA, using the same term employed by Japanese gays and lesbians when coming out of the closet.[9] He explained that he had recently and explicitly told those he regularly interacted with that he was now an alcoholic, in AA, and this membership meant he could no longer drink any alcohol. Reizo's decision to make this disclosure had been exceedingly difficult, taking weeks for him to gather the requisite courage and still a sensitive topic he spoke about with obvious difficulty. He ended by saying that while his disclosure had been met positively, he remained concerned with how it might impact his relationships, particularly at work, in the coming weeks and months.

Such overt admissions of alcoholism are also far from commonplace in Japan, alluded to in Reizo's use of terminology associated with public declarations of homosexuality, and speak to the difficulties and concerns many in AA and Danshūkai harbor at how a public disclosure of alcoholism will be received by family, friends, and co-workers (McLelland 2000: 197). Reizo was also in the minority, as many in sobriety group members keep their alcoholism a secret from all but their most intimate family and friends, a practice with parallels among Japanese gay men when "selectively" coming out to others (*ibid*). However, it must be emphasized that feelings of secrecy and hesitation among both groups are often rooted in concern at "letting one's friend and family down by failing to conform to society's expectations" (*ibid*). Reizo "outing" himself to co-workers and friends is noteworthy for its rarity among Japanese men, as it represents a break with convention that also highlights the power of cultural expectation to confine and marginalize the many men who feel unable to make such disclosures. While Reizo's disclosure is commendable for the individual courage it demanded, its significance lies in illuminating a frequently unsaid reality of muted social interaction and unrealized life changes among sobriety group members.

An Ohashi Danshūkai meeting in February, immediately after St. Valentine's Day, further illustrates this depth of concern and the extent to which men avoid disclosing their alcoholism outside meetings. Junichi, a salaryman nearing retirement and resigned to his middle management status, said he had been on edge all week avoiding the offered Valentine's Day chocolates from young women in his office as they often contained alcohol. His comment during the meeting of "because it's impossible to say, 'I'm an alcoholic,' I said I had a tooth removed" was received with knowing nods of the head from others in the room. For Gen, Junichi, and many other men at the Central Group and Ohashi Danshūkai, an admission of alcoholism and sobriety group membership remains frequently impossible, as alcohol consumption continues to dictate Japan's cultural definitions of manhood and emasculate sober men.

The consequences of living sober not only weigh heavily upon many Central Group and Ohashi Danshūkai members, it also dictates talk of alcoholism around frequent expressions of unhappiness and frustration mixed with nostalgia and humiliation. Carole Cain notes that a core component of AA's success in North America has been aiding members in "com[ing] to understand why, and how, they are alcoholics" (1991: 244), facilitating a transformation from destructive drinker to sober and recovering alcoholic. Yet AA's vision of alcoholism's why and how struggles to find credibility in Japan, in part because oppositional societal constructions favoring drink and drunkenness remain pervasive and disruptive, leaving few options for individuals confronting addictive behavior. Tokyo's alcoholic community is thus marked as "a world that dwells in the space of the gap, in a logic of negation . . . and perpetual incompletion" (Stewart 1996: 17). In AA and Danshūkai, group members have been given a new "guide" to charting a happy and sober life, yet too often they find the prescribed path in conflict with their daily lived realities.

Additionally, AA and Danshūkai have largely failed to confront the difficulties many Japanese men face when trying to permanently reimagine how they understand themselves, and accepting that they can never drink again. Japanese physicians advocate definitions of successful recovery that mandate lifelong abstinence and label any relapse, even the tiniest sip of alcohol, as a failure requiring the individual to begin their sobriety anew. This recovery protocol consistently divides those finding fulfillment and meaningful interpersonal transformation in AA or Danshūkai from those struggling to accept the group's principal message. In short, required sobriety without comprehensive acknowledgment and change to the societal and cultural perception of alcoholism and addiction throughout Japan does allow some men to get sober and reassert an absent control over their lives, but it does so with the too-frequent sacrifice of their ability to openly identify as alcoholics and an often absent transformation of self.

PERFORMING SOBRIETY

Living sober and in recovery for AA and Danshūkai members means forging and performing a new identity in adulthood by reinterpreting past experiences and memories of individual alcohol use, particularly dramatic or shocking moments of drunkenness. Fear of disclosing one's alcoholism to those outside meetings can also motivate a performance of identity during groups meetings, as a demonstration of competence with organizational conceptualizations of alcoholism and addiction. Returning to Carole Cain's work, she notes that "the self-understandings of the individuals joining AA must come to reflect and incorporate the knowledge organized by the AA system of beliefs; cultural knowledge must become self-knowledge" (1991: 211). For the individuals discussed here, internalizing the belief system of either organization is essential to becoming an AA or Danshūkai member. It is part of a process whereby an individual member comes to see "not only his drinking as alcoholic, but his self as an alcoholic. The disease is a part of one's self" (*ibid*: 214). Acceptance of organizational ideology signals an internalization of group concepts and an aligning of those ideas with new interpretations of self and identity.

Coming to view oneself as an alcoholic is thus a process of layering AA's Twelve Steps or Danshūkai's Oath onto past behavior and transgressions committed while drinking. Demonstrating engagement with this process occurs through meeting speeches which are displays of expertise and familiarity with group history, literature, governing principles, the disease model of alcoholism and addiction, and how all of these now explain and structure individual memories of consumption. As such, it is a system of incorporating the language of AA or Danshūkai into one's sense of identity, and thereby coming to reinforce that understanding of alcoholism as the only viable interpretation of a successful recovery (Carr 2011). Experienced group members speak about their past through the language of AA and Danshūkai, most frequently seen when invoking admission, belief, and surrender—the major principles of the first three steps, and how they are now governing life principles. Through such acts members demonstrate their investment in sobriety group participation and the depth of their transformation from destructive drinker to sober and recovering alcoholic.

However, such a transformative process also manifests in frustrations that are voiced alongside members' use of sobriety group language, resulting in a fragile yet consequential performance. For Japanese members, a reinterpretation of past drunkenness now viewed in hindsight through the lens of sobriety group ideology becomes possible by sharing personal stories during meetings—personal stories that are now colored as alcoholic, differentiating them from the actions and decisions a non-alcoholic would have taken and creating a shared pool of experience upon which others in the meeting can draw. This process allows members to connect personal experience to a collective "social memory" of alcoholism, yet offers little recourse to disseminate such discourse beyond the confines of the meeting (Antze and Lambek 1996: xx). Finally, it is a process that does nothing to stem the uncertainty and secrecy many Tokyo AA and Danshūkai members feel when the meeting adjourns and they rejoin a city and nation flush with alcohol and largely indulgent of its consumption.

A Central Group meeting in late November neatly illustrates the power of social memory among group members. About twenty minutes into the meeting an older man arrived, noticeably underdressed for the winter cold, and stood outside of the windows glancing cautiously into the meeting room. Shortly after his arrival another late arriving member walked past and they talked briefly before the member opened the door and quietly called Yoshi to join them outside. The three talked and smoked cigarettes outside for a few minutes before Yoshi rejoined the meeting. He waited for the speaker to finish and then announced that the older man was a lapsed member and, it appeared, had been drinking before coming to tonight's meeting. Yoshi wanted to ask if there were any objections to his presence before inviting him in to warm up against the cold. There were none and the older man spent the rest of the meeting sitting quietly, hunched so low only the top of his head was visible, against the far wall of the meeting room. Those sitting to his left and right comforted him throughout the meeting with a constantly refilled coffee mug and pats on the back.

The older man was a living example for many that evening of sobriety's fragility and the inescapable temptation that structures an alcoholic's life in Tokyo. Motivated in part by his presence, the evening's original theme, one day at a time, was quickly ignored in favor of speeches that throughout the meeting build upon a shared social memory of loss and destruction to emphasize how fragile and easily lost sobriety is for many members. One man spoke of his loss of control over his bowels, experienced as a result of decades of heavy alcohol consumption. His condition became so grave in the weeks immediately before getting sober that he could not leave the house for long periods of time, and soiled himself once during a quick trip to the corner convenience store for more beer and sake. As he finished speaking he quietly added, "the day we crash comes eventually," an apt metaphor given the presence of a lapsed former member. Thus, the reinterpretation in Japan of past drinking experiences are manifest in frequent invocation of language depicting sobriety as inherently fragile, frustrations with the wider perception of alcoholism among the Japanese public, cautious questioning of the disease model of alcoholism, and the considerable effort undertaken to conceal one's alcoholism and sobriety group membership from others. In the end, frequent challenge of an individual's alcoholism by those around them leads many to hide this major aspect of their daily life, resulting in conflicted performances of sobriety during meeting that frustrate while also enabling members to continue living in recovery.

"Hitting bottom," reaching one's absolute lowest point of despair and drunkenness, is understood as a necessary condition in AA and Danshūkai before an individual can begin to hear and appreciate the group's message of recovery. Importantly, this structuring of recovery allows AA and Danshūkai to displace any responsibility for their recovery program failing someone, as it was not the organization's shortcomings but the individual. In AA parlance they were not yet able to "hear the message," an important critique returned to in the upcoming chapters. As already noted, hitting bottom in Japan is most often experienced as an impossible to ignore physical breakdown, shaking hands, organ failure, inability to control one's bladder or bowels, or an alcohol-induced coma being frequently raised examples. The presence of such an affliction or moment enables individuals to receive a diagnosis as an alcoholic that also bring accompanying challenges to their understandings of masculinity. "The loss of work identity, social roles, and the sense of isolation that can accompany the physical and mental effects of serious illness can present significant challenges to men, resulting in a 'loss of self'" (O'Brien et al. 2007: 179). A consequence then of the medicalization of alcoholism in Japan, to the point that men frequently feel emasculated for seeking treatment, is how it motivates many to hide and endure their sobriety instead of embracing group membership.

The next chapter examine alcoholism and the self in greater detail, particularly the frequent use of disparaging language and phrases when speaking about alcoholism as an emergent and conflicting aspect of identity. Language used by members, especially men, that mentions the "moral failings" they feel as a result of being alcoholics is particularly prevalent in Tokyo AA and Danshūkai meetings. The consequences of this language use, made all the more significant in a setting many feel is the only outlet and options to pursuing recovery and sobriety, are explored in detail. Finally the chapter considers national and institutionalized victimization in an attempt to further clarify "why me?" questions—"why must my family suffer?"—consistently and rhetorically raised by individual members during meetings.

NOTES

1. See http://www.aa.org/en_pdfs/smf-53_en.pdf for AA collected data on membership numbers, distribution, and growth.

2. Danshūkai's website gives its own historical account of the organization's founding and expansion (http://www.dansyu-renmei.or.jp /). Additionally, Richard Chenhall and Tomofumi Oka have written extensively on Danshūkai's history (Chenhall and Oka 2006, Chenhall and Oka 2014, as well as this informative pamphlet http://miya.cc.sophia.ac.jp/oka/papers/2011/newlife05.pdf are a good selections of their writings).

3. Kyūshū/Okinawa, counted together in AA's membership survey, also have a large number of AA members disproportionate to their share of Japan's population. This is perhaps due to the presence of several American military bases, numerous military personnel, and several English language meetings across the two regions.

4. The AA office in Tokyo was quick to note that American AA typically gives the Big Book and other printed materials away for free. While they would like to do the same it is not feasible with Japan's high printing costs and the organization's scant financial resources, as the sale of books and other material goes to cover such expenses. As such, book sales also generate little income for the organization.

5. In the United States Al-Anon/Alateen are the outlet for family and friends impacted by the drinking and alcoholism of others. As already noted, Al-Anon/Alateen have a minimal presence in Japan. This can also result in non-alcoholic family members participating in Japanese AA meetings, often when the alcoholic in their life does not accept such a diagnosis and continues to consume.

6. He said "contractor" at our first meeting with an emphasis I only later understood. It meant he stood around construction sites, looked tough, and made himself available should those higher up the organized crime ladder need him.

7. Giants are the Tokyo Yomiuri Giants, by far Japan's most popular baseball team and a particular favorite for many Ohashi Danshūkai members.

8. *Gambaru*, typically translated as "endure," here implies that they will earnestly strive to do their best at staying sober. Its use is noteworthy as it is an easily relied upon set phrase many members invoke during meetings, as well as a powerful cultural ideal of total commitment and effort to a given task.

9. The phrase "coming out" is written and spoken using katakana, the Japanese alphabet reserved for foreign loan words, as *kamingu auto* (カミング・アウト).

Chapter Five

Moral Failures

A popular description of addiction frames the condition as a "disease of the will" that commandeers an individual's ability to control or regulate their substance use (Carr 2011, Valverde 1998: 23). Yet, interestingly, addicts entering recovery programs are asked to begin a process of reinterpreting past life events in order to recast themselves as sober individuals and learn to understand their past actions as those of a sick individual who lacked control. Recovery becomes a "matter of coming to terms with, or *discovering*, one's true inner self that is purportedly denied in active addiction" (Carr 2011: 92, italics in original). Speaking about drunken experiences through the language of sobriety group ideology is offered to new members as the means to finding salvation and beginning a renewed life lived happily "in recovery." Thus, alcoholism within the context of recovery and the sobriety group is not so much a disease of the will as it is a process of self-reflection and discovery, reliant on a model of addiction as a chronic and incurable disease where individuals are unable to control their desire for consumption. Further, it is a process "invented under historically and culturally specific conditions, promulgated by particular actors and institutions, and internalized and reproduced by means of certain discursive practices" (Reinarman 2005: 308). In short, being an alcoholic means residing within a confusing mix of beliefs and practices drawn from divergent medical and psychological motivations that manifests in culturally specific ways. Of consequence then for Japanese sobriety group members are the ways in which these practices promulgate around a narrow range of treatment options.

Along these lines, AA and Danshūkai work to give members throughout Tokyo and across Japan a new descriptive vocabulary, with the expectation that it will enable them to reject offers to drink, find happiness, and manage lingering desires for alcohol. But the adoption of this new vocabulary is predicated on acceptance of numerous and often fundamentally new principles and reinterpretations of past memories. These include an individual's history of drinking now deemed personally destructive, the presence of humiliating or gravely felt memories that must now be dissected and rectified anew, as well as acceptance of governing sobriety group principles, most notably spiritual salvation and belief in God, as you understand Him, or at the very least some form of a "Higher Power."

As such, AA and Danshūkai are striving to create in Japan a membership of self-governing alcoholics, yet struggle when confronted with established, and not easily dismissed, norms of consumption, drunken comportment, and masculinity. AA's contention is that happy, sober, and self-governing alcoholics result from a circumvention of the physician's diagnostic authority and a transfer of power to the alcoholic, who by weight of experience is the only one capable of understanding, appreciating, and confronting the strength of alcoholism's grip on their psyche. Lost in such an approach are the struggles felt by many Japanese men as they begin to navigate sobriety, on top of the complex layering of gendered consumption expectations, alcohol comportment norms, and Japan's popular renderings of the alcoholic. Thus, while physicians lend authoritative heft to sobriety group methodology through hospitalization programs, they also often stumble in accounting for the complicated engagement required of Japanese men as they wrestle with accepting sobriety, changing masculine expectations, and group institutional tenets. These circulating forces in turn foster an environment inside meetings where failures and frustration become the convention through which many group members discuss and live their alcoholism. Meeting speeches and reinterpretations of past memories at the Central Group and Ohashi Danshūkai are filled with language and statements concerning who individual group members have become with sobriety and how the impact of their alcoholism on others continues to ripple outward. The focus then of this chapter is looking at how members at both meetings speak about their alcoholism, as these admissions offer insight into the sometimes diverging relationship in Japan between sobriety group renderings of a success recovery and individual lived experience—individual admissions and struggles with recovery ideology that, in my view, demonstrate the need to reconsider how alcoholism and addiction are diagnosed, treated, and lived as meaningful categories of identity.

For AA and Danshūkai members in Tokyo and across Japan, becoming conversant and comfortable with a new descriptive vocabulary of self, which makes significant assumptions about the stability and cohesiveness of individual member's worldview, situation, and relationship with spirituality, is a major part of joining either group. Members must be comfortable and accepting of a recovery model mandating surrender to a supernatural power beyond themselves and accept this power's ability to bring about meaningful interpersonal change. An inability or unwillingness to embrace this view as a major component of self-identity clashes with much of the sobriety group program, complicated further in Japan by the dearth of alternative options for confronting problem drinking. Additionally, addiction as a diagnostic process relies on faith, intuition, and feeling—both of the attending physician and patient—alongside standardized assessment models and instruments to determine who is abusing, dependent upon, or addicted to alcohol and other psychoactive substances. Ethnographically, what rises to the surface throughout these practices are the ever shifting understandings of addiction, alongside established recovery methodologies for living in recovery that confront Japan's entrenched popular ideas of alcoholism and drunkenness. The result is a slippery confluence of opinions and conceptions whirling around the individual group member's quest for interpersonal stability after typically years, if not decades, of anguish and destruction brought on by alcohol consumption.

FAILED FATHERS, HUSBANDS, AND SONS

As noted earlier, the bulk of Japan's sobriety group members are men, more than seventy percent according to AA's member survey and likely almost ninety percent in Danshūkai. This organizational gendering has two immediate consequences: it has largely failed to give alcoholic Japanese women a voice and outlet for their struggles—itself a topic worthy of greater attention yet beyond the scope of this book—and it has made the difficulties facing male alcoholics *the* major concern among those suffering from alcoholism. Simply put, the concerns of alcoholic men constitute the bulk of sobriety group meeting content across Japan. The irony of course is that while alcoholism as experienced through sobriety group membership is largely undertaken by men, it is also regarded by many within the groups as an emasculating process that also simultaneously limits the voice of Japanese women and their alcoholic struggles.

This gendering comes prominently to the fore at Ohashi Danshūkai where the gender neutral format of non-alcoholic family member meeting participation alongside individual alcoholic partners often turns into a back and forth between now sober men and long suffering women. Tatsu, a slight, now retired man in his late sixties, was emblematic of such a gendering process when he stood to speak at a meeting in early summer. Generally concise in his speeches that typically made heavy use of set phrases that revolved around a continued vigilance regarding his sobriety, tonight Tatsu took a different approach. He spoke at length about his children, asking rhetorically what kind of future they could possibly have or expect after being so poorly raised by a chronically drunk father. His speech was motivated by recently witnessing his daughter's inability to "properly" fold and store the family's *futon*, a task that generally falls to women. As he saw it, he had failed his family as a father because of his drinking, raising children now incapable of living "normally," just as he was unable to do for so many years because of his drinking. Tatsu's attributes his alcoholism to being unable to drink normally, meaning getting drunk regularly with other men as long as that drinking was not destructive and took place at "proper" hours or moments of the day and year. His inability to first drink "like everyone else"—he would frequently become so intoxicated he was a violent and chronic burden to others—and now his inability to participate in any aspect of this normal male ritual, marks Tatsu and his children as, in his view, deficient and morally suspect. They are all, in Tatsu's mind, "abnormal" and "strange," hopelessly divergent because of his past drinking from the standards of normality he still desires for his children.

Tatsu continued, speaking of himself and his children as *dame ningen* (bad people) and *gomi* (garbage), seemingly forever corrupted by his alcoholism. Instead of finding a newfound sense of happiness and freedom at Danshūkai, he sees himself and his family as permanently broken, necessitating that he endure and suffer through his sobriety to prevent any further damage. Tatsu, like many others at Ohashi Danshūkai as well as at meetings across Japan, relies on the group and organizational structure to help in staying sober, but also professes feelings of anger and frustration at having to do so. The prominence given these feelings of frustration also leaves little room for optimistic talk of the future or the "new happiness" AA and Danshūkai sets forth as resulting from sobriety. As became clear during my time with Ohashi Danshūkai, these interpersonal frustrations are due, in part, to the limits sobriety places on individual men and lingering popular resistance in Japan to major portions of sobriety group ideology. The ability of AA and Danshūkai to offer a space for individuals to work through their struggles with addiction is only effective if it exists alongside active efforts to ensure popular opinion of addicts in recovery is one of acceptance and inclusion. And for many Japanese members such a coexistence is fleeting or absent. Thus, while the promised transformative potential of group membership is very real and powerfully meaningful for some members, it remains a marginal experience doing little to increase awareness of what it means to live as an alcoholic. As such, the struggles of many Japanese men at AA and Danshūkai also illustrates what happens when one side of the recovery equation between interpersonal transformation and popular acknowledgment of one's struggles and accomplishment is neglected.

Member struggles and frustrations were on consistent display during my time with Ohashi Danshūkai, particularly in the speeches of Kazu and Satomi, a long married and well-known couple who almost never missed a meeting. Satomi, a serious yet kind woman in her early fifties, often sat stoically throughout meetings, even when her husband took umbrage with her comments on his past drinking. Kazu, tall and lanky with an animated face and a few years older than his wife, enjoyed weaving humor into his typically poignant meeting speeches. As the non-alcoholic family member, Satomi always speaks first during meetings, giving Kazu an opportunity to respond to her comments several minutes later when he is called to speak, yet leaving her no recourse for a rebuttal. While they are rarely overly contentious, this arrangement resulted in several heated exchanges, including one of particular importance, during my time with the group. At this meeting Satomi spoke of her ongoing frustrations with Kazu for constantly talking about the loneliness he continues to feel now that he is sober. "I cannot understand how he can feel alone and unloved when he is surrounded by family, co-workers, and everyone we know and see regularly at Danshūkai"—individuals, she added, that have all been tireless in their patience and efforts to help Kazu get and stay sober. She ended her speech saying it is "*wagamama*" (selfish) that he continues to feel this way, constantly complaining about feelings of loneliness to her, and blaming such feelings on his alcoholism. It means he has not changed from the aggressive and violent drunk he used to be, as this is also what he wants and feels is denied him by others.

Several minutes later it was Kazu's turn to speak and he rose purposefully, staring piercingly at his wife as she sat still, eyes locked on the open space in front of her. He began aggressively, "you still, after all these years, don't understand that I'm *sick*!" His feelings of loneliness, he emphasized, come from the absence of alcohol in his life, and all the associated drinking and revelry that went with it, and no amount of family affection or sober socialization with group members can fill that void. He continued, emphasizing how she still fails to appreciate that he is *byōki* (sick) and *futsū ja nai* (abnormal) meaning, he added, that he is unable to find total fulfillment in the love and attention she and their children offer. Yet as an active and now long sober group member this is precisely what Kazu is charged with working towards, finding interpersonal happiness and satisfaction without alcohol. His admission of the absence of such feelings stands as powerful evidence for lingering difficulties facing Japan's sobriety group members. It is not enough to simply get sober, because once sober the individual, and this remains particularly the case for men, must confront a bleak social landscape that reinforces their voiced frustrations and perceptions of failing to conform to recognized cultural norms. Kazu, like other men at Ohashi Danshūkai, finds himself caught between sobriety's stable and physically healthy existence, alongside the loneliness and disconnection he continues to feel because he cannot consume alcohol, and thus cannot share in the camaraderie of consumption with other men.

Asami, the petite and unfailingly polite wife of Eiji, another Ohashi Danshūkai alcoholic, spoke the next week about how many group members still crave the mainstream and struggle with their feelings of denied participation in ritual practices that accompany sobriety. At this meeting in late December she said she knew her husband wanted to drink the bottles of sake arriving at their home as gifts, a traditional practice throughout Japan between companies and colleagues around the New Year holiday. "He feels it is wasteful," she said, not to drink them and potentially problematic if he is later asked how a particular sake tasted, as he feels he cannot divulge his alcoholism to those sending the bottles—a concern so powerful, albeit also wrapped within a greater fear of disclosing his alcoholism to others, that Eiji increasingly took to the Internet and online sake forums to research flavor characteristics and taste in case he ever needed to comment on a particular bottle. Instead of his marginal alcoholic existence, Eiji desired the conventional, represented in the sake bottles delivered to their home as a gesture intended to maintain convivial relationships between business associates. His inability to fully participate in this social exchange marks both his and the Japanese male alcoholic's ambiguity and systematic elimination from ritual participation that can result from sobriety.

Naomi, a recently divorced woman in her late thirties, spoke of these frustrations with not conforming to convention, not being able to drink "normally," at a Central Group meeting on a bitterly cold February evening. Unusually, she had not lost her job due to her drinking, despite months of erratic attendance and minimal productivity, and had recently returned to work after being hospitalized in a three month recovery program. Her return to the office alongside attempts to stay sober and active in AA were also becoming a constant source of tension between herself and her co-workers. Many she worked with felt that leaving the office for a stay in hospital and then returning meant she was cured, and could not understand why Naomi now rejected their offers to go drinking. She recounted at the evening's meeting an exchange with a male co-worker who earlier in the week had interrupted her tentative explanation of sobriety and AA with the "condescendingly" expressed question "but, you're better, right?" (*demo, naotta jyanai ne*?). As open admissions of sobriety group membership are already unusual among Japanese members, Naomi's encounter only strengthens concern among the meeting-goers that sobriety group ideology is too often seen as incompatible with Japan's prevailing attitudes on alcohol consumption. Naomi's reluctant yet forthright openness about her alcoholism was largely met with derision and dismissal from her co-workers, most of it in skepticism at how a three month stay in hospital did not result in a cure and comprehensive recovery. Naomi's experience is reflective of the wider challenge many at AA and Danshūkai face when confronting not only their own interpersonal struggles with addiction and trying to stay sober, but also a dismissive and even patronizing Japanese public.

LANGUAGE

Meeting discourse, particularly the linguistic performance of members while speaking, plays a major role in an individual's transformation from active drinker to group member at Tokyo AA and Danshūkai meetings. Much has been made of this process in North America, including how it is used, and manipulated, to chart an addict's progress through a recovery program (Carr 2011). For Japan's alcoholics the relationship between the language of addiction and recovery is often more ambiguous. AA and Danshūkai ask Japanese members to recast past experiences and memories of drinking and drunkenness along specific linguistic lines that render these events the actions of a diseased individual in need of help. Religion and spirituality are prominent in this process as members are tasked with being honest and open, while also making sincere admissions of powerlessness, swearing an oath of perseverance and effort, and confessing to others their wrongdoings or other harmful acts they may have committed while drinking. Yet instructive gaps emerge from such linguistic practices as faith, however defined, at the center of the recovery process abuts individual frustrations of self, community and ultimately nation. The result is prevailing linguistic competence with the conventions of AA and Danshūkai among Japan's sobriety group members, yet a competence frequently used alongside expressions of frustration, self-loathing, and anger.

AA and Danshūkai encourage members to speak about anything they want during meetings without fear of reprisal or critique, and speeches often reflect the liminal cultural position of alcoholics and gender-based frustrations many of them maintain at no longer being able to drink. During a Central Group meeting in October, one member said, "I hate myself, I want to commit suicide, I am weak, and I am selfish." Later that month another meeting attendee stated, "I want to return to good society, I want to be normal." Several months later Yoshi, the lanky unofficial Central Group leader, asserted, "[I want to] escape reality."[1] His statement referred to his reasons for initially starting to consume alcohol, yet he added that it is a desire for escape he still feels with sobriety today. Finally, at a Ohashi Danshūkai meeting in early spring a visiting hospital patient who for many years had consistently struggled with long term sobriety and cycled in and out of meetings said, "I want to die!" in a loud voice that briefly startled those at the meeting not paying close attention to the speakers. Notably, all of these statements, as well as similar admissions at other meetings, were typically met with limited and muted reactions from the other assembled participants. When the long suffering hospital patient almost bellowed, "I want to die!" several Ohashi Danshūkai members who had dozed off or let their minds wander to other thoughts snapped back to attention, but the majority of attendees listened stoically and without any obvious display of emotion.

They had all heard such declarations many times already, and uttered similar statements themselves during the course of their sobriety. It is language initially startling to the meeting outsider, notably myself the first several times I heard such blunt admissions, that quickly dulls and becomes conventional, eliciting minimal reactions from others while neglecting the larger concern of deep, unaddressed frustrations with sobriety.

Additionally, the broader significance of such blunt statements is their infrequency among Japanese men for, as Cindi Strutz Sreetharan notes, "descriptions of Japanese men as silent, taciturn, or at least verbally restrained are not uncommon" (2004: 277). Men in Japan are told to *gaman*, to endure and persevere, not proclaim their weaknesses for all in attendance to hear. Richard Light has made note of the strong connection between Japan's norms of masculinity and "ideals of self-control and the notion of *gaman*" (2003: 114–115)—connections evident in the frustration many Japanese men at the Central Group and Ohashi Danshūkai expressed when they dutifully commit themselves to group ideology and staying sober, but as a result feel they are cast outside the normal conduct of men. Further, these blunt statements on individual men's relationship with their sobriety emphasizes the consequences of a disconnection between specific behavior expectations for Japanese men, drinking alcohol with other men, and the linguistic strategies used to assert what such behavior is representative of, "*tsuyoi* 'strong' at drinking alcohol" as appropriately masculine (Strutz Sreetharan 2004: 277). In essence, men's gruff and blunt meeting declarations ring hollow because the men making these assertions are denied one of Japan's principal channels through which a recognized form of masculinity can be asserted.

A few days after he spoke of wanting to flee reality in the meeting, Yoshi recounted his mentioning of a desire for escape, and its role in his alcoholism, during a conversation we had over coffee. We met at a small inexpensive coffee shop attached to a Yamanote line train station, the central loop line that rings Tokyo's core, convenient for both of us. When we arrived Yoshi asked if we could sit in the smoking section and was rarely without a cigarette throughout the nearly two hours we spent chatting. Yoshi was the oldest son in a family that struggled tremendously for financial stability during the years of Japan's bubble economy, when everyone around them seemed to be getting rich. Frustration at not finding financial success eventually became too much for his father and he committed suicide when Yoshi was in high school, saddling his son, as the oldest child, with feelings of responsibility to provide for the family. At nineteen Yoshi suddenly found himself burdened with tremendous expectations from his family, compounded by lingering grief and shock at the grisly nature of his father's suicide. Not coincidentally, he added, this was when he began to drink heavily and regularly, a practice that continued until he was almost forty. Initially drinking and intoxication deadened him to the pain and burdens he faced, yet it quickly came to overwhelm all other aspects of his life until it was all he knew.

Escape continues to mark Yoshi's alcoholism as the major descriptive metaphor. During his more than twenty years of heavy alcohol consumption he was drinking to escape from the unhappiness and expectations he felt to provide for his mother and younger siblings. Yet it also became a growing source of strain and division within his family. As the years progressed Yoshi's health steadily declined and his behavior grew increasingly unpredictable. His family's patience was finally exhausted when late one night, so drunk he thought he was in the bathroom, Yoshi urinated on his younger brother's head while he slept. In the morning he was told to move out of the family home. He quickly found an apartment, only to also discover that having never lived on his own, he did not know how to cook, clean, do laundry, sort and take out the garbage, or perform any other basic household task.[2] His new apartment quickly and unsurprisingly descended into squalor while he continued drinking heavily. As we sat talking he paused between drags on his cigarette when telling me this, before saying purposefully that for nearly a year he was "like an animal," constantly drunk and living in filth.

While Yoshi's account of the drinking that preceded his sobriety and eventually forced him into AA is not unusual among group members, his thoughts and descriptions of group membership in Japan are revealing. He sees AA in Japan as a "closed society" of *kurushin de iru* (suffering) individuals who have nowhere else to go for support or comfort. In his succinct phrasing, "people who can quit [drinking] come to AA, many others just die," implying both that those in AA have a higher capacity to endure, whether it is drinking or sobriety, and that many others across Japan never find productive help for their addiction before it is too late. Instead of happiness in a new life, Yoshi regards sobriety group membership as an extender of life through the elimination of destructive drinking, but little else. AA helps him not bring harm to himself and others, yet does little else to alleviate his interpersonal struggles with the consequences of addiction or the outcomes of living sober. As such, his desire to escape reality has not abated with sobriety and he remains wary of those outside AA, minimizing social interactions he might have with such individuals in order to avoid frustration and embarrassment.

Making his feelings of greater and revealing significance is Yoshi's standing as a respected voice among AA members throughout Tokyo. Beyond his work with the Central Group, Yoshi is a full time volunteer with MAC, a boarding house in San'ya for alcoholic men recently discharged from hospital who have nowhere to go. He is both an AA advocate and an activist for alcoholism, addiction, and treatment and recovery efforts across Tokyo. Yet Yoshi also questions the extent of change and transformation possible when following the Twelve Steps and living in recovery. Hence his continued frustrations with AA as a "closed society," alongside his unwavering commitment to the organization as the only lifesaving and sustaining tool available to those in Japan struggling with addiction.

Not surprisingly, Yoshi's outlook on sobriety has also resulted in limited employment opportunities, and he lives austerely on monthly welfare payments he is eligible for as a diagnosed alcoholic. As we stood outside the coffee shop saying goodbye I asked how he came to organize Central Group meetings. Yoshi smiled and said it was because his absence of a work schedule ensured he would never miss a meeting due to his job, and he could thus be counted on to always unlock the room and arrange the chairs every week. Reflected in the descriptive language he uses to talk about sobriety—escape, suffering, and burden—is AA membership as a heavy responsibility Yoshi carries constantly—a worry predicated on knowledge that a return to drinking will likely result in his death, but one that also closes him off as abnormal and incompatible with Japan's conventional expectations of masculinity. Escape, never realized, serves then as an apt metaphor to describe Yoshi's struggles with alcoholism, as well as those of many other group members.

Like escape, *modoru* (return) is another term and theme sobriety group members frequently use to talk about their alcoholism. Men at the Central Group and Ohashi Danshūkai, burdened by frustration and questioning how they can assert a sense of masculine vitality without alcohol, and now active in organizations endeavoring to give them a new existence through the "*self*-governance" of their soul, routinely expressed a longing for return to a past when drinking was possible and unproblematic (Valverde 1998). During meetings this stated desire for return was also to an undetermined and undistinguished past. Return was to "good" or "normal" society, where their alcohol consumption was neither destructive nor debilitating, a place that for some likely never existed. At meetings these expressions of return were also often uncritically raised during meeting speeches, an unproblematic reaction to the loneliness of sobriety. Men would speak happily and nostalgically during meetings of past drinking *omoide* (memories) when they had frequented favorite bars around Tokyo with other men from work or longtime friends from school or their neighborhood. And while reminiscing about the past is certainly not taboo or banned by AA and Danshūkai, to continue remembering these moments as happy and fulfilling sits in absolute opposition to conventional understandings of healthy group membership. AA labels this as being a "dry drunk," someone who is sober yet unchanged from the person they were while drinking, a condition regarded in both AA and Danshūkai as destined for failure and an eventual return to drinking.

Metaphors of return also emerge frequently among individual members enduring their sobriety instead of finding a sense of solace, relief, or self-transformation. Many members struggling with this methodological inconsistency express frustrations with their current sobriety and a desire to return to an undefined past. "(I) want to go back to normal society" was how Takeo, a strong stocky man in his fifties who typically wore the heavy work boots and jacket of a laborer to meetings, discussed his sobriety at a spring Ohashi Danshūkai meeting, the time of the year he found particularly problematic for the outpouring of temptations it offered to drink. Many members often speak of wanting to have or at least return to a "normal way of drinking," lamenting their inability to drink "normally" like those they encounter outside AA and Danshūkai, a topic returned to in chapter 7. What is evident here is that sobriety is not, for many, the sought after outcome of group membership. Instead, many express a desire to drink again, if only they could somehow ensure it was done in a manner not destructive to themselves or their family. Takeo and countless other men at Ohashi Danshūkai and the Central Group are unable to let go of their past, when alcohol consumption was not yet prohibited, or reconstruct previous experiences within the group framework that presents itself as allowing these men to find a spiritual transformation of self and release from the temptations of alcohol.

This was evident as Takeo continued that evening, speaking about the coming *hanami* (flower viewing) parties, known across Japan more for the heavy drinking that transpires than an appreciation for the ephemeral beauty of cherry blossoms. He said "[I] don't want to forget that [good] feeling" he still associated with such gatherings. Following Takeo, others that evening also expressed a nostalgic longing to return to the fun they continued to link to the drinking and revelry of hanami parties, as well as the sadness many feel as sobriety now denies them participation in these gatherings. As another Ohashi Danshūkai member noted several speakers later, the space of hanami and its myriad temptations to drink was now "*kiken*" (dangerous), an area into which alcoholics could not venture. But this feeling of danger and need to avoid such public spaces is not due entirely to the heightened opportunities and temptations to drink. Instead, the alcoholic is an unrecognizable figure at hanami parties, an anomaly so counter to the purpose of gathering together in Japan's parks at this time of year that their very presence would tear at the social fabric. The result then for these men is their alcoholism, instead of signifying an identity transformed through a profound spiritual experience and ensuing happiness in sobriety, is experienced as a burden endured at great personal and social cost that excludes them from large swaths of Japan's public spaces. Parks, the setting of most hanami parties, are made inaccessible to many alcoholics during numerous festivals throughout the year as drinking and drunkenness feature prominently and expectantly in these social gatherings. More importantly, alcohol treatment programs ignore the ways in which the burden of being sober relates to yearning for a substance. In short, AA, Danshūkai, and Japan's network of hospitals devoted to treating alcoholism pay insufficient attention to the power and importance inspiring the sense of nostalgia for the social relationships forged through drinking within these public spaces.[3]

Finally, hate, of self and others, as well as thoughts of suicide mark numerous meeting speeches that confront sobriety and constitute a major vein of descriptive meeting language. Hate, as well as shame, often stems from thinking back to past drunken acts that continue to linger and exert contemporary consequences. Gen often spoke during Central Group meetings of his arrest record, multiple times for stealing bicycles to ride home after spending all his money on drink and missing the last train, as well as his restraining order, for stalking a woman from a favorite bar he became obsessed with, as lingering scabs constantly inducing feelings of self-hate and shame. More importantly, Gen is unable to forgive himself, despite this being a crucial aspect of working the Twelve Steps. During one of our conversations he spoke about taking a "searching and fearless moral inventory," as AA asks of all group members, yet continues to feel unable to ask forgiveness from those he wronged, or absolve himself of his previous behavior. Gen is also keenly aware that such an inconsistency, deep engagement with the Twelve Steps yet an inability to fully carry out specific components, is looked upon in AA as likely ruinous.

Yasu, a slightly statured Ohashi Danshūkai member with teeth darkly stained from years of smoking, spoke of how he wrestled with feelings of hate, directed towards himself and those he knew from the horse racing track near his home. Yasu, now in his early sixties, spent most of his adult life drinking and sporadically gambling at the track with, as he described it, "other degenerates" before his failing health finally forced him to enter hospital. The final episode, the moment he "hit bottom," came one afternoon while driving home drunk after several hours at the horse races. While driving he suddenly lost control of his bowels and soiled the seat of his car. Yasu's hate around this incident is directed towards the "degenerates," those who he now regards as for years having encouraged his drinking and gambling—or failed to do more in stopping him on his slide into ill-health—as well as reflected back upon himself for so thoroughly destroying his body. It is a hate that today also mixes with Yasu's still raw shame around his final moment of bodily breakdown. Unable to afford a new car, Yasu continues driving with a badly stained driver's seat, a constant reminder of his alcoholism and motivator to remain sober. However, the unremarked aspect of Yasu's graphic road to sobriety is his ongoing inability to forgive, either himself or those he once spent so much time with at the racetrack, for contributing to his current condition.

Finally, feelings of hate and shame came painfully to the fore during an AA meeting I attended with Aki in a working class Tokyo neighborhood near Ikebukuro. This meeting was more socioeconomically diverse than the Central Group, and also counted among its regular members several young alcoholics, men in their late twenties and early thirties who were trying to live sober. One of these men, Makoto, stylishly dressed in jeans and a t-shirt printed with nonsensical English words, spoke that evening of his lingering feelings of shame and hate for himself and for the person he was while drinking. He traces most of these feelings back to an evening shortly before he got sober. Makoto had been out drinking most of the night and in the early morning his friends left him, drunk and unable to stand, in front of the apartment building where he lives with his parents. He does not remember it, but he managed to climb two flights of stairs before collapsing and then beginning to vomit. His mother found him several hours later after following his trail of regurgitation that by then extended back down the two flights of stairs and out into the building's lobby. The shame he still feels several years later stems from his mother having seen him in such a pathetic state, and then unquestioningly and lovingly getting him home, clean, and into bed. Such feelings are coupled with a gnawing sense of hate he feels towards himself, and his friends, for allowing him to become so dangerously drunk, and then leaving him for his mother to find. He sighed and ended his speech with a bit of macabre humor, saying that at least some good came from everything: he collapsed in such a way that he didn't asphyxiate "like Jimi Hendrix" and leave a corpse for his mother to find, just a still drunk and barely conscious son.

The importance in each of these sometimes explicit examples lies in how they linger deep into the tenure of each individual's sobriety, persisting as memories that cannot be forgiven or reinterpreted anew in the light of recovery. Yasu, Gen, Makoto, and numerous other AA and Danshūkai members harbor simmering resentment and anger towards themselves, as well as family, friends, co-workers, and even the Japanese state over their past disregard for what they now remember as the destructive consumption of a sick individual. At issue, however, is how such linguistic practices, the use of terminology that invokes hate and a desire for return to an ambiguous state of "normalcy," also thwarts recovery and leaves individual sobriety group members frustrated and marginalized while also limiting the avenues of meaningful exchange between themselves and those outside the group. Anger at the "normalization" of heavy alcohol consumption in Japan, to the degree that health concerns, excessive consumption, and bodily harm are easily masked, pervade and fester at Tokyo sobriety group meetings while simultaneously stifling dialogue on alcoholism as an issue of national importance (Borovoy 2005: 44).

ALCOHOLIC BODIES AND THE PARADOX OF SPIRITUAL STRENGTH

The final element of failure explored in this chapter centers on the bodies of alcoholics, a major locus of attention, as the body is the vessel through which the effects of alcoholism both pass and are outwardly manifest. Bodily consumption and the breaking down of ingested alcohol into first intoxication and then hangovers are "inescapable in the construction of masculinity," making sober, alcoholic bodies a major definitional and diagnostic tool shaping constructions of identity for Japanese men at AA and Danshūkai (Connell 1995: 56). Moreover, a desire to maintain the "representational—and illusionary—boundary of the Japanese nation-state and of the (heterosexual) male body as (im)permeable and (in)penetrable" makes disclosures of alcoholism problematic as they challenge such assertions concerning the status of male Japanese bodies (Kazama and Kawaguchi 2003: 180). The result is individual male alcoholics made vulnerable in Japan as their inability to consume alcohol means they are also excluded from drinking as the most prominent and visible ritual of masculine bodily performance (Connell 1995: 54). In short, for Japanese men to live sober is to also have their claims to heteronormative gender norms made problematic and suspect.

Additionally, many men at the Central Group and Ohashi Danshūkai see their bodies as failing, or at least to have individually failed them, and this becomes a basis for then perceiving their alcoholism as a bodily dysfunction. Imagined links between the body and alcoholism among these men are particularly problematic, as they are symbolic of a perceived lack of bodily spiritual strength, a perception of deficiency compounded by its prohibiting of "normal" alcohol consumption and assertion of vigilant sobriety as the only possible recovery option. Sabine Frühstück in her work with soldiers from Japan's Self Defense Force writes that while physical strength was important, "'as Japanese' they would particularly excel as soldiers with the 'spiritual strength' to persevere" (2007: 65). Spiritual strength, the ability to gaman (endure), is here understood as a quintessentially Japanese characteristic and its absence, or at least such a perception, marks alcoholics as that much more broken and outside the recognized cultural norms of social interaction. Ironically, when considering drinking, the normalized quotient of spiritual strength is that which allows men to drink heavily yet still arrive at work the next morning despite their hangover. Thus, the deficiency many men at sobriety groups speak of is really their having taken the recognized norm, shared drinking with others within a set of culturally sanctioned limitations, to an unsustainable extreme—an irony not lost on sobriety group members during meetings, yet rarely acknowledged in other broader contexts. The result then is perceptions of individual deficiencies of spiritual strength among Japanese men as a basis for criticizing these alcoholics' inability to control and maintain "normal" alcohol consumption levels. Because of past excesses, alcoholic bodies have been made somehow deficient, leaving many men isolated and with limited recourse to reassert a masculine disposition once alcohol consumption becomes problematic.

Naoki, a short and pudgy man in his late thirties, who typically spoke hesitantly at first but gained confidence while talking at Central Group meetings, embodies this unsustainable extreme of expectations surrounding male bodies in Japan. When speaking at meetings Naoki often invoked the bodily impact and impulses he linked to his alcoholism. His most revealing comments came at a meeting in late March, when he addressed the approximately thirty other assembled group members that week. The meeting's theme was gaman, and Naoki chose to speak about his past and frequent trips to "Filipina bars," inexpensive hostess clubs where women from the Philippines entertained men with karaoke, flirting, and paid companionship. Naoki attributes his patronage of these bars to his alcoholism as, in his words, "women are *zurui*" (sly/cunning) and, blinded by drunkenness, he was powerless to resist their requests for him to consume more drinks and spend more money. The result was Naoki quickly becoming so drunk he didn't know what he was doing, and only able to stop drinking when he ran out of money and was unceremoniously removed from the bar. He ended his speech with the addition that after a night of drinking with co-workers he would often, if he still somehow had any money left or could find a 24 hour ATM, visit a brothel by himself before going home, typically one providing prostitutes also brought from the Philippines to Japan.

Naoki's outlined cycle of drinking—initially and typically with co-workers, followed by a solitary visit to another hostess club and then a final stop at a brothel—led eventually to his firing as he was constantly late, sick, or incompetent at work, as well as a persistent fear of contracting a sexually transmitted disease. Yet his fears of bodily harm and contamination did little to stop him from continuing to drink and frequent brothels for several more years, until his savings and the patience of family and friends was fully exhausted. Now sober and a Central Group member, Naoki has gradually rebuilt and reimagined these past actions as those of a sick individual uncomprehending of the polluting dangers he was subjecting himself to. His final statement that evening was to marvel at how he had managed to avoid "getting AIDS" before wondering aloud why he was so lucky.

Naoki's conduct and comments on bodily exposure to potential pollutants, while taken to an extreme infrequently matched by other Central Group members, fit with wider conversations on the alcoholic body, bodies that many members regard as abnormal and deficient, contaminated and sullied by an invisible affliction. Naoki frames his statements as a story of triumph over the unseen dangers of alcohol and contamination in a narrative that borders, at least in his telling, on the personally heroic. Not only do the prostitutes he frequented remain nameless and contaminated, condemned to an even darker recess of Japan's societal margins than alcoholics, but Naoki's position in his narrative is one of perseverance in the face of personal challenge and the perceived deception of others. This process of reinterpretation allows Naoki to reconcile what he regards as his past personal and moral transgressions, as he now frames them as the conduct of a sick man in need of help. His body, while still somehow abnormal, is in sobriety free from the pollutants and contaminants he was powerless to resist while drinking. Yet despite such a reconciliation, Naoki is also reluctant to disclose his alcoholism, and the behavior that accompanied it, to others, leaving him wanting for a wife, children, and other hallmarks of middle class stability, the absence of which he often raises during meetings as evidence of his continued abnormality and masculine shortcomings.

The sobriety group meetings as the setting where frustrations and opinions on bodily normalcy and consumption norms are aired further complicates the experiences of Tokyo alcoholics, in part because it is a setting where individuals display tremendous willpower and spiritual strength to resist temptations and opportunities to drink, while tasked with speaking of their inherent "powerlessness" as alcoholics. R. W. Connell notes that as "the constitution of masculinity through bodily performance means that gender is vulnerable when the performance cannot be sustained," Japanese men who identify as alcoholics must acknowledge their paradoxically applied and socially ascribed deficiency of spiritual strength, the vulnerability of their gendered identity, and their ensuing inability to perform a masculinity that demands alcohol consumption as a component of masculine bodily practices (1995: 54). Yet spiritual strength here acts as a tool reinforcing the status quo of shared alcohol consumption among men, and ensuring through Japan's domestic infrastructure that those men are also on time to work the following day despite how they may physically feel, while neglecting the efforts of AA and Danshūkai members to maintain their sobriety. Japan's alcoholics, by virtue of having pushed a convention of alcohol consumption to an extreme that renders them economically unproductive and culturally deviant, are made to suffer a systematic denial of claims to a recognized masculinity. The bodies of Japan's alcoholic men are first broken through excessive consumption and catastrophic breakdown that demands sobriety, and then renders them abnormal and tainted, while any recourse to recoup a lost sense of manhood remains elusive.

Such catastrophic breakdowns, moments of loss of bodily control, often after spurning long-lingering symptoms, are explicitly seen in episodes similar to those noted earlier and divides conventional and problematic drinking in Japan. If the individual male is most "*otokorashii*" (manly) when drinking, a cultural position frequently reinforced on television and in other forms of mass media, then his claims to being otokorashii are also wholly diminished in such moments of bodily failure (Borovoy 2005: 47). These heteronormative discourses reinforce "Japanese educative strategies" that strengthen views of masculinity as constituted through a bodily performance marked by consistent alcohol consumption and drunkenness (Castro-Vázquez and Kishi 2007: 173). For the membership of AA and Danshūkai then, the consequences of this are alcoholic bodies understood as possessing diminished spiritual strength—tainted bodies that are also called upon in group ideology to surrender themselves to a higher spiritual authority in order to transcend any desires to consume alcohol and find "happiness in sobriety" (Alcoholics Anonymous 2001: 50). The result, in Yoshi's words, is the alcoholic's body as the site of a "vicious circle" marked by struggle, disconnect, questioning, and shame that many men invoke during meetings, as by joining a sobriety organizations and working to stay sober, they face of tremendous opposition urgings.

Toru spoke at length of spiritual strength and its role in sobriety group membership when I made a return trip to Tokyo in the summer of 2012. Since we last saw each other he had continued working to blend AA with elements of "Japanese spirituality" including Zen Buddhism, Naikan meditation, and various elements of Shintōism, practices that are discussed in greater detail below. His own meditation regimen, he said, allowed him to function actively each day despite sleeping for just a few short hours each night. Particularly evident in Toru's efforts, and a consistent presence in sobriety group literature and teachings, are ideas of the spiritual, and the central importance it is given in the recovery process. AA and Danshūkai are similarly conceptualized organizations that at their core maintain the necessity for spirituality, in some capacity the individual finds meaningful, in order to maintain long term sobriety. Such an emphasis on the spiritual derives, in part, from the need for "absolution from guilt mediated by a 'power greater than ourselves' [that] provides an alternative to alcohol and becomes an important part of the alcoholic's healing process" (Vaillant 2005: 433). The ability to sustain long term sobriety is predicated in both groups on seeking out and, more importantly, finding forgiveness for past transgressions by accepting spiritual forces as a source for interpersonal transformation. Because of such outlooks on recovery, both groups also struggle for widespread recognition and legitimacy, and, in the case of especially AA, contend with suspicion from some that organizationally they are cultish in origin and practice. Yet ideas concerning spirituality and spiritual strength also circulate widely in Japan, particularly as a vehicle for notions of Japanese exceptionalism (Befu 2001, Frühstück 2007). Thus, AA and Danshūkai's rejection of alcohol consumption comes prominently to the fore as a major source of disconnect between the sobriety groups and the larger Japanese public, as the rendering of the need and purpose for the spiritual clashes with how many view the use and purpose of such concepts.

WHY MUST MY FAMILY SUFFER?

Tomomi, the doting mother of Kenji, an Ohashi Danshūkai member in his late thirties whose alcoholism prevented him from leaving home or marrying, stood to speak at a meeting in early spring. Nervously clutching a handkerchief as she spoke, Tomomi asked aloud why her family must suffer so much, why first her husband and now her son are alcoholics when so many others around them drink without having to ever endure such hardship. What had they done wrong? For Tomomi, as well as many other Tokyo Danshūkai members and their families, individual struggles with the presence of alcoholism in their life reflect a deeper disharmony, a persistent grappling with a diagnosis as an alcoholic and the necessity of self-confession and "the obligation to produce words that are true to an inner reality, through the self-examination that precedes and accompanies speech" as a core part of the recovery process (Rose 1999: 244). Surrender and allowing a new form of self-governance to emerge, allowing oneself to become "a subject for oneself," is consistently challenged by the pathologization of treatment and the emasculation of manhood surrounding admissions of alcoholism, expressed in Tomomi's feelings of victimization and uncertainty, unfairly heaped upon her family (*ibid*)—struggles that manifest generally when, despite membership in AA or Danshūkai, consistent meeting attendance and identification as an alcoholic, many individuals and their family still chafe at wholly accepting sobriety group ideology and continue to question why they are subject to addiction's cruel influence.

While Tomomi asked her question rhetorically and out of frustration at her son's ongoing struggles to find interpersonal stability, the relevance of her frustrations are far more extensive. Tomomi, along with many of Japan's current sobriety group members, are a generation that in service to the nation did all that was asked of them. Most attendees in the room for that particular Ohashi Danshūkai meeting, and many others at AA and other Danshūkai groups meeting across Japan, were born in the immediate aftermath of World War II. Tomomi and nearly everyone else that evening remember a childhood in a Japan laid waste by war. And in the ensuing postwar years they were asked to collectively strive and sacrifice to rebuild the nation. Like Tomomi, many Ohashi Danshūkai members entered the workforce in the late 1960s, 1970s, and early 1980s, at the height of Japan's postwar prosperity. Drinking for many attendees listening sympathetically to Tomomi that evening had been tacitly understood as not only a requisite part of employment but also rehabilitative, how men recovered and restored themselves at the end of grueling workdays. Yet within this social arrangement alcoholism and addiction are much more than destructive personal afflictions; they invoke "excessive self-questioning of causes and meanings" that erode individual feelings of worth and purpose while doing little to challenge the status quo

(Kitanaka 2011: 138). Tomomi's feelings of anger and frustration stem in part from she and her family having spent a lifetime doing all that was asked of them by employers, the community, and even the Japanese state, helping rebuild a broken Japan into an economic power of global significance, only to see her husband and son debilitated through their participation in these efforts. For their efforts and sacrifice many alcoholics of Tomomi's generation feel ignored or excluded, and the voiced frustrations that litter meeting speeches at AA and Danshūkai reflect such feelings of exclusion and neglect.

Failure and victimhood mark the experiences of many Tokyo sobriety group members as they work to fit their alcoholism into Japan's national postwar history. Many who gather at Central Group and Ohashi Danshūkai meetings made significant contributions of time and labor to Japan's rapid postwar recovery—labor that was in turn rewarded with after work drinking, as well as an unproblematic view that the resulting drunkenness was requisite and deserved. Such an arrangement leaves little room for conversations on alcoholism or addiction, and the result is alcoholics, particularly Japanese men, regarded as nonpersons, unrecognizable entities so divergent from cultural norms of socialization even their presence is felt to be disruptive and detrimental to group harmony and cohesiveness.

All this begs a seemingly simple question. Why can't alcoholism better integrate into Japan's popular consciousness? Why do so many Japanese men feel such difficulty in refusing a drink or telling someone they are an alcoholic? In the summer of 2012 I traveled to Kōchi, a city in Shikoku and the home of Danshūkai's founder, Harushige Matsumura. In Kōchi I attended a meeting with Kōchi-kai, one of Japan's longest running Danshūkai groups. Kōchi-kai's meeting, held in a collection of low-slung aluminum sided buildings that have served as the group's headquarters for many years, was attended by six alcoholics and four non-alcoholic spouses. I came early to the meeting with Megumi and her husband Yasuo, both group members and tireless advocates for Danshūkai throughout Kōchi and Shikoku. As everyone chatted while waiting for the meeting to begin at 7:00 pm, I asked another attendee, a man in his late sixties, how had he created a new *seikatsu* (life) for himself after he stopped drinking. Laughing at the broadness of my questions he said, "well, that's the difficult part, isn't it!" Always "saying no" to a drink, he added, is the real challenge. For him at least, a drink, or more accurately many drinks, remains something he not only wants, but that is also everywhere one goes in Japan, from sidewalk vending machines to the convenience stores and small shops on seemingly every street corner. It is also not typically something a man always refuses, especially, he added, in Kōchi, a city famous throughout Japan for its hard drinking residents.[4] Thus, for a Japanese man, particularly this now retired Kōchi laborer, to always say no to a drink is the result of typically years of struggle and anguish that, once achieved, also remains constantly in opposition to widely held norms of conduct and male comportment. The next chapter explores this difficulty by looking at how individuals talk about working to transform themselves into sobriety group members and the rare yet powerful moments of transformation experienced by some at AA and Danshūkai.

NOTES

1. 現実逃避 (*genjitsu tōhi*) Escapism, escape from reality.

2. As anyone who has spent time in Japan knows, household trash is rigorously sorted into a variety of categories, burnable or non-burnable, recycling for cans, plastic bottles, tetra packs, bulk garbage, etc., with different days of the week and month designated for pickup. Being unable or unwilling to follow these rules ensures that one's waste goes uncollected and even returned to one's front door, where Yoshi's trash would typically accumulate for weeks.

3. Tremendous thanks to Laurence Ralph for excellent comments at the American Anthropological Association annual meeting in 2013 that helped strengthen the idea and material in this section.

4. Kōchi's reputation throughout Japan as a city of tough, hard-drinking men is evident in numerous local practices and oddities, including some peculiar sake cups. These cups come in several designs, one with a small hole at the bottom, another with a rounded bottom that cannot be placed on a flat surface, all to ensure constant and rapid sake consumption during drinking sessions. Danshūkai members pointed to the existence of these cups as evidence of Kōchi's love of drinking and the difficulty in staying sober in such a city.

Chapter Six

Ten Yen Coins

The promise of AA and Danshūkai, a profound transformation of self and happiness without alcohol, as well as the means to forgive oneself for past transgressions, are seductive but often unfulfilled among the group members I worked with in Tokyo. These promises retain relevance through the speech acts of a minority of Central Group and Ohashi Danshūkai members who can attest, often in powerful and detailed language, to having had a profoundly moving experience as a result of active sobriety group participation. Yet for many others such a tangible moment of change remains elusive and unattained. Significantly, the struggles of group members to find a deeply moving moment of transformation also become acutely consequential when Japan's lack of alternatives to AA or Danshūkai for those questioning their alcohol consumption is considered. This chapter looks at how some AA and Danshūkai members have experienced a moment of transformative conversion that they then try to share with other, often frustrated and struggling, sobriety group members—struggles that also highlight the need, not only in Japan but globally, to reconsider how alcoholism and addiction are conceptually framed and how treatment is approached, as the effectiveness of current methods relies on an individual surrendering to a spiritual authority, thereby accepting and then "freely" entering into a process of self-transformation in order to mold themselves to fit established comportment norms, despite not always fully accepting or deriving meaning from these often sweeping notions of spirituality and faith (Rimke 2000: 63, Rose 1996: 77).

To look at how the spiritual is maintained as an essential yet uncertain aspect of membership in AA and Danshūkai, this chapter starts with the exceptional, an account of an explicitly felt and comprehensively transformative moment of individual conversion from struggling drunk to happily sober. It is important because when the experiences of individual alcoholics align with prescribed sobriety group practices, it can produce a powerful narrative on the transformative potential of group membership—narratives that make it impossible to forget how both AA and Danshūkai help and heal many individuals who would otherwise have likely died due to their alcohol use. The first and most explicit example I encountered on the transformative potential of sobriety group membership came from Toru, the volunteer leader of the beginners meeting and a highly active AA member throughout Tokyo.

Toru's adult life is unmistakably demarcated by his transitional moment of conversion from heavy drinker to recovering alcoholic, giving substantial yet, as noted in previous chapters, not unchallenged authority to his words. As such, his narrative account below is significant for two reasons. First, for the neat connection he makes between his sobriety and acceptance of group ideology, and second, for the rarity of such a transition process in Japan, as Toru's deeply moving moment of transformation is the exception instead of the norm. Born almost a decade after the end of World War II, Toru has faint memories of Japan's poverty and struggle in the immediate postwar years. What he remembers more from his adolescence and early adulthood are optimism, opportunity, and a collective belief in the provisional power of the Japanese government. Today Toru is in his late fifties and employed as a lawyer with one of Japan's major automobile companies, a job he has held since entering the workforce as a young law school graduate, and one that has given middle class stability and comfort to him and his family.

Toru also drank heavily throughout his years as a student and into his thirties. As he entered his forties the physical and emotional toll of such heavy consumption could no longer be ignored and he, as well as his family, still bears many scars from his years of heavy drinking. Like nearly all alcoholics in Japan he came to AA and sobriety through hospitalization—the three month recovery program that typifies many members' transition to sobriety group membership. He was first hospitalized due to his drinking at forty-two, solely for detoxification, and upon being discharged after a few days began drinking again for three more years until his second stint in hospital. It was during this period of hospitalization that he was encouraged by the attending physician to try AA, something that had not happened the first time despite ample evidence of Toru's chronic heavy drinking and numerous associated health complications. He began going to AA meetings while still in hospital and quickly stopped drinking for a year and a half before slipping and returning to alcohol for a short period of time. Finally, at forty-five, he found a sustained sobriety that continues today, a tenure that has now grown to more than ten years.

I first spoke to Toru on a cold February afternoon at a "family restaurant" near the hospital where the beginners AA meeting he was leading was going to be held a few hours later. Seated among the high school students and retirees idly enjoying the restaurant's warmth and bargain prices with friends, we both ordered the "drink bar" option, unlimited soft drinks and juices for a nominal amount, and began chatting. I started by asking my set of loosely structured interview questions, and Toru indulged me with thoughtful answers. Finally, with a wry smile he said "do you want to know how I really feel about AA?" My enthusiastic "yes" was met first with a review of the Twelve Steps, emphasizing the importance of Steps Eleven and Twelve. These Steps are as follows:

> 11. Sought through prayer and meditation to improve our conscious contact with God, *as we understood Him*, praying only for knowledge of His will for us and the power to carry that out.
> 12. Having had a spiritual awakening as the result of these Steps, we tried to carry this message to alcoholics, and to practice these principles in all our affairs.

Toru added that they are also the components of AA membership many Japanese members struggle with as they systematically "work the steps," but often fail to find the "spiritual awakening" AA's ideology outlines. And as noted earlier, Toru's experience with AA ideology and the Twelve Steps makes him the rare exception. After reviewing these Steps with me he talked about being home one night reading the "Big Book," AA's primary text, after his wife went to bed. While reading, he said, a calm began to wash over him and he saw a light, initially the size of a ten yen coin (roughly the size of a U. S. quarter) that slowly grew, projected against the wall in front of him, until it filled the entire room, wrapping him in a comforting warmth he had never before felt. As he continued to read the words went "directly into my heart," and he finished the book and then sat all night in his kitchen, overwhelmed by a feeling of calm and release. His wife came into the kitchen in the morning to begin breakfast and found him still in his chair. Her face initially registered anger as her first assumption was he had been up all night drinking, but when Toru said "*ohayō*" (good morning) she stopped, overcome by the serene tone of his voice. They sat together talking and he said any remaining desire to drink was gone, he was reborn as a "recovering alcoholic."

Thus, the importance of Toru's account of conversion and rebirth is its neat conformity to the distinguishing pattern of alcoholism in Japan: frequent short-term hospitalization until encountering a doctor who recommends joining a longer hospitalization program and a sobriety group, neatly fixed to a deeply emotional narrative about his sobriety and conversion experience that mirrors AA's advocated and idealized position. Toru has melded two seemingly incompatible extremes, Japan's heavy medicalization of alcoholism and the centrality of individually realized spiritual transformation, in a successful recovery. This powerful moment of self-transformation, spurred on through the use of AA's ideological language to reinterpret memories of past drunkenness, gives ideological heft to Toru's lectures and efforts at spreading the group's message to those in hospital. However, and more importantly, such a process remains the exception for many of Japan's sobriety group members. As such, Toru's moving account of self-transformation also emphasizes the ongoing ambiguity felt by many in Japan questioning their drinking or trying to stay sober, as well as the limitations created by entangling requisite hospitalization with a sobriety program ideologically rooted in finding spiritual recovery.

Peter Stromberg's work among evangelical Christian groups in the United States highlights the ambiguity surrounding conversion narratives and the experiences such moments engender. He notes that "the conversion narrative enables the believer to forge a sense of coherence by using the ideological language to embrace intentions which . . . persist in spite of being denied. It is this sense of coherence that signals, both to the believer and to the observer, a transformed identity" (1990: 54). Stromberg adds that "emotional ambivalence was not resolved once and for all in the original conversion experience, but rather persists in the present" (*ibid*: 43). While reliance on an ideological system, here the governing principles of AA or Danshūkai, can allow an individual struggling with their alcohol consumption to create meaning "where previously there was none," it offers no assurances that such meaning will find relevance or resonance within a given cultural context (*ibid*: 53). Put differently, AA gave Toru the means to find a profound "spiritual transformation" that inspired his now more than ten years of happy and productive sobriety; it did not however convey any assurances that others could hear, accept, or be moved to action by such a message, despite assurances from AA and Danshūkai that this is what would happen.

Since his conversion experience, Toru has continued working to bring AA to those in Japan who might not otherwise encounter the group; something AA members call "Twelfth-stepping." He and other group members volunteer at a large hospital in northwestern Tokyo, leading the already mentioned beginners AA meeting one evening each week. The group uses a textbook, cobbled together by Toru and the other volunteers from a range of material that includes a detailed explanation of the Twelve Steps, inspirational essays from primarily American group members found online and translated into Japanese, and a brief history of AA and its founders Bill W. and Dr. Bob. The goal of this text is to help those in Japan previously unaware of sobriety group ideology understand and accept a fundamentally new interpretation of themselves, and their relationship to alcohol, through a spiritual transformation. This means that Toru and the other volunteers' work at the beginners meeting is proselytization of the sobriety group message, given a degree of authority through his and the others' deeply moving moments of conversion and commitment to the organization, but also marked by skepticism from many of the patients required to assemble at the beginners meeting as part of their treatment program.

It is to these beginners meeting patients that our attention again turns. At the meeting group I attended all patients were men, generally in their fifties and sixties, and several were "dually diagnosed" with alcoholism and other mental affliction including depression, anxiety, and schizophrenia.[1] While the attention to serving dually diagnosed patients makes this meeting a bit unusual, other beginners meetings often have patients who chronically cycle through the hospital program and struggle with other mental and physical conditions. Many of the men at this meeting were in poor health, the result of years of heavy drinking, and soft yet hacking coughs from moist chests are heard constantly during every hour and a half meeting. The patients enter as a group promptly at 7:00 pm, shuffling from the lounge down the hall in hospital issued slippers and rarely speaking at a volume higher than a whisper. Once assembled the AA volunteer leader calls the meeting to order and things begin by everyone taking a turn reading aloud from a section of the textbook that is relevant to the lecture to follow. Several struggle with this task, having trouble with the book's small text or stumbling over the proper reading of more complex kanji, and are quickly helped by those seated around them. Once finished Toru or another AA volunteer begins their lectures on the day's topic, generally trying to construct a narrative that explains a three-step section of the Twelve Steps in a manner the volunteers felt would be relevant and applicable to the patients once discharged.[2]

Despite the committed effort of all the AA volunteers, skepticism—particularly over the role and need for spirituality in the recovery process—pervades throughout most meetings. While the already mentioned "it stinks of Christianity" moment makes such feelings overtly obvious, most beginners meetings at various hospitals across Tokyo reminded me of a high school classroom where a teacher barely holds control over unruly and disinterested students. While not an entirely fair generalization—a number of individual patients, particularly those attending Ohashi Danshūkai meetings, spoke earnestly about a desire to quit drinking and regain control over their lives—a large number of patients chronically drift between hospitalization and heavy alcohol consumption without ever finding lasting change, transformation, or sobriety.

These struggles were painfully evident during my visits to a different hospital, this one in western Tokyo with Masa, who like Toru consistently volunteers to bring AA's message to those in hospital. Despite their shared commitment to AA and spreading its message, Masa openly bears the struggles and frustrations with trying to bring the group's message to those in hospital. I accompanied him for the first time on a rainy May afternoon and he felt it necessary to warn me in advance about the meeting. "They are very quiet," he said dispiritedly as we huddled under our umbrellas while walking from the train station to the nearby hospital, and for the next hour and a half I watched him strain to elicit minimal responses from a disinterested group, many previously hospitalized numerous times for alcohol related problems. Several patients that afternoon stated flatly that they "did not believe" in reflecting on or critically sharing past drunken experiences with others, while others simply said they had nothing to say when called upon to speak, a de facto rejection of sobriety group ideology. As Clare Moynihan notes in her work on health care and masculinity, "it was crucial for men to be controlled and silent about their emotional life," a trend particularly evident among those in Japan hospitalized for alcohol related issues (1998: 1074).

After my first meeting with this group Masa and I had coffee in a small restaurant next to the station. While trying to remain upbeat and energetic, this meeting had clearly taken a toll on him, and he struggled to frame the patients' attitudes in a positive light. Despite his frustrations he did manage to remain optimistic. "I was like them" he said, adding "it takes a long time to hear the [AA's] message. It took me years to hear [accept] AA's message and acknowledge I had a problem with alcohol, and only with this 'honest' admission can I begin to 'truly' work the steps." Masa's tireless devotion to volunteer work with AA comes out of his struggles with accepting his alcoholism and once he did finding interpersonal happiness, and the hope that even reaching one patient makes his efforts worthwhile. He volunteers for the one person he might be able to help, not the many others dismissive of AA and the spiritual nature of personal transformation it demands.

While in hospital many patients hear, often quite extensively, about AA and Danshūkai. They are also typically asked to join one organization as the most effective means to maintain their sobriety after being discharged. Yet the majority of patients fail to do so. Statistical support is difficult, for numerous reasons, in tracking anything resembling accurate retention and success rates in AA, Danshūkai, or hospital programs for alcohol treatment. This is due in part to how AA and Danshūkai allocate responsibility, as individuals shoulder the burden of accepting their alcoholism in a system that renders "power and mastery" over addiction as "matters of the self's free will" (Rimke 2000: 65). Yet the logic here is also circular, as admission of a lack of control over one's drinking is demanded before self-control and sobriety can be cultivated with meeting attendance. The result is many Japanese patients struggling to accept AA or Danshūkai's initial premise, while finding no alternative forms of treatment, and cycling through periods of hospitalization and then a return to drinking. As Dr. Mori estimates, roughly eighty percent of the patients she sees never find sustained sobriety, and many of the patients she treats have been through her program before. AA and Danshūkai do not keep records of retention rates, but informal member estimates suggest that about two-thirds of individuals who attend a meeting in Japan do not stay sober for more than a year—observations that are consistent with the findings of others looking at AA membership in the United States and elsewhere (Brandes 2002, Laudet 2003, McIntire 2000).

All of this begs two obvious questions. The first is open to a greater range of interpretation and individual variance. Why does the sobriety group model of AA and Danshūkai work so well for some, as Toru's story demonstrates, but leave a larger number in Japan struggling to find the promised "transformations" that will allow them to live without alcohol? The second question is more straightforward. Why and how are AA and Danshūkai the dominant, and it could be argued the only, recognized recovery options in Japan for confronting alcoholism and addiction? The rest of this chapter looks at these two questions in detail, focusing first on the socialization of individuals into group members and the emphasis given to "healing the self" in both groups.

HEALING THE SELF

Becoming an AA or Danshūkai member is a process, often a quite lengthy one, of transforming the self into someone fundamentally different from the person one was before starting to attend meetings. It is a movement from being a "drunk" to someone who is "living in recovery," and it requires not just incorporating numerous new concepts and terminology into how one talks about and remembers past experiences, it is also a process of healing, whereby wrongs are amended, forgiveness is sought—both from oneself and others, and recovery constantly "worked." "It [alcoholism] is a transformation of their [members'] identities, from drinking non-alcoholic to non-drinking alcoholics, and it affects how they view and act in the world. It requires not only a particular understanding of the world, but a new understanding of their selves and their lives, and a reinterpretation of their own past" (Cain 1991: 210). Yet, as a specifically constructed and carefully tailored view of alcoholism and addiction it is also rigid, allowing little room for challenge or questioning of its methodology. Each member must not only come to the group of their own volition, but once present must accept and conform to the organizational dictates.

AA and Danshūkai occupy the dominant position in dictating how alcoholism and sobriety are framed, conceptualized, experienced, and talked about in Japan. Both groups envision sobriety "not [as] a cure, but a special state of being unique to recovering alcoholics, one that demands a certain amount of mindfulness and vigilance" (Swora 2001: 65). The ambiguity and uncertainty surrounding alcoholism and addiction in Japan is also what makes such vigilance necessary. Both AA and Danshūkai make claims to heal the self, to move individuals away from their past destructive drinking by remaking them into better people who are happy without alcohol. Yet what exactly is being healed is unclear. Alcoholism and addiction are the end result of years of heavy drinking. How one arrives at such a place, the myriad causes of each individual's alcoholism, is complex and poorly understood.

Thus, it is an individual's acceptance of this uncertainty that divides those in AA and Danshūkai from the multitude of patients throughout Japan who return to drinking after their stay in hospital concludes. Nakamura recounted a moment from his past at an Ohashi Danshūkai meeting in February, emphasizing the difficulty many have with acceptance their addiction. He remembers waking up in a hospital to a doctor screaming "you're an alcoholic!" and shaking him, with no memory of how he got there or the events that brought about his stuporous state. He had been brought to the hospital after being found in the early morning hours lying semi-conscious in front of a Seven-Eleven convenience store. He acknowledged the doctor's comments at the time, promising to "cut back" on his alcohol consumption, but continued to drink heavily for nearly a year. He ended his speech that evening by emphasizing the difficulties he sees in others, including some long sober Ohashi Danshūkai members, concerning acceptance, whether it be to a Higher Power, the sobriety group, God, or another meaningful entity. As Nakamura recognized that evening, simply acknowledging that one is an addict is itself a difficult admission, doing so in a cultural context that is largely indulgent and encouraging of alcohol consumption makes it all the more challenging, for both experienced Ohashi Danshūkai members and those just beginning to attend meetings.

This is also where the genius of sobriety group ideology resides. In the view of many group members the ideology of AA or Danshūkai is an infallible program for healing the self, provided one freely accepts and then works the program with the requisite diligence. Any failures or shortcomings are not the program's fault but that of the individual, who was either unable or unwilling to hear the message at that particular moment. Thus, healing the self means seeking treatment and recovery in a program that mandates first acceptance of a loss of control and then individual diligence and constant self-control. Such a structuring speaks to the necessity of submission to a higher authority, yet within an institutional framework build to usurp the physician's diagnostic gaze, while also mandating tremendous self-transformation as a requisite component of success. This control is made possible through the adoption of a lexicon of terminology to help facilitate reinterpretation of past events and experiences in a format conducive to the mores of AA or Danshūkai. As James Clifford notes, "communities can and must reconfigure themselves, drawing selectively on remembered pasts. The relevant question is whether, and how, they convince and coerce insiders and outsiders, often in power-charged, unequal situations, to accept the autonomy of a 'we'" (2001: 479). As communities, Japan's AA and Danshūkai groups exist in a corresponding manner, dominantly positioned as the source of authority on alcoholism and recovery. My contention is that due in part to the dominance AA and Danshūkai wield in dictating how alcoholism is defined and lived, those in Japan reluctant or unwilling to accept sobriety group ideology while confronting their own alcoholism and addiction face a limited number of alternative treatment and recovery options—limitations and constraints that are deeply consequential for not only members but also those at the group's margins, a topic returned to momentarily.

To summarize, alcoholism as a lived identity is experienced as a process whereby individuals freely accept the governing sobriety group principles and actively work to integrate them into their lives. As such, it is a comprehensive methodology predicated on equally comprehensive acceptance of sobriety group interpretations of the characteristics that govern a diagnosis of alcoholism and addiction. Yet, as Junko Kitanaka expertly demonstrates in looking at depression in Japan, how an affliction enters public discourse is as important as the tangible realities that affliction carries (2012: 37). It is undeniable that alcoholism and addiction are often destructive at an interpersonal and societal level. What the experiences of Japan's alcoholics demonstrate is how this destruction is understood, interpreted, and lived in ways that often fail to neatly align with the established sobriety group principles, making AA or Danshūkai membership and meeting participation, for some, an exercise in frustrated endurance instead of the promised spiritual awakening and transformation of self into a new person happy without alcohol.

SPIRITUALITY—GOD AS YOU UNDERSTAND HIM

"He fools himself. Inwardly he would give anything to take half a dozen drinks and get away with them. He will presently try the old game again, for he isn't happy about his sobriety. He cannot picture life without alcohol" (Alcoholics Anonymous 2001: 152). This passage at the beginning of chapter 11 in AA's Big Book begins to outline for the newly sober, the process of becoming an active group member. It goes on, noting the likely response of the reader: "You say, 'Yes, I'm willing. But am I to be consigned to a life where I shall be stupid, boring, and glum, like some righteous people I see? I know I must get along without liquor, but how can I? Have you a sufficient substitute?'" (*ibid*: 152). The next paragraph offers a solution, noting "Yes, there is a substitute . . . it is the fellowship of Alcoholics Anonymous. There you will find release from care, boredom and worry. Your imagination will be fired. Life will mean something at last. The most satisfactory years of your existence lie ahead. Thus we find the fellowship, and so will you" (*ibid*: 152). These passages, never invoked during my time with the Central Group and Ohashi Danshūkai in Tokyo, set forth the significant promise and transcendent potential of AA (as well as Danshūkai), yet in Japan the expressed everyday reality of group member seldom matches the printed ideal.

This chapter of the Big Book ends by detailing how this transformation of self is possible and will be experienced for individual members. "Our book is meant to be suggestive only. We realize we know only a little. God will constantly disclose more to you and to us. . . . The answers will come, if your own house is in order. But obviously you cannot transmit something you haven't got. See to it that your relationship with Him is right and great events will come to pass for you and countless others" (*ibid*: 164). "Delight in sobriety," the stated outcome of group membership, is also presented as possible only through an admission of *muryoku* (powerlessness) and surrender of oneself to God, albeit *"God, as you understand Him*" (Alcoholics Anonymous 2001, italics in original). Permanent sobriety is thus presented and understood as the only acceptable means through which this requisite surrender and acceptance of ensuing spiritual guidance is possible, a position muting any cultural, linguistic, and religious diversity or difference. AA and Danshūkai are bound by their methodological adherence to spirituality and self-surrender as the fundamental components of achieving and, more importantly, maintaining sobriety. And while some, like Toru, find this transformative and necessary, it causes others in Japan to reject membership in AA or Danshūkai out of personal aversion to its religious and spiritual elements, or the permanence of change it demands. As a result, an unwillingness to accept self-surrender to a spiritual or religious power is deeply consequential in Japan, as it limits who joins AA and Danshūkai, going so far as to categorize, for some struggling with their alcohol consumption, acceptance of group membership as in opposition to normative interpretations of Japanese cultural values and identity.

The conflating of religion and spirituality within the recovery process is often a source of tension and a basis for rejection by many hospital patients when being encouraged to join AA or Danshūkai by attending physicians and group volunteers. Much of this stems from AA's strong association with Christianity, a worldview regarded by many Japanese patients as foreign and personally incompatible with their own views on the world. While Danshūkai is not as overtly religious in terminology or philosophy as AA, members must still give themselves over to a power greater than themselves and admit, to themselves and others, a lack of control over their ability to regulate their alcohol consumption. Ultimately, sustained participation in a sobriety group is predicated on the assumption that freely surrendering to a power greater than oneself, and faith in that process to provide guidance, is a proposition individual members find meaningful. When this is not the case, when calls to give oneself over to a Higher Power for help and guidance fall upon deaf, disinterested, or disbelieving ears, little progress in how Japan approaches and treats alcoholism and addiction is made. Such a conflating of the factors that govern treatment not only carry broader implications for the classification and treatment of addiction globally, they also sustain static and inaccurate popular views of Japan's addicts as somehow unworthy of compassion and care.

Spirituality, here concerned with "concepts of God, the divine and transcendent and also sacred objects, time and places," is used to differentiate sobriety group practices from religion (Morjaria and Orford 2002: 229). If religion is bound by "institutionalized dogma," spirituality within the sobriety group context is the search for "connectedness with the transcendent" (*ibid*: 228). It is a deliberate construction, done to make participation in a sobriety group as open and inclusive to as many people as possible. Yet in the case of AA and, I would contend, Danshūkai, it is also one that cannot be divorced from the underpinnings of the original source of spiritual inspiration, in this instance a worldview deeply influenced by Christianity. While this recovery format has brought salvation to many struggling with alcoholism, its reliance on culturally and religiously specific practices also restricts acceptance of this approach to treatment. And Japan's absence of alternative treatment options leaves many facing a choice between two ill-suited options, continued alcohol consumption or participation in an organization that demands difficult reinterpretations of self and past actions.

Toshi, the former patent clerk who now volunteers at the AA office, was able to fuse Christianity and spirituality, as he interprets the term, into his sobriety and participation in first Danshūkai and now AA. While he rejects Christianity as a component of how he wants to identify himself, he speaks of having found relevance and meaning in concepts he regards as Christian. This is evident when he speaks of "admission and devotion" (*mitomeru to yudaneru*) to something greater than himself. For many years these were concepts Toshi rejected while drinking; it took the near total destruction of his life and family, he says, for him to acknowledge an inability to control his drinking. He feels his resistance to admitting powerlessness stems from discomfort with the very notion of surrendering oneself to a Higher Power. Yet unlike Toru, no deeply moving moment of spiritual transformation marks Toshi's acceptance and engagement with these principles or his sobriety. Instead, he simply accepts that he cannot control his drinking, "I'm different from everyone else," and "endures" (*gaman suru*) his sobriety as a necessary condition he believes he must tolerate. This was particularly evident when he talked about how much he disliked going to AA meetings, adding that he only does so regularly because he knows it is the only way he will stay sober. For Toshi sobriety is a burden he must bear for the rest of his life, a failing he fights against, and going to AA meetings offers reminders of the destruction that can come from slipping. What AA does not impart, largely because it is not something Toshi regards as possible or realistic, is the spiritually guided transformation of self into a new and happy person without alcohol.

However, while Toshi, Toru, and many other sobriety group members draw comfort, to varying degrees, from the spiritual relationships they cultivate in the name of their sobriety, others are uncertain about how to attach meaning to the recovery principles structuring group membership. When surrender to something beyond one's self is requisite in order to "live in recovery" and a concept many in Japan contemplating sobriety group membership for the first time find foreign and without meaningful application, struggle is not an unexpected result. At a broader level, these concerns of conceptual and religious compatibility also contribute to AA and Danshūkai's legitimacy struggles against accusations of cultic behavior linked to the rise of "new religions" in Japan's postwar era (Gordon 2008: 261).[3] Aki mentioned several times during my visits to the AA JSO the harried phone calls the office received, typically from family members concerned about a loved one's drinking and desperate for help, yet also apprehensive of the organization's "true intentions"—feelings and fears of organizational claims to spiritual transformation that she worries also keep many from ever calling.

Like AA, Danshūkai struggles with religious associations that members fear turn some away from participating in the group. The most common critique is that Danshūkai is overly dogmatic and hierarchically structured, while also drawing heavily from religious sounding language and ritualistic meeting practices. While Ohashi Danshūkai is an exception, as noted earlier, due primarily to the absence of organizational paraphernalia in the meeting space, many other groups make heavy use of such accessories. These usually include and revolve around a large and now iconic photo of Harushige Matsumura, typically displayed prominently at the front of the room and alongside group flags, often adorned with ribbons acknowledging various achievements, as well as banners printed with Danshūkai's oaths of sobriety, inner strength, and family. The Danshūkai Oath and other prayers for ongoing sobriety are also often recited at the beginning or end of meetings. Many in Danshūkai regard these images as paramount, and certainly bordering on sacred, to a meeting environment as they stand as testament to the dramatic change sobriety has brought to their lives. Members also recognize how this could be problematically interpreted when observed by those outside the group. During my visit with Kōchi Danshūkai in the summer of 2012, several members made a point of telling me they were not a cult or any other type of "odd religious group" before and after the meeting I attended, despite also knowing that I was familiar with the Danshūkai and its governing principles, as well as deeply interested in gaining a better understanding of the meaning and significance members draw from such practices.

This section looked at the role of spirituality and surrender to a Higher Power in AA and Danshūkai as major impediment to the expansion of sobriety group membership in Japan. As a source of tension and disagreement among group members, as well as in their interactions with nonmembers outside the groups, differing understandings of spirituality, particularly feelings of a connection to Christianity and concepts regarded as "foreign," are often linked to resistance and sometimes rejection of AA or Danshūkai. Yet they can also help sobriety thrive among some individual members in a way that leads to deeply meaningful and transformative experiences. The result is acceptance and cultivation of an active and vigorous spirituality as a point of division between those who accept the principles of AA or Danshūkai and those unwilling or unable to do so. While the depth of engagement with interpretations of spirituality is unevenly felt among group members, and can result in membership being an act of enduring or something profoundly transformative, the consistently voiced view is that some amount of spiritual cultivation is necessary to sustain sobriety.

When disagreement and frustration had been frequently voiced, Nakamura often tried to end Ohashi Danshūkai meetings on an upbeat and optimistic note. He felt it was his job as group leader to remind everyone of the importance and power in regular meeting attendance and participation, particularly when members had collectively aired feelings of frustration and struggle with living sober in Japan. Just showing up every Friday, he often added, showed a commitment to sobriety that had been rewarded by another day shared with sympathetic friends and without alcohol. These moments at the end of meetings also gave him the opportunity to chastise those who were absent and emphasize the importance of regular attendance. He also encouraged everyone to pursue whatever methods or practices helped them stay sober. If that included also going to AA, reading the Big Book or online diaries about other's alcoholism, incorporating different religious elements into one's life, going to different Danshūkai meetings, or anything else members found helpful, then it was something they should embrace. I heard Nakamura emphasize this message many times during my time at Ohashi Danshūkai, always immediately followed by "and the most important thing is to stay sober." Yet despite the successes at Ohashi Danshūkai, the group's message is shared every week with numerous hospital patients who remain unable or unwilling to make the requested transformation of self.

OTHER OPTIONS

AA and Danshūkai loom large in any discussion of alcoholism and addiction in Japan. Both organizations have integrated themselves into the standard treatment options for anyone questioning their alcohol consumption, ensuring that most in Japan today who are hospitalized for alcohol-related health complications will at least hear about both organizations, including the governing principles, and be encouraged and sometimes required to attend meetings. I outlined earlier some of the consequences of this arrangement, the most prominent being a thwarting of discussion or consideration for forms of treatment that differ from those AA and Danshūkai set forth as "correct" (Room 2001, Singer and Baer 1995). These include consideration of total abstinence as potentially not a requisite condition of recovery, as well as the possibility of moving from "living in recovery" to recovered, greater consideration given to the context and cultural environment where drinking occurs, and a questioning of the prominence given spirituality, particularly in a format that draws heavily from Christianity, within the recovery process (Hunt and Barker 2001).

Despite AA's global prominence, efforts at diversifying treatment approaches and methodologies are unevenly evident.[4] Yet, despite AA and Danshūkai's dominance of Japan's approach to treating addiction, there are other active methodologies and practices concerning the diagnosing and treating of alcoholism that strike at the heart of how addiction is defined and treated, itself an ongoing and contentious designation fraught with "social and cultural significance" (Campbell 2007: 2). While limited in scope, these efforts not only challenge and question how Japan should treat alcoholism and addiction, they also work to insert a degree of cultural sensitivity into the diagnostic and treatment process surrounding such afflictions (Marutani and Miyazaki 2010). The most prominent sobriety group alternative draws heavily from *Naikan,* a meditation technique derived from Buddhism, and often done in tandem with blogging, use of social networking websites, online forums and other forms of Internet enabled communication. The remainder of this chapter explores these peripheral and emergent aspects of treatment and recovery in greater detail.

While working with AA and Danshūkai in Tokyo I heard several physicians mention Naikan as a distinctly Japanese approach to treating alcoholism, as well as addiction generally. However, this intriguing approach to treatment is offered on a limited scale across Japan, and one of the largest centers for Naikan therapy is about as far from Tokyo as one can venture in Japan. This center of activity for Naikan therapy is Takemoto Hospital, located an hour south of Kagoshima in Ibusuki on the far southern peninsula of Kyūshū. It is a naturally beautiful part of Japan, marked by a jagged coastline of black sand beaches carved around deep bays dotted with small islands and small fishing villages. It is also isolated and rural, requiring interested patients to undertake a significant journey to reach the hospital. As such, many of the patients come from throughout Kyūshū and the hospital struggles to attract patients from farther afield.

Naikan, often translated as self-observation psychotherapy, is an "individual psychotherapeutic method which has its origins in Japanese Buddhism" (Suwaki 1979: 15). While not used exclusively to treat addiction, this is likely one of its most common contemporary application, and patients struggling with alcohol, other drugs, and gambling afflictions fill Takemoto Hospital's crowded Ibusuki campus. The Ibusuki center is the largest of several Naikan treatment programs for addiction spread across Japan, many in rural areas and nearly all tracing their philosophical roots back to Dr. Takemoto's program, the hospital's founder, namesake, and Japan's leading advocate for Naikan therapy. A trim, healthy man in his late sixties, Dr. Takemoto speaks of Naikan's healing potential in deeply reverent tones, emphasizing that while AA and Danshūkai have their place, Naikan delves to the root cause of individual struggles and afflictions.

In treating addiction, Naikan therapy consists of multiple sessions of intense self-reflection, often lasting over an hour, followed by individual counseling with a therapist to reflect back upon the previous meditative session. At Takemoto, patients do their treatment sessions in a large house next to the hospital's dormitory. The house is built using traditional Japanese architecture, with tatami mat floors and shoji sliding screen doors and walls throughout its spacious interior. Patients sit in the corner of a room, behind folding screens put in place for added privacy, and are asked to meditate silently on a specific topic. At their first session patients are instructed to begin their meditative work by focusing solely on their initial memories of school, as this is likely an easily recalled event from early childhood. From this they move progressively through their life, reflecting deeply and intensely on specific episodes and incidents of importance. Naikan therapy is less concerned with alcohol, or any other substance of abuse, instead emphasizing how patients' actions have hurt or burdened others—actions that often resulted because of their alcohol or drug use and intoxication. As patients progress through their lives the treatment goal is to foster a recognition of the harm addicts caused those in their life to whom they are most indebted, primarily their parents.

As such, Naikan as a treatment approach is rooted in Dr. Takemoto's and other therapy advocates' reading of Takeo Doi's *The Anatomy of Dependence* (1971), a major work of psychoanalysis in Japan and abroad that introduced and popularized the concept of *amae* to a broad international audience. Doi presents amae, most often translated into English as dependence, as a "key concept" in understanding the Japanese psychology and society as a whole (*ibid*: 28). The focus in Doi's work is on the structuring of Japanese interpersonal relationships and how they are understood as rooted in a dependence and debt, particularly between child and parent that can never be entirely repaid. As such, its use in treating addiction lies in getting patients to recognize their amae, their incalculable debt owed to others for giving them life and carc as children, and how their drinking or drug use impedes any attempts at repaying this fundamental cultural burden. Addicts, it is hoped, will recognize through Naikan's focused meditation how they have harmed those to whom they most indebted, and the strength of this realization will enable them to overcome their addiction. It must then be emphasized that this is an approach to treatment fundamentally rooted in a particular and increasingly challenged understanding of the Japanese family structure that privileges a stable domestic environment.

Like Doi's work generally, Naikan therapy is an approach to treating addiction likely to invite criticism outside Japan for being overly essentializing and rooted in notions of Japanese exceptionalism and *Nihonjinron* (theories of Japanese-ness). It is also an approach largely unable to aid those coming from traumatic or dysfunctional home environments, which is sadly the reality for a substantial number of Japan's alcoholics. However, while such criticisms are accurate, and Naikan therapy is also largely dismissive of addiction as a powerful biological and psychological force upon afflicted individuals, Takemoto Hospital's program recognizes the need for comprehensive environmental change in an addict's life, and emphasizes the need for reasserting hope into patients' lives. Many patients live and work on the hospital grounds in a variety of small industries that provide job training and cultivate a sense of individual worthiness. These include a bakery and cafeteria that feeds everyone staying at the hospital and sells bread and box lunches to the surrounding community, as well as a small retail shop staffed entirely by patients. These endeavors are set up to give purpose and meaning to individual addicts. They also represent perhaps the most tangible aspect of the hospital's recovery program. While Naikan, with its links to Buddhism and specific interpretations of a distinctly Japanese identity, garners much of the popular attention, an emphasis in this treatment regimen on giving addicts a job where they are individually empowered and can cultivate a talent is, I argue, a practice other recovery groups and programs too often overlook.

Finally, a number of Japanese alcoholics use the Internet, particularly online diaries, as a tool to help them manage their addiction. These diaries often take the shape of daily blogs, and many alcoholics use Livedoor and Ameba—two of Japan's largest blogging hosts—as their online platform.[5] Diary instead of blog, however, better captures the tone of these online posts, as they are typically updated daily, quite often with mundane details of the day's events, yet with the occasional post of tremendous emotional depth and poignancy on life as an alcoholic in Japan, all undertaken as a form of therapy to aid with recovery. Japan's long established historic propensity of diary keeping allows it to act as "a medium of communication to increase the intensity of friendship" (White 1994: 137)—a practice that today is increasingly visible online as these diaries take on a recognized form where confession, communication, and exchange can take place within a historically and culturally vetted format.

Several sobriety group members talked about using an online diary to supplement meeting attendance, sometimes at a doctor's urging, as the blog acted as a different outlet for their struggles and ensured a higher degree of anonymity. Others who had rejected joining AA or Danshūkai instead used their online presence as the primary mechanism to aid in controlling their drinking. More than anything else, use of the Internet by Japanese alcoholics is an attempt to create and build community among a group that often feels isolated and incompatible with mainstream life (Oka et al. 2011: 532). The importance of online diary keeping for alcoholics rests in its potential for positive change at the meeting point of technological innovation and human subjectivity (Katsuno and Yano 2002). If "healing the self" is a primary objective of treatment for alcoholism and addiction within current paradigms, then emergent technological forms of human expression are also the next frontier in trying to better understand and shape recovery. Online diaries allow individual alcoholics across Japan a meaningful outlet for vocalizing their struggles with addiction, as well as the frustrations they feel with those around them, giving it the potential to alter established views on recovery and offer access to a place of comfort and support to those with nowhere else to turn.

This chapter argued that AA and Danshūkai's emphasis on spirituality enables some alcoholics in Japan to experience a profoundly moving moment of self-transformation, allowing them to regain and reassert a lost sense of interpersonal control and purpose. For these individuals the transformation is often dramatic, a catalyst for comprehensive change in their actions, feelings of self-worth, and relationships with others. As Toru's narrative illustrated, it can allow for a near total reversal of one's life path resulting in a cessation of any desire to consume alcohol, repaired interpersonal relationships, improved physical health, and a reassertion of purpose and self-worth. However, the experiences of Toru and Masa are largely the exception in Japan and many others at AA and Danshūkai chafe at accepting that they cannot control their alcohol consumption and must surrender to a power greater than themselves in order to indefinitely live "in recovery." Thus, the importance of spirituality in the sobriety process, and acceptance of AA and Danshūkai's methodology as the only means to a recognized and accepted recovery, cause many in Japan to reject group membership outright or endure their sobriety in the absence of alternative programs.

NOTES

1. Women were not restricted from entering this treatment program, but in the year of meetings I attended not a single female patient came to a meeting. Dr. Mori noted that this was most likely due to men still being the ones to eventually seek out treatment for their drinking, while too many women of a similar age continue to hide their consumption from others.

2. These blocks of three steps, 1–3, 4–6, 7–9, and 10–12 correspond to larger thematic points in AA. Steps 1–3 emphasize admission and surrender, 4–6 are a chronicling of wrongdoings and transgressions, 7–9 outline a process of seeking forgiveness, and 10–12 speak of a spiritual awakening and the mission of carrying AA's message to others.

3. Japan's history of new religious movements during the postwar era, with Aum Shinrikyo, perpetrators of the Tokyo Subway sarin gas attack in 1995, being among the most well-known, have left many Japanese skeptical of organizations claiming to bestow religious or spiritual salvation through institutionalized practices. Such sentiment, Aki feels, restricts AA's ability to attract new members as many harbor concerns that the organization is "just another cult" eager to reap financial gain from vulnerable members.

4. Motivational interviewing is one method gaining prominence in the United States yet, to my knowledge, not used in Japan for treating addiction (see Miller and Rollnick 2012 for more on this treatment technique).

5. While blogs have a tendency to be indefinite, disappearing without warning or suddenly not updated regularly, several long running and active examples include http://syousuke.livedoor.biz /, http://ameblo.jp/ippozennsinn/ , http://sirafudeikou.jugem.jp /, and http://ameblo.jp/komomonokoto/ .

Chapter Seven

Futsū or *Fushigi*

Normally Drunk and Oddly Sober

This chapter confronts an important polemic that surrounds alcoholism in Japan, Tokyo AA and Danshūkai members' understanding and use of the terms *futsū* (normal) and *fushigi* (strange/mysterious) as conceptual categories. As previous chapters have shown, discussion of normal are common among alcoholics, and both *futsū* and *fushigi* are frequently used during group meetings, as they reflect a pervading desire among many members to reestablish a sense of normalcy in their lives and confront the perceptions of abnormality they and others often ascribe to them. However, before looking at the use and meaning given these terms, several major assumptions and prevailing positions on alcoholism and addiction generally must be revisited. This review is crucial because, when considering Japan, such an unpacking requires looking more at the secrecy that often surrounds alcoholism and sobriety group membership, as well as the links formed to other afflictions—notably depression, the gendering of this process, and the power addiction can wield over individuals. As such, the chapter first looks at major popular elements contributing to how an alcoholic identity is experienced in Japan, including how this contrasts with the United States and other areas influenced by sobriety group ideology, before returning to *futsū* and *fushigi* as important descriptive categories.

For readers in North America, particularly the United States, two important assumptions related to alcoholism and addiction must be initially considered. The first deals with the prevalence of the AA meeting as a standard component of not only the recovery but also the popular culture landscape, evident in its use across countless television shows, films, and other forms of media that all rely on the assumption that viewers immediately recognize the meeting for what it is. Specific examples are too numerous to list, and instead what is important to keep in mind is the unproblematic use in particularly American popular culture of AA or AA-like meetings and other recovery settings, as it reflects pervasive comprehension and familiarity with the sobriety group framework.[1] Whether a viewer or reader has attended a meeting is largely irrelevant, as simply residing in North America has likely imparted an awareness of AA's existence and conveyed the importance given meetings in the organizational structure. However, despite the prevalence of American popular media in Japan, the sobriety group meeting as a conventional trope within popular entertainment remains relatively unknown as a domestic practice.[2]

The second assumption concerns how addiction is understood and perceived by non-addicts. While addiction is recognized by many, in and out of Japan, as a legitimate and powerful affliction, many of the particulars surrounding its manifestation are far less clear. In part this is due to the individual specificity of addiction. Prevailing contemporary biomedical understandings label addiction a disease of the brain that has physical, psychological, and environmental manifestations (Koob and Volkow 2009). Such understandings also increasingly rely on a fundamental differentiation between drug use and abuse along a continuum of diagnostic criteria. While these ideas increasing leach out from academic publications into popular definitions of addiction, they remain unevenly distributed and inconsistently applied. Such shifts are away from earlier and far less nuanced definitional attempts that reflect not only how addiction remains a fluctuating category of inquiry, but also an area of research into human behavior where conclusions and research directions sometimes reflect prevailing societal norms and political dictates as much as conclusions derived from biomedical research (Campbell 2007, Levine 1978).

What is clear is that many of Japan's addicts at AA or Danshūkai are fundamentally changed by their addiction, to the degree that many of their actions and behaviors before joining a sobriety group are no longer possible. Moments of what can best be described as "risky behavior" illustrate this process of individual change. Kazuko, an AA member in her mid-thirties, who periodically came to Central Group meetings, often recalled her multiple arrests for unpaid taxi rides. After spending all of her money drinking, she would hail a cab, tell the driver to take her to a well-known landmark or station near her apartment building, and when they arrived flee the scene as quickly as possible, leaving behind a fare that typically approached ¥10,000 (about $100.00). As Kazuko did this with greater frequency, her description also circulated among Tokyo's taxi drivers, as she was told one night after trying to run but falling immediately when her high-heeled shoes and intoxicated sense of balance caused her to slip on a wet sidewalk. She was arrested that night, and several other subsequent times for similar criminal acts, behavior she now understands as inconceivable and the actions of a sick woman in need of help. Additionally, the power addiction is said to wield over afflicted individuals renders not only a variety of public spaces "dangerous," as discussed earlier, it also permanently alters how addicts interact with their immediate milieu and the people within it. As many of Japan's addicts feel they do not have the power to refuse an offered drink, or once they begin drinking cannot stop, they must also avoid temptation as completely as possible. Thus, much of the secrecy and struggles recounted so far among the men at AA and Danshūkai is a response to a shifting relationship with their lived environment, particularly an inability of those around them to understand or appreciate such a transition.

The secrecy surrounding many group members' alcoholism stems from the difficulties many feel in explaining or discussing their addiction and the changes it necessitates in their life. Reizo, Naomi, and Takashi—a younger Central Group member who frequently discussed fights with his girlfriend about his sobriety during meetings—as well as numerous other meeting attendees, spoke often of the need to decline invitations to class reunions, friendly meetings with former schoolmates, and other customary social events. Meeting past classmates in particular, a common occurrence in Japan that often takes place at bars or izakayas, came with the expectation that everyone gets drunk and reminisces about their time together in school. Yet for Central Group members such gatherings are a source of persistent stress and dishonesty as their unwillingness to tell people they have known for many years, in some instances since elementary school, of their current alcoholism means they must now lie about why they feel they can no longer attend reunions or meet for drinks. With sobriety Takashi, Naomi, and many others at the Central Group have changed who they now are, but struggle with how or if they can disclose this transformation to others, a decision they often measure with great care and only make known to a small and typically unavoidable number of individuals.

Takashi's case is particularly tragic and revealing of the turmoil that can result when Japanese alcoholics reveal their addiction to others, as the girlfriend he lives with refuses to accept his sobriety and AA membership as legitimate, productive, or even necessary. In his late twenties, Takashi is younger than most at the Central Group, yet can also recount interpersonal struggles with alcohol that far outpace his youth. At many meetings over several particularly difficult months he discussed his girlfriend's constant verbal abuse and aggression towards him, as well as her ongoing heavy alcohol consumption in their small apartment, all stemming from her disdain for his sobriety. She finds his sobriety emasculating and "stupid," he said, typified in her screaming one night while drunk "which is more important, AA or me!" before throwing an open beer can at him. Her unwillingness to accept Takashi's sobriety reflects not only the broader difficulties many Japanese men face when electing to no longer drink, and finding that others frequently regard such a decision with suspicion and derision, it is also representative of larger cultural forces in Japan structuring comportment norms and impacting how alcoholism is lived in ways not fully anticipated by AA or Danshūkai's recovery methodology.

Takashi's struggles, and the larger links that can be made to admissions of alcoholism among Japanese men, mark these disclosures as "about the human body and society's perception of normal and abnormal," making those who elect to no longer consume alcohol somehow abnormal (Dennett 1996: 325). Takashi's decision to abstain from alcohol gives his girlfriend cultural ammunition to question and delegitimize his position and performance as a boyfriend and man, framing sobriety as a problematic and easily derided condition. Japan's dearth of cultural recognition and therapeutic sympathy or understanding for alcoholism, addiction, or AA and Danshūkai make sobriety group membership incompatible with prevailing constructions of masculinity, and leave men like Takashi adrift in how to confront or challenge their ongoing difficulties. The result is conflict, sometimes aggressive and violent, as alcoholism is understood by AA and Danshūkai as a disease that can only be managed and overcome through active meeting participation, while outside this context addiction is regarded as an abnormality inconsistent with the cultural expectations placed on Japanese men. Takashi's girlfriend does not see him working towards personal betterment or struggling with interpersonal issues of control and substance abuse, instead he is a failure as a man and an easy, unproblematic target for her abuse and typically drunken aggression.

The paradox here is that for Japanese men, many of the "crises of masculinity" noted elsewhere, an inability to financially provide for one's family or a systematic denial of a productive masculine identity by outside colonizing forces, are not immediately or oppressively acute concerns (Brandes 2002, Pine 2008, Tengan 2008). While limited or unfulfilling employment and economic stagnation remain inescapable issues, Japan also remains collectively among the world's wealthier nations (Allison 2013). And even within Japanese feelings of widespread "precarity" about the direction of national affairs, alcohol consumption remains a constant, available to assuage individual concerns as much as celebrate triumphs or solidify bonds of friendship (Allison 2012). Thus, alcohol is not only a tool through which homosocial male bonding is made possible, it persists as a core component shaping a Japanese masculine identity. This, in part, helps explain recent mass media infatuation and processes of crisis creation around the purported rise of "herbivorous" men, young adult Japanese males who reject alcohol consumption and are labeled as uninterested in sex and averse to competition (Bardsley 2011: 133). Like alcoholics, herbivorous men stand as a challenge to convention, in that they explicitly clash with root understandings of what a Japanese man should be. What unites alcoholics, herbivorous men, and Japan's other societal outliers are their struggles with challenging or changing the persistently pervasive strength behind the importance given alcohol consumption—because as the historical trajectory of postwar Japan has privileged alcohol consumption as a means of dispensing reward for hard work, it also continues to encourage its use in solidifying bonds of friendship and trust between men. Thus, to challenge such positions today is to do much more than decline an invitation to drink—it is to call into question the roots of Japan's status quo and the implied necessity of shared alcohol consumption.

Takashi's struggles with his girlfriend, or Reizo and other members' apprehension at broadly disclosing their alcoholism, reveal deeper fears than the individual concerns of the embarrassment such an admission could bring. They reflect how deeply embedded alcohol consumption and drunken comportment are in defining and shaping Japan's understandings of masculinity. With sobriety, Japanese men who no longer consume alcohol must comprehensively renegotiate and reinterpret how their sense of masculinity is imagined, defined, and lived. While this definition of masculinity is by no means permanent, and I have argued elsewhere how challenges can be found in some corners of Japan's drinking landscape, it remains the dominant and structuring thread concerning the nation's popular conceptions of masculinity (Christensen 2012). To be a man in Japan still means you periodically drink and get drunk with other men, in order to assert not only a homosocial male intimacy between friends and acquaintances, but to also confirm and conform to a powerful set of expectations governing normalcy. As such, the norms of alcohol consumption continue to marginalize Japan's alcoholics and addicts in ways that offer few avenues to pursue or enact meaningful change.

The strength of these constructions is also, in part, what makes the meeting space so important for group members hoping to achieve lasting sobriety. Sobriety group meetings are the space in which disclosures and frustrations are vocalized without fear for the reaction they might generate or concern with how alcoholism is perceived. And while AA and Danshūkai meetings, despite the minor methodological differences already discussed, maintain the same goal of creating a space and place within which a life devoid of alcohol consumption is possible, the liminal nature of the meeting space and the difficulties many express in transporting the content and tenets of the meeting to non-alcoholics also mark it as a space of frustration. Yuka captured this discrepancy between the comfort of the meeting room and the callousness of the outside world when asked to moderate a meeting in early October. Unemployed, she said she deliberately spends most days alone at home, often waking early in the morning and then lying awake in bed until nearly noon, telling herself over and over again that today she will not drink. Several daily tasks fill her with dread, checking her mobile phone and email for messages being the worst, as she fears receiving a message from a former "drinking friend" that could trigger a return to consumption. On this day the only thing that got her out of the house was the 7:00 pm meeting, and while she had tried to convince herself several times that she did not need to go, in the end her desire to feel the warmth and rejuvenatory power she draws from attending won out. But, she added, fear of losing her sobriety also drove her to the meeting that evening, and her biggest concern for her sobriety is that fear often fades with time.

Like Yuka, many at AA and Danshūkai regard meetings as a kind of home where alcoholism is openly discussed without concern for the questions or judgment that frequently come from nonmembers. However, the openness of the meeting rarely extends beyond the comforting confines of the meeting rooms, offering little challenge to the social and occupational marginalization and diminished claims to masculine gender norms felt by many of Japan's sobriety group members. As a result, the meeting sites of the Central Group and Ohashi Danshūkai are cultivated as alternative homes, *ibasho* (good places) in the language of group members, where feelings and opinions impossible to express elsewhere are aired. Yet without any cultural assurances of a comprehensive challenge or end to group member's feelings of ambiguity, the sense of disconnection between the meeting space and the wider Japanese public continues to influence the content and tone of members' in-meeting speeches. Takashi's struggles, noted earlier, poignantly convey such difficulties as his efforts to stop drinking, motivated by the destructive influence he feels alcohol is having in his life, are met with mocking and scorn from his girlfriend at home. For Takashi the meeting space becomes the only place where he can feel "at home," comfortable and with a sense of normalcy, unafraid that his actions and decisions will be met with anger and ridicule (Allison 2013: 47).

Also keenly felt by many at AA and Danshūkai is a sense of ambiguity around addiction, and Japan's as yet unrealized potential to change or challenge such notions. Interestingly, this is seen most prominently in discussion of depression and its growing acceptance among the Japanese public as a legitimate and recognized affliction. Sometimes this is done during meeting speeches, but more often it occurs outside the room before or after the formal proceedings when many attendees gather to share in casual conversation over canned coffee and cigarettes. As one attendee at a Central Group meeting exasperatedly pleaded one night, "why can't we be like depression!," after telling everyone gathered around the walkway's communal ashtray about a young woman in his office who was now being given a lighter workload and constant sympathy after telling their boss she had been diagnosed as depressed. His frustration stemmed from Japan's growing acceptance of depression's popular legitimacy, thereby warranting sympathy and compassion from others instead of the skepticism and suspicion he feels typically meets a disclosure of alcoholism and addiction. After that same meeting Naomi stood quietly with others in the outdoor walkway, a cigarette ignored and slowly burning down between her fingers, before angrily mentioning to no one in particular an incident similar to the one brought up earlier, where an acquaintance at work recently told everyone she was depressed and received an outpouring of compassion in response. "Those who know I'm in AA," she added caustically, "never acted like that."

As Junko Kitanaka's recent book demonstrates, the transformation of depression into an accepted affliction, complete with shelves of self-help books on the topic given prominent display at major bookstores, emanates from specific linguistic practices within Japan's medical and psychiatric institutions (2011). Kitanaka adds that diagnostic and institutional authority concerning depression and psychiatry were maintained "not because its knowledge was accepted as cultural common sense, but because it was able to monopolize medical knowledge and exercise its jurisdiction for treatment of those diagnosed as mentally ill" (*ibid*: 109). This makes straightforward comparison of diagnostic and treatment processes between depression and alcoholism difficult, as AA and Danshūkai also seek to frame alcoholism and addiction as a "perfectly normal illness," yet do so by divorcing the physician from their monopoly on diagnostic authority. However, AA and Danshūkai also rely in Japan upon the authority physicians wield to impart legitimacy to their organizations. Additionally, both groups employ their own linguistic and methodological conventions, many adopted by, not initiated from, Japanese physicians focusing on addiction, that have since come to dictate the tone and direction of recovery. What is thus largely evident in the speeches and comments from many group members is a frustration at the ongoing inability of Japan's sobriety community to shift popular opinion on alcoholism and addiction in a sympathetic or more informed direction, despite tremendous ongoing reliance on traditional channels of medical authority.

THE POWER OF ADDICTION

No matter the region of the world under consideration, addiction is a problematic subject of scientific and cultural inquiry. Bodies, neighborhoods, and communities all bear the typically graphic reality of addiction's destructive potential, yet alcohol, tobacco, and other potentially habit forming substances also remain readily available for purchase and consumption. Further complicating this arrangement is the seemingly indiscriminate nature of addiction, how it can fully consume some, while others imbibe periodically and without the destructive side effects. Research on addiction is, and has largely been, the domain of the medical sciences, yet this work is also often dictated by shifting political policy overseen through the punitive power of police forces and other apparatuses of the state typically more interested in stopping the behaviors associated with addiction than understanding how it develops (Garriott 2011: 72)—a reality starkly evident when the tolerance and availability of alcohol, a legal yet powerful psychoactive drug, is contrasted with Japan's aggressive illegality towards marijuana and other illicit narcotics.[3] Even much of the research on addiction comes out of specific cultural contexts that structure how conclusions are discussed, disseminated, and given legitimacy. As Nancy Campbell elegantly notes, "no one definition of addiction has integrated enough levels of analysis to achieve universal acceptance or even survive very long" (2007: 6). Yet addiction, despite invoking collective definitional struggles, is everywhere, a pervasive cultural, medical, and political phenomenon that cannot be ignored and demands to be better understood as a medical, social, emotional, punitive, and cultural phenomenon.

Nowhere is this uncertainty more evident than in the widespread classification of addiction as a disease. Turning again to Campbell's work, "calling something a 'disease' appeals to scientific conventions and clinical vocabularies but generates a cascade of questions" (2007: 1–2)—questions that are as thorny to answer as they are numerous. If addiction is a disease is it curable or incurable? How does it mark its victims? Is it contagious and if so in what ways? Is it chronic and lifelong or episodic? All are relevant questions examined earlier in discussion of the disease model of alcoholism. What remains unclear, in Japan and elsewhere, is how such questions can be answered and the consequences, particularly in varying cultural contexts, of such efforts—issues that become particularly pronounced when, as is the case in Japan, the primary means of treating alcoholism and other addictions derive from integrating sobriety group ideology, much of which has its roots in a decidedly different historical and cultural context, coupled with intense medical scrutiny and extended periods of hospitalization.

Additionally, it is crucial to keep in mind David Courtwright's now well-circulated reminder that "what we think about addiction very much depends on who is addicted" when considering how Japan frames addiction, particularly to alcohol (2001: 4). Addiction as a distinct field of study garnered little attention in postwar Japan as the government's response to psychoactive substance use was aggressively punitive towards methamphetamine, marijuana, and other narcotics deemed illicit, while largely indifferent of alcohol and drunkenness (Alexander 2013b, Vaughn et al. 1995). A tolerance for alcohol was also the consistent practice among Japan's physicians, with many of them often instructing patients with alcohol-linked problems to drink less for a little while in order to let their livers recover, but rarely raising the possibility of addiction (Borovoy 2005). Dr. Higuchi, of the National Alcohol Center at Kurihama Hospital, noted during one of our meetings that the addiction curriculum in most of Japan's medical school does not exceed a "half hour" of instruction, leaving too many nurses and doctors ill-equipped to recognize or treat an addicted patient. While his offhand remark, said with a smirk and a tone of exasperated indifference, is an obvious and deliberate oversimplification of the curriculum, it also reflects his well-informed frustration at the lack of attention paid to addiction by those in Japan who should be motivated to enact change. As one of Japan's senior physicians and researchers on alcoholism, Dr. Higuchi's statement also carries substantial heft as a critique and demand that greater attention be paid to addiction, as what positive changes have taken place in recent years have been slowly and sometimes reluctantly enacted. His critique is also supported by a slew of recent work highlighting Japan's deficient infrastructure for dealing with persistent methamphetamine addiction (Matsumoto and Kobayashi 2008), the overall lack of drug treatment facilities across the country (Kondo et al. 2000), and ongoing popular opposition to abstinence as the only effective treatment method (Higuchi et al. 2014, Kimura et al. 2013).

Yet addiction is also starting to garner greater levels of attention in Japan, evident in shifting linguistic practices across the medical and sobriety landscape. Amy Borovoy highlights the recent linguistic shift in medical literature when describing how alcoholics are moving away from the term *arukōru chūdoku* (literally, alcohol poisoning), that means both "the condition of alcoholism and chronic drinking," to *arukōru izonshō* (alcohol dependency syndrome), a less pejorative term steeped in medical authority (2005: 52). This transition is evident at Central Group and Ohashi Danshūkai meetings, as participants are typically split in how they describe their alcoholism when giving self-introductions. Members of both groups make use of *aru chū* (the abbreviated version of arukōru chūdoku) and arukōru izonshō when introducing themselves and speaking about past drinking at meetings. Additionally, differences in what term of description is used also can reflect a conscious decision from the speaker, with aru chū imparting a sense of informality, while arukōru izonshō conveys awareness of the medical aspects of alcoholism, including likely having received and accepted a physician's diagnosis as "alcohol dependent."

While these small adjustments in terminology use may seem trivial, as both identify the individual as an alcoholic, how they are used reveals ongoing struggles among Japan's alcoholics concerning the ways in which they feel it best to present themselves to those outside AA or Danshūkai. Aru chū is the conventional term, recognized by all, yet heavy with negative implications of homeless drunks in Tokyo's ignored corners and margins. An aru chū is understood by many as either a hopeless drunk or is used jokingly by those with a reputation for, and love of, heavy drinking.[4] To invoke it with all the seriousness and implications that the word commands is to challenge its very use and popular imaging among many in Japan. In contrast, arukōru izonshō carries the weight and authority of medicalization; to use this as a descriptor of self implies illness, given legitimacy through a physician's diagnostic authority. Yet living with an illness is most often followed by either recovery or death; to absorb and assume that illness as a permanent part of one's existence also challenges how most people understand and interpret sickness. Thus, while arukōru izonshō carries more linguistic heft and institutional authority, it is also, to those in Japan unexposed to AA or Danshūkai, an odd way to structure one's existence.

Despite these changes Japan's popular renderings of addiction remain largely metaphoric and, in some instances, unproblematic. As discussed earlier, overly simplistic notions of a Japan afflicted by "workaholism," or students being addicted to studying, are not only inaccurate generalizations of the nation, they also conceal the pain and difficulty facing Japan's alcoholics and other addicts. In short, these culturally inflicted notions of the addict in Japan make consideration of addictions damaging physical aspects difficult, contributing to the expressed feelings of alienation among AA and Danshūkai members. As such, what cannot be denied, and must increasingly come to shape understandings of addiction, is the destructive potential and pervasive power addiction wields over afflicted individuals. Crucial to this recognition process is increased awareness of how individual suffering can be exacerbated through culturally specific contexts, evident in Japan in the reluctance to broadly consider addiction as something personally destructive that can befall anyone, a reality that makes recognition of the addict's pain exceedingly difficult. Japan's addicts are conditioned to speak about their addiction as a loss of control over their ability to regulate the consumption of psychoactive substances, resulting in the need for comprehensive sobriety. By making such an admission they submit themselves to addiction's definitional apparatus as framed by AA and Danshūkai, making the intricacies of their lives fit within group ideology. And while such efforts integrate group members into transnational recovery communities, they simultaneously hamper inquiry into the "cultural aspects of drinking," as well as sobriety, and the lived impact for individual members of adopting such radical interpersonal changes (Douglas 1987: 7).

As such, "loss of control" must now be grappled with, as it is a major force structuring prevailing contemporary understandings of addiction. Sobriety group members at AA and Danshūkai speak frequently of how they would immediately "lose control" upon beginning to drink alcohol, leaving them powerless to regulate the amount they consumed despite awareness of the physical and social consequences. Gen, the Central Group's treasurer, spoke frequently of his past inability to control his level of consumption during meetings. "For years I would go drinking with colleagues after work, despite having earlier promised myself I would not drink that day, and now justifying this reversal by telling myself I would only have 'a beer or two.'" The need for such a promise was rooted in his persistent heavy consumption, "I always had a hangover," and the growing toll it was taking on his health. When recounting his past behavior at meetings, Gen scoffed at how ridiculous he now regards his promises to not drink. Adding that each time he was out drinking he would quickly have one beer, "I always finished it before everyone else," and then a second, before dismissing his earlier plan for restraint and continuing to drink until he "blacked out" and usually had to be helped into a cab home by a co-worker. He did this with such regularity that colleagues began avoiding him or conveniently "forgetting to invite me" for outings at the bar. This only spurred Gen to invite himself or act as the one organizing after work drinking sessions, and pressuring others until they felt obliged to attend. Eventually things became so bad that everyone he worked with found sometimes elaborate ways to avoid going drinking with him, and Gen took to imbibing alone. Only increasingly severe tremors in his hands and an inability to focus on even the simplest tasks at work drove Gen to seek help from a physician, nearly three years after he first began to question his consumption and tell himself he would "take today off," or only have "one or two beers."

Gen's account of struggling with control is also not atypical among sobriety group members. An older man who periodically attended Central Group meetings spoke of a similar drinking pattern after hearing Gen's account of absent restraint and control. "I would always drink too much" when out with co-workers and have to spend the rest of the next day with a terrible hangover and "lowering my head" while apologizing to everyone in the office. "I went around saying *ayamare! ayamare!* (apologies) to everyone in a loud voice all day"—a scene he says he repeated several times each week for over a year before succumbing to alcohol-related health complications and entering hospital. Thus, control, or lack thereof, over an individual's desired level of consumption is the major variable in these and an abundance of other meeting accounts of past struggles with drink. Yet control in this context is also a highly variable concept. While Gen and others speak often of being "out of control" while drinking, they were also drinking, at least initially, at the invitation and behest of colleagues and co-workers—individuals who later avoided them out of frustration with their drunken excesses instead of intervening out of concern for their well-being. So, in the case of Japan, to whom is responsibility for control over drink and drunkenness bestowed? AA very deliberately emphasizes a language of control as "a basic Protestant virtue" that could "prevail over the scientific and psychiatric ones" (Valverde 1998: 125). Japan's sobriety movement has taken up such linguistic conventions, including incorporating them into the medical apparatus for treating alcoholism and addiction, yet done little to absorb and account for the lived daily realities of men across Tokyo who struggle with alcohol-related problems, and find those struggles firmly rooted in the expectations and exigency of the workplace.

This structuring places inquiries into addiction at the intersection of culturally influenced scientific understandings of the addict, and the lived moments of struggles and despair each individual carries with them in sobriety. As my examples from Japan illustrate, emphasis has often focused on the scientific side to this equation. One need only consider the importance of accepting the disease model of alcoholism to sobriety group membership, at the expense of individual frustrations, as well as the dearth of culturally specific conversation on how Japanese men might confront addiction or assert a domestically productive masculine identity in the absence of alcohol. This imbalance is borne out of Japan's heavy reliance on sobriety group ideology and teachings, without fully considering how such positions are received and viewed by those outside or unfamiliar with AA and Danshūkai. To accept sobriety group membership and its accompanying diagnosis of alcoholism, individuals agree to rearrange their sense of self around a set of rigid principles meant to govern addiction, a chaotic and wholly unpredictable affliction, yet are also required to confess a lack of control or ability to regulate their actions. This begs the question: Does the manner in which Japan approaches and engages with addiction exacerbate its destructive potential? I return to this issue in the next chapter.

FUTSŪ OR *FUSHIGI*

As Japan's economic bubble was bursting in the early 1990s, more than ninety percent of Japanese households identified as "middle class" (Allison 2012: 351). Beyond a reflection of Japan's permeating affluence, such statements of self-identity reflect a high level of faith and investment in the instruments of the Japanese state, a pervading commitment among Japan's citizens to the status quo. While a generation of economic stagnation has eroded this high level of trust and belief in the state's provisional power, it has not been as successful in undermining the strength of the status quo in dictating notions of the acceptable and unacceptable. Within such a context the importance of *futsū* (normal/ordinary) as not only a descriptive term but also an influential definition categories becomes evident. *Futsū* implies mainstream, unproblematic, and accepted, containing in its use "the implication of conformity" to established norms (Clammer 2013: 34). *Futsū* is comforting, both in its familiarity and predictability. It implies an anticipated condition that, if not met or received, is then potentially viewed with suspicion and derision. *Fushigi*, in contrast, implies strange, unusual, and mysterious—a comprehensive deviation from the expected or anticipated. And this is also, in part, what makes it such a revealing dichotomy when its use in the context of sobriety group meetings is considered. Group members understand and describe their alcoholism as both something that deviates from the norm, but also as something mysterious and poorly understood, an affliction of uncertainty governed at AA or Danshūkai by concrete rules and protocols.

The strength of *futsū*, the tyrannical power of normal in Japan, pervades and structures not only wide ranging notions of comportment and conduct, but also discussion of illness and health, albeit in ways recognized in the context of Japan as culturally valid (Lock 1984, Ohnuki-Tierney 1984). This layering of *futsū* erects what I see as the "contradictory conventions" of the status quo, conventions that then derive meaning through transgression. As an example, drunkenness is largely tolerated in Japan, despite numerous individual objections or dissatisfactions, because at its widest level of interpretation it is seen as normal conduct, particularly for men after the workday ends. To be drunk periodically is *futsū*, and everything from the ubiquity of outlets selling alcohol to a sophisticated Tokyo infrastructure built to accommodate the consequences of overconsumption—look closely and you find canisters of sawdust on train station platforms to help clean the nightly vomit from over-indulging commuters—make deviation from such practices strange and abnormal. Drunkenness as *futsū* also makes it far harder to "pathologize" or even critique such behavior, as anything but the normal conduct of men (Borovoy 2005: 66). Inversely, a rejection of alcohol, even if entered into out of a concern for one's health, confines these individuals to the cultural margins and makes integration with the *futsū* problematic.

This rendering of the *futsū* is often graphically evident in the regularity with which one finds vomit and severely, shockingly, drunk individuals in various states of semi-consciousness across Tokyo's train cars, station platforms, sidewalks, and park benches. While this is sometimes painted as a positive—Japan is so safe you can get falling down drunk in central Tokyo and still have your wallet and mobile phone when you wake up—it is an oversimplification of the reality that ignores the far more important question of why are there so many deeply inebriated individuals on display across Tokyo and Japan each night? Why, as one particularly frustrated Central Group member asked rhetorically at a meeting, is the *futsū* being dead drunk while the *fushigi* is being sober?

I kept thinking of this question during one impossible to forget train ride home through some of Tokyo's busiest rail stations. I and my roommate were returning home from our part time job tending bar, exhausted after the busy Saturday night shift. Eager to sit down for the twenty minute ride, we were thrilled to see a nearly empty car as the Yamanote line train entered our station. Our happiness was short lived as we bounded through the doors only to be hit with the nauseating punch of vomit's unmistakable odor. Seated in the middle of the car was a man who looked to be in his thirties, covered to soaking in his own regurgitation, while all around him the chunky liquid sloshed back and forth in a slowly expanding pool on the floor. We, like nearly everyone else, quickly moved to the adjacent car, escaping the full impact of the smell but now packed in tightly with everyone else who had fled the contaminated scene. As I listened to those around us, I was struck by how they discussed our drunk companion. While a few grumbled about being forced to cram into other parts of the train, everyone was mostly sympathetic or commiserate, remembering and reminiscing about their own experiences with intoxicated train travel, and how they had never been that bad, or so they hoped, on a trip home. Finally, we arrived at Shinjuku Station and the man who had vomited across now nearly the length of the train car got up and left as if nothing had happened, leaving behind his mess for someone else to clean.

Futsū's strength is not only evident in such moments of tolerated transgression, like the one above, but also in more mundane conversations on past moments of required consumption, often done at the urging, and many would say ordering, of bosses and other associates. Nobuki, a kind and energetic man in his sixties, is a now retired president of a major highway bus company based in Kanto. While not an AA or Danshūkai member, he has been sober for several years and is often invited to speak at group meetings. His choice to live sober comes after years of heavy work-related drinking left him angry at the importance given alcohol in corporate Japan, and also made him a vocal volunteer with several Tokyo-based NGOs working to strengthen alcohol related legislation throughout the country. During one of our conversations he talked about the drinking he had to do as the boss during company retreats and parties. Nobuki said he would routinely drink more than twenty-five cups of sake in an evening, mostly while individually toasting with each of his employees, yet also maintained the *shiikari* (steady, sturdy) demeanor he felt mandatory for someone in his prominent position. He did this for nearly ten years as company president, as well as many other years of somewhat less intense consumption prior to his promotion as a vice president, all because it was, he felt, required of him as the company's leader.

Reflecting back on these years, he feels the strength of drinking practices are catastrophically damaging to Japan, particularly for the men required in take part in such consumption. Yet, he added, it is also nearly impossible, at least in the context of company retreats and parties, for individual men to refuse offers, although orders is probably more accurate, to drink. Nobuki remembers "things quickly becoming *kimochi mazui*" (unpleasant, awkward) if one individual on a company outing genuinely tried to not drink, as others were unsure of how to respond to someone not as drunk as everyone else, or unwilling to continue participating in the festivities. In Nobuki's view this is part of the reason for Japan's collective disinterest and dismissal of sobriety, as even entertaining the possibility of a social gathering without alcohol for middle-aged Japanese men is largely inconceivable. The enduring necessity of "*nomyunikēshon*," a term that combines the Japanese verb "*nomu*" (to drink) with the English loan word "communication" and carries the implication that heartfelt interpersonal exchange is impossible without alcohol, is too strong to consider such a shift. Furthermore, feelings of kimochi mazui are directly tied to violations of the *futsū*, as they derive from discomfort with individual divergence from what is expected. As Nobuki added, those who don't drink are often seen as "*kuroi*" (dark, wicked) by others, and their refusal to consume condemns a practice many regard as fun, worthwhile and, most importantly, requisite.

These understandings of *futsū* also transcend generational categories. Kentaro, an Ohashi Danshūkai member in his thirties, invoked distinctions made between *futsū* and *fushigi* at numerous meetings. A still strong and stocky young man who wore thin wireframe glasses and always kept his hair closely cropped, Kentaro was a rugby player in college and then for his company's team. He talked often about his time as a rugby player when speaking at meetings, joking that in Japan it is a sport revolving more around the heavy and "mandatory" drinking after each match than the level of athletic performance displayed on the field. Now sober and retired from rugby, Kentaro marveled when speaking during meetings at how the excessive alcohol consumption, often to the point of nearly everyone on the team vomiting or losing consciousness, was regarded as normal and expected by everyone, including coaches and other team staff. The strange or abnormal among his teammates would have been a refusal to drink or consumption in moderation, and he was often among the heaviest drinkers and strongest pushers of others to imbibe more.

In contrast, *fushigi* is used by alcoholics to articulate and emphasize feelings of uncertainty and ambiguity frequently felt by many sobriety group members. It is not simply the case that as alcoholics their past actions and sense of self are now divergent and different from the expected, or that their behavior somehow contradicts Japan's accepted and anticipated norms of comportment. Instead, sobriety is *fushigi* because it disrupts the *futsū*, and as such, it challenges the established status quo. It is not that alcoholics are strange or mysterious, instead they potentially undermine established conventions the majority in Japan are reluctant to see altered or dismissive of why such actions are necessary. Thus, in a Japan increasingly described as "precarious," the use of *futsū* and *fushigi* by alcoholics highlights ongoing tension between an individual's ability to assert a divergent self-identity and shifting understandings of cultural acceptability (Allison 2013). The result is sobriety in Japan regarded as an affront to convention, yet the presence of group members is also demanding change to comportment norms that have thus far only been reluctantly considered by the mainstream. As such, the degree of challenge to popular perceptions of alcoholism is unclear, and the reality for many at the Central Group and Ohashi Danshūkai is paralysis concerning how those outside the meetings understand their addiction, albeit one mixed with hope that change in the popular perception of the alcoholic is eventually possible.

Thus, Japan, considered broadly, offers an example of the power normative constructions of cultural comportment can wield over individual lives. Drinking and drunkenness, while not unchallenged, sits squatly as the norm, the *futsū*, influential over a wide range of behaviors and conventions. In doing so, it makes alcohol the requisite substance to creating moments of social intimacy, particularly between men. It is also a construction that renders questioning or rejection of alcohol as strange, and marks moments where such refusals take place as socially awkward and uncomfortable. Group members are caught between *futsū* and *fushigi* as definitional categories, reflected in their use of both terms as major descriptors of their experiences with living sober. Having joined AA or Danshūkai in order to restore normalcy to their own as well as the lives of those around them, group members' sobriety now marks them as decidedly outside the norm. As such, without widespread recognition of alcoholism and addiction, Japan's sobriety group members remain caught between a set of untenable cultural norms and their desire to escape the destruction and damage caused by their past alcohol consumption.

Finally, hope for such change is often linked to the possible emergence of a charismatic and inspirational leader. Toshi spoke often of former American first lady Betty Ford as such a figure in the United States, and the need for a similar Japanese individual in order to fundamentally change popular views of addiction.[5] In his view, Betty Ford's forthrightness about her struggles with alcohol and prescription pain medication changed American perceptions of the addict toward one of greater sympathy and understanding. Toshi feels the absence of such a figure in Japan has stunted popular understanding of the condition and allowed addiction to remain a taboo and easily derided topic. Interestingly, Danshūkai cultivates an organizational reverence around Harushige Matsumura, the group's founding figure (Oka and Chenhall 2014). As noted earlier his photo is often prominently displayed at meetings, although not at Ohashi Danshūkai, and his biography acts as an inspirational guide to living sober, filling a role similar to that of the Big Book in AA. Yet he died in 1970 and while his writings, most prominently the *Matsumura Goroku* or fifty maxims of Matsumura, still circulate widely among Danshūkai members, they rarely move beyond the group's sphere of influence (Oka 2011: 22).[6] A moment of hope for change came with the 2007 announcement from Prince Tomohito of Mikasa, a first cousin of Emperor Akihito and fifth in Japan's Imperial line of succession, that he was an alcoholic. The prince's candid public admission was met with hopeful yet hesitant optimism among many at AA and Danshūkai—an optimism that quickly faded, as the next chapter explores in greater detail.

This chapter argued that a source of the struggles and frustrations felt by Japan's alcoholics is due in part to cultural constructions of normal and unusual. Drinking and drunkenness enjoy a well-established position in contemporary Japan as normal conduct, especially for men. The result of this is sobriety and refusals to drink as often poorly understood practices among the majority of Japanese unfamiliar with AA or Danshūkai. Refusing a drink strikes many of Japan's drinkers as strange, the behavior of a socially awkward individual resistant to mainstream sensibilities. Stasis emerges from such pervasive views on the necessity of drinking and drunkenness, and sobriety group members struggle for acceptance and legitimacy in a Japan generally disinterested in their struggles. While this stasis is not comprehensive or unassailable, evident in the emergence of "herbivorous men" and other challenges to the necessity for shared drinking, this chapter highlighted how in the absence of wider acceptance, Tokyo's alcoholics continue to face an uncertain future. The next chapter concludes the book by first returning to Prince Tomohito of Mikasa's public disclosure of alcoholism, before looking outward and considering the significance of Japan to the study of addiction as an aspect of lived identity.

NOTES

1. Prominent recent examples include HBO's *The Wire* which made frequent, and by the account of many addicts, accurate use of a Narcotics Anonymous meeting, AMC's *Breaking Bad* in a somewhat critical look at meeting effectiveness, and Fox's *The Simpsons'* use of AA meetings numerous times during the show's long history, often for comedic purposes.

2. This raises the obvious and intriguing question of how these scenes are interpreted by Japanese viewers when watching American movies and television. While I do not explore this in any more detail, it is an interesting subject for future study.

3. This includes typically heroin, methamphetamine, and cocaine that have all witnessed fluctuating use levels in the postwar era. Notably, Japan's aggressive anti-drug laws are facing increased pressure as arrests for use continue to rise: http://online.wsj.com/article/SB123612257155123461.html#articleTabs%3Darticle.

4. The typically response when explaining my work to people in Japan unfamiliar with AA or Danshūkai, and usually saying initially that I was researching alcoholism in Japan, was "I'm an alcoholic (aru chū), interview me!" This was generally followed by a declaration of love for beer, sake, cocktails, or whatever else was their favorite type of drink.

5. The open and candid manner in which Betty Ford discussed her struggles with addiction, including while serving as first lady of the United States, was raised several times by Japanese members as an example of the kind of public figure they needed to begin changing public perception of alcoholism and the seeming impossibility of finding such an individual.

6. To give a sense of how important this is, several of AA's idioms are now a part of the everyday American lexicon, to the degree that they are rarely recognized as originating in AA. Two of the better known examples are "one day at a time" and "easy does it."

Chapter Eight

The Imperial Drunkard

CRITICAL DIFFICULTIES

AA and Danshūkai save lives and help an alcoholic population that is too often ignored and maligned by the rest of Japan. Japan's alcoholics are ignored, in part, because it is easy to do so and the accounts voiced by AA and Danshūkai members during meetings are often sad, jarring, and unpleasant to hear. Yet when viewed from a different perspective these same accounts are also deeply moving and beautiful, containing in the spoken words evidence of the power a community can wield in helping individuals find peace and stability in their lives. Aki, Toshi, Toru, Masa, Kazu, Gen, and everyone else introduced in this book stated at some point while I attended meetings that without AA or Danshūkai they would be dead. Each of them strongly feels that they would not have been able to stop drinking without AA or Danshūkai and that drinking would have eventually killed them, either gradually through progressively failing health or suddenly in an accident that likely would have also harmed others. As such, it would be irresponsible of me to offer academic scrutiny and criticism of these organizations, or the prevailing views on alcoholism and masculinity in Japan, without again acknowledging that AA and Danshūkai have, and continue to save and salvage countless lives in Japan and across the globe. And it must also be noted that I was deeply changed by my exposure to AA and Danshukai. I remain profoundly impressed, in awe even, of many of the accounts I heard during meetings, the confidently expressed tales of utter desperation followed by a slow, steady march to recovery that restored a degree of stability and interpersonal peace to so many lives. In short, AA and Danshūkai are impressive and necessary organizations that Japan would be much the worse without.

However, I also understand the purpose of scholarship, particularly ethnographic fieldwork, as one of posing questions and inquiry into why an unassailable truth, AA and Danshūkai are *the* way of treating alcoholism, is really so unassailable. As such, I look to strike a balance in this final chapter between once again highlighting the impressive and often overlooked work done by Japan's sobriety group members to help themselves and those around them get and stay sober, and then regain a sense of control and purpose in their lives, alongside what I see as a need for critical inquiry into how alcoholism and addiction are broadly understood, treated, and experienced. Aki's history of drug and alcohol use speaks precisely to such a need for balance between these often conflicting views. She spent many years as a young adult drinking heavily and using heroin, methamphetamine, and other illicit narcotics, while also being periodically hospitalized, attending Narcotics Anonymous, Danshūkai, and AA meetings during her brief periods of sobriety, and then returning to use. As she candidly said one afternoon at the JSO when talking about her past alcohol and drug use, "I was slowly killing myself."

It also took death for Aki to find sustained sobriety, interpersonal peace, and meaningful work. Her boyfriend died of a drug overdose while they were both using, and the trauma of being so close to this moment of death allowed her, like many other committed AA members, to "hear" for the first time the group's message and find lasting sobriety. Yet this raises an important questions, why could Aki not hear and meaningfully engage with AA before this moment of abject despair? Why is success when treating addiction predicated on so much failure? Aki was able to go on after her boyfriend's death because of AA. But not everyone confronts such a startling moment of choice, or is ever able to hear the message of either group despite the trauma and hardship their drinking creates. This uncertainty surrounding who will benefit and who will reject the sobriety group model is a large part of what makes addiction a vexing and important area of study. Aki, Toshi, and thousands of other AA and Danshūkai members across Tokyo and Japan are alive because in a moment of despair they were able to hear the group's message and take away something that allowed them to find long-term sobriety. For all of these members AA and Danshūkai are wonderful and necessary organizations that saved their lives. Yet, there is also another and likely much larger group of individuals that, while equally troubled by problematic alcohol consumption and likely addiction, have not yet been able to hear or continue to reject outright the sobriety group's message, and few if any alternatives exist to potentially aid in confronting their struggles with alcohol and other addictive substances.

WHY JAPAN?

The complications that persist for those who structure and define their life around their addiction extend beyond the interpersonal. Many in Japan find themselves caught between addiction as a biomedical certainty and the cultural dissension such a diagnosis inspires. Addiction is viewed today and treated as a biomedical certainty, albeit one flush with uncertainty and divergence concerning cause, treatment, and permanency—uncertainty that is rife with concerns of cultural identity and local expectations. As such, this certainty can often overwhelm, much to the detriment of afflicted individuals, aspects of culture, gender, and identity that are inescapable in the daily lives of Japanese AA and Danshūkai members. At no point was this more evident than on an afternoon I spent with Ryota, the sober "ACA" or Adult Children of Alcoholics who also helps the AA office with computer issues.[1] Tucked into a corner table at a small cafe above Ikebukuro Station, we digressed from my prepared questions as Ryota talked about how he came to be an ACA. Both his parents drank heavily and daily for as long as he can remember and as a child his memories are of a filthy home overrun with empty beer cans and shōchū bottles. And while Ryota suffered tremendously in such a household, often being neglected for days at a time or having to make his own way to his grandparents' house for several weeks when his parents would temporarily disappear, the anger he still carries today is not with his mother and father. Instead, he wonders why their neighbors did nothing when they must have heard him crying amid the yelling of his parents' drunk and violent arguments. Why was his parents' incessant drunkenness not regarded as cause for concern or intervention? Particularly in a home that contained a young child? These feelings are the reason for Ryota's sobriety as well as his view of Japan as a "sick" society unable and unwilling to acknowledge the depth of its problem with alcohol.

Japan's abundance of alcohol makes Ryota's comment all the more biting, as it shows how stuck many "nots," those who cannot or will not consume alcohol, feel between the conflicting extremes of "biomedical certainty" structuring addiction and the societal expectations to imbibe they face daily. And much of the struggle and frustration Ryota and other sobriety group members feel finds root in the "idea that we are inescapably shaped by our dependence on other human beings" (Garcia 2010: 203). Japan's "nots" rely heavily on each other for support, guidance, and often friendship, but this alone is insufficient when they are also thoroughly excluded from so much of contemporary Japanese life. As Garcia goes on to emphasize, addiction is almost never anonymous, and in Japan the centrality of drinking and drunkenness is rooted in it being an activity typically shared with others. Thus, the shortcomings of treatment for those in Japan struggling with alcoholism is its neglect and disregard for human interdependency as fundamentally important, and the difficulty felt in confronting the "complex set of dependencies that expose something of shared human vulnerability" (*ibid*).

For Japanese men this sense of being trapped between two conflicting extremes is felt in struggles and difficulty with finding a place that does not deny sober men a sense of masculine worthiness. While contemporary Japan is increasingly described as fractured by different social groups and expressed identities, little space is afforded the sober and alcoholic male. The numerous examples from earlier chapters of secrecy and individual feelings of an inability to tell those outside the meeting of one's alcoholism speak to a powerful sense of disconnection among many Japanese men at AA and Danshūkai between the feelings of sanctuary felt at meetings and the illegitimacy of their sobriety elsewhere. Put simply, not drinking cuts many men off from others. So while it also allows these men to heal and stop bringing harm to themselves and others because of their drinking, it leaves them adrift in a nation largely tolerant of drunkenness. Toshi was not alone in hoping that all Japan needs is a charismatic and candid addict, "our Betty Ford," to begin turning public opinion in a sympathetic direction and allowing alcoholic men to be more open and forthright about their addictions. Yet it must also be considered that such a moment already came and went with little tangible change.

THE DISAPPEARING DRUNKEN PRINCE

In early July 2007 Prince Tomohito of Mikasa, a first cousin of Emperor Akihito and fifth in line to Japan's Chrysanthemum Throne, addressed a welfare services meeting in Sendai, a city in northern Japan. The Japan Times article from July 8, 2007 quotes the prince as saying "I am Prince Tomohito, dependent on alcohol," a deliberately similar statement to those made by AA and Danshūkai members before beginning a meeting speech (Japan Times, July 8, 2007). The same article quotes the prince as saying, "The Imperial Household Agency had told me not to say outright that I am dependent (on alcohol), but I hated being made a topic of talk based on speculation" (*ibid*). The day this and numerous other articles were published on Prince Tomohito's admission of alcoholism, news that dominated the headlines of the evening papers, coincided with the early stages of my time in Tokyo.

Prince Tomohito's alcoholism was also expectantly discussed by AA and Danshūkai members in the weeks following his admission as the possible beginning to raising societal awareness of alcoholism and addiction in Japan. During one of my visits to the JSO after the news broke, Toshi excitedly linked the events to Betty Ford's work in the United States that brought alcoholism and addiction into greater and far more sympathetic public discourse, adding that he saw Prince Tomohito's candor as following a similar trajectory. He hoped the result would be not only increased public awareness and sympathy for Japanese alcoholics, but also provide an inspirational leader members could point to when telling others of their own struggles with addiction. But then the headlines faded. What had just been front-page news quickly slipped from the newspapers. A major earthquake in Niigata prefecture on July 16, 2007, became the dominant story over the ensuing weeks and Prince Tomohito's alcoholism was largely forgotten. Despite the prince's willingness to publicly identify as an alcoholic, the larger Japanese public was not ready or not interested in hearing or considering his admission and reporting on the story quickly dissipated. Prince Tomohito, after an extended period of sobriety, also returned to drinking and on January 13, 2010, was again admitted to hospital and then a rehabilitation program for ongoing health complications stemming from a lifetime of heavy alcohol consumption and cigarette smoking. The Japan Times article that day was four one-sentence paragraphs buried deep in the newspaper, announced with little fanfare and quickly forgotten. Finally, on June 6, 2012, Prince Tomohito died of multiple organ failure at the age of 66. He had been in hospital at the time receiving treatment for multiple cancer-related health complications, and while his alcoholism was not listed as a cause of death, it certainly contributed to his poor health near the end of his life.

Prince Tomohito's admission of alcoholism, and the relative public disinterest that followed, offer one final example to the challenge facing AA and Danshūkai members in their efforts to reduce the stigma and disapproval that surrounds addiction in Japan's popular consciousness. It is not that addiction is unheard of in Japan, even Prince Tomohito described himself as a "workaholic" in a 2007 New York Times profile, but that it is widely regarded in a manner at odds with the position advocated by AA and Danshūkai (New York Times, October 20, 2007). Challenging and changing such entrenchment by the sobriety groups continues to be a struggle, in part because much of the organizational structure relies on accepting a worldview easily cast as at odds with elements of a "traditional" Japanese identity. And while traditional is as much "invented" and constantly challenged in Japan as elsewhere, the ongoing ability of patients to resist calls to join AA or Danshūkai by invoking claims of tradition also reveals the power such broad statements continue to exert. Prince Tomohito briefly thrust alcoholism into the public arena with force and flourish, yet it was a short lived conversation that ultimately resulted in minimal change to how addiction as an aspect of individual identity is regarded across Japan.

FUTURE CHALLENGES

Addiction and alcoholism are a challenge at countless individual and societal levels, no matter the context in which they are considered. Yet unlike two decades of a stagnant economy or growing feelings of national anxiety among many Japanese, addiction is a national challenge thus far ignored at numerous institutional and popular levels. This is particularly unfortunate because Japan can serve as a highly illustrative example of the ways in which conventional thinking on the diagnosis and treating of addiction should be challenged and potentially changed. As I noted in chapter 1, there is a tight logical circularity to how AA and Danshūkai structure and determine success and failure for anyone wanting or feeling they need to stop drinking. This approach, with fundamental reliance on the disease model of alcoholism and the mandated necessity for surrender to a Higher Power, admission of a loss of control, and emphasis on the immutable permanence of the condition, has saved and helped many in Japan when nothing else worked. However, many more also reject this way of defining addiction, labeling it foreign, overly religious, incompatible with being Japanese, or some combination of all three. For these individuals, particularly men who continue to struggle with how they might assert some sense of masculinity without alcohol, alternatives ways of addressing addiction must be considered, ways that dare to venture outside the tight logical circle and disrupt some of addiction's heretofore unassailed truths.

In 2012 I returned to Ohashi Danshūkai after an absence of nearly four years. While everyone, including myself, had visibly aged, little else was different and walking up to the sign-in table, writing my name, and dropping my 100 yen coin into the small plastic tray was familiar and comforting. I felt happy listening to everyone speak that evening, many of them familiar voices I had heard many times before, as well as a few new ones who had joined Ohashi Danshūkai since I left Tokyo. The two hours passed quickly and it was soon Nakamura's turn to conclude the meeting. Smiling as he got up from his chair he said "Ohashi Danshūkai is really great. Don't you think? Look at everyone here, it's great." As he paused and looked around the room, smiling at everyone, I found myself agreeing with him. Ohashi Danshūkai, as well as the Central Group and many other AA and Danshūkai meetings throughout Japan are indeed great. Yet they are great not because of the program on recovery they follow or the dictates on living sober and in recovery established by Bill Wilson, Bob Smith, or Harushige Matsumura. They are great because they exist as a collection of individuals determined to confront a life of often horrific memories brought on by their past alcohol use in order to ensure they do not again suffer through such hardship or inflict it upon others. The programs of AA and Danshūkai help make this desire for change possible, but addiction is rooted in the knowledge and experiences each individual carries and shares with the larger group.

And this is the final point on which I wish to end. For Japanese men who struggle with addiction, like all men and women throughout the world wrestling with similar interpersonal demons, it is a highly individual set of experiences that have shaped their path through periods of heavy alcohol, or narcotic, use and often periodic sobriety, to addiction. AA and Danshūkai exist in Japan as possible options to help these men, as well as a growing number of women, in their efforts to resist any feelings of temptation to drink, yet ultimately their addiction, despite its biomedical designations and characteristics, is an affliction rooted in their life story. Addiction is, in short, an impossibly complex set of memories, thoughts, feelings, and engagements with the world around them that is too often treated as a steadfast certainty to be confronted and treated in a consistently similar manner from person to person. For some such an approach works, and to see it work is amazing, just as hearing Toshi, Aki, Kazu, and countless other AA and Danshūkai members speak about who they once were when drinking and who they are today was a powerful experience difficult to put into words. Yet continuing to view and treat addiction through these established treatment programs, lionizing them as the only approach available for those questioning their alcohol use in Japan, is asking the individual to fit their experiences into the dictates of the group. Such an approach abandons many alcoholics and addicts, as it fails to fully consider the myriad other aspects shaping addiction as a lived category of identity, making the comfort and interpersonal stability of a life lived in recovery incompatible with much of daily life in Tokyo.

NOTE

1. ACA, sometimes shortened as AC (Adult Child or Children), are in Japan typically young adults who grew up in households with at least one alcoholic parent. However, rare is the case where the parent acknowledged their alcoholism, and many ACs, like Ryota, trace their own struggles back to parental unwillingness to admit or address their substance use.

Appendix

The Twelve Steps, Twelve Traditions, and Danshukai's Oath

THE TWELVE STEPS OF ALCOHOLICS ANONYMOUS[1]

1. We admitted we were powerless over alcohol—that our lives had become unmanageable.
2. Came to believe that a Power greater than ourselves could restore us to sanity.
3. Made a decision to turn our will and our lives over to the care of God, *as we understood Him.*
4. Made a searching and fearless moral inventory of ourselves.
5. Admitted to God, to ourselves, and to another human being the exact nature of our wrongs.
6. Were entirely ready to have God remove all these defects of character.
7. Humbly asked Him to remove our shortcomings.
8. Made a list of all persons we had harmed, and became willing to make amends to them all.
9. Made direct amends to such people wherever possible, except when to do so would injure them or others.
10. Continued to take personal inventory and when we were wrong promptly admitted it.
11. Sought through prayer and meditation to improve our conscious contact with God, *as we understood Him*, praying only for knowledge of His will for us and the power to carry that out.

12. Having had a spiritual awakening as the result of these Steps, we tried to carry this message to alcoholics, and to practice these principles in all our affairs.

THE TWELVE TRADITIONS OF ALCOHOLICS ANONYMOUS

1. Our common welfare should come first; personal recovery depends upon AA unity.
2. For our group purpose there is but one ultimate authority—a loving God as He may express Himself in our group conscience. Our leaders are but trusted servants; they do not govern.
3. The only requirement for AA membership is a desire to stop drinking.
4. Each group should be autonomous except in matters affecting other groups or AA as a whole.
5. Each group has but one primary purpose—to carry its message to the alcoholic who still suffers.
6. An AA group ought never endorse, finance or lend the AA name to any related facility or outside enterprise, lest problems of money, property and prestige divert us from our primary purpose.
7. Every AA group ought to be fully self-supporting, declining outside contributions.
8. Alcoholics Anonymous should remain forever non-professional, but our service centers may employ special workers.
9. AA, as such, ought never be organized; but we may create service boards or committees directly responsible to those they serve.
10. Alcoholics Anonymous has no opinion on outside issues; hence the AA name ought never be drawn into public controversy.
11. Our public relations policy is based on attraction rather than promotion; we need always maintain personal anonymity at the level of press, radio and films.
12. Anonymity is the spiritual foundation of all our traditions, ever reminding us to place principles before personalities.

DANSHŪKAI'S OATH[2]

断酒の誓い

1.　私たちは酒に対して無力であり、自分ひとりの力だけではどうにもならなか ったことを認めます。 **2.** 私たちは断酒例会に出席し、自分を率直に語ります。 **3.** 私たちは酒害体験を掘り起こし、過去の過ちを素直に認めます。

4. 私たちは自分を改革する努力をし、新しい人生を創ります。 5. 私たちは家族はもとより、迷惑をかけた人たちに償いをします。 6. 私たちは断酒の歓びを、酒害に悩む人たちに伝えます。

心の誓い

私は酒害から回復するため、断酒会に入会しました。これからは例会に出席して　酒を断ち、新しい自分をつくる努力をいたします。多くの仲間が立ち直っている　　のに私が立ち直れないはずはありません。私も完全に酒を止めることができます。　私は心の奥底から、酒のない人生を生きることを誓います。

家族の誓い

私は夫(息子・妻)の酒害に巻き込まれて、悩み、苦しみました。アルコール依　存症は家族ぐるみの病気です。病気だから治さなければなりません。また、治す　ことができます。これからは酒害を正しく理解し、互いに協力して心の健康を回　復します。私は断酒会の皆様とともに、幸せになる事を誓います。

ENGLISH TRANSLATION:

Sobriety Oath

1. We admit that alone we do not have the strength and are powerless over alcohol. 2. We speak frankly and participate in regular Danshūkai meetings. 3. We reclaim our harmful personal experiences with alcohol and admit our past errors honestly. 4. We make a strong effort to reform ourselves, creating a new life. 5. We atone to our family and those we have wronged from the beginning. 6. We delight in sobriety, conveying this to others worried about the evil influence of alcohol.

Oath of Inner Strength

I joined Danshūkai to recover from the evil influences of alcohol. From now on I will make a great effort to become a new person by attending a regular meeting and abstaining from alcohol. With the help of our many fellows there is no reason to lose our way. I can also completely quit alcohol. I swear from the bottom to live as a new person without alcohol.

Family Oath

I am the spouse (son/daughter, wife) who suffered and was troubled by the evils of alcohol. Alcohol dependency syndrome is an illness of the entire family. As an illness, it must be cured. And it can also be cured. In understanding the evils of alcohol, mental and physical recovery occurs. I pledge, in Danshūkai meetings with everyone, to be happy.

NOTES

1. AA's Twelve Steps and Twelve Traditions are taken from the organization's website. See http://www.aa.org and http://www.aa.org/pages/en_US/twelve-steps-and-twelve-traditions for more on these organizational principles.

2. Danshūkai's Oath is also available on the group's website at http://www.dansyu-renmei.or.jp/susume/danshu6.html. Additionally, see Tomofumi Oka's 1994 paper on Japanese Self-Help Groups for more on the purpose and use of the Oath during meetings at http://pweb.sophia.ac.jp/oka/papers/94/danshukai1994.pdf.

References

2005. *The Kojiki: Records of Ancient Matters*. Translated by Basil Hall Chamberlain. London: Tuttle Publishing.
Alasuutari, Pertti. 1992. *Desire and Craving: A Cultural Theory of Alcoholism*. Albany: SUNY Press.
Alcoholics Anonymous: The Story of How Many Thousands of Men and Women Have Recovered From Alcoholism. 2001. Alcoholics Anonymous World Services.
Alexander, Jeffery. 2013a. *Brewed in Japan: The Evolution of the Japanese Beer Industry*. Vancouver: University of British Columbia Press.
——— 2013b. *Japan's Hiropon Panic: Resident Non-Japanese and the 1950s Meth Crisis. International Journal of Drug Policy.*
Allison, Anne. 1994. *Nightwork: Sexuality, Pleasure, and Corporate Masculinity in a Tokyo Hostess Club*. Chicago: University of Chicago Press.
——— 2012. "Ordinary Refugees: Social Precarity and Soul in 21st Century Japan." *Anthropological Quarterly* 85, no. 2 (2012): 345–370.
——— 2013. *Precarious Japan*. Durham: Duke University Press.
Antze, Paul, and Michael Lambek. 1996. *Tense Past: Cultural Essays in Trauma and Memory*. New York: Routledge.
Arkowitz, Hal, and Scott Lilienfeld. 2011. "Does Alcoholics Anonymous Work?" *Scientific American* 22, no. 1: 64–65.
Arno, Andrew. 2011. *Alarming Reports: Communicating Conflict in the Daily News*. New York: Berghahn Books.
Arukōru Yakubutsu Mondai Zenkoku Shimin Kyōkai (ASK). Available at http://www.ask.or.jp/index.html (accessed August 10, 2013).
Aston, W. G. 2011. *Nihongi: Chronicles of Japan from the Earliest Times to A.D. 697*. London: Tuttle Publishing.
Bardsley, Jan. 2011. "The Oyaji Gets a Makeover." In *Manners and Mischief Gender, Power, and Etiquette in Japan*, eds. Jan Bardsley and Laura Miller. Berkeley: University of California Press: 114–135.
Befu, Harumi. 1974. "An Ethnography of Dinner Entertainment in Japan." *Arctic Anthropology*, 196–203.
——— 2001. *Hegemony of Homogeneity: An Anthropological Analysis Of "Nihonjinron."* Melbourne: Trans Pacific Press.
Benedict, Ruth. 1946. *The Chrysanthemum and the Sword: Patterns of Japanese Culture*. Boston: Houghton Mifflin Harcourt.
Bestor, Theodore. 1989. *Neighborhood Tokyo*. Palo Alto: Stanford University Press.

——— 2003. 'Inquisitive Observations: Following Networks in Urban Fieldwork.' In *Doing Fieldwork in Japan*, eds. Theodore Bestor, Patricia Steinhoff and Victoria Lyon Bestor. Honolulu: University of Hawai'i Press.

Bride, B. E., and L. Nackerud. 2002. "The Disease Model of Alcoholism: A Kuhnian Paradigm." *Journal of Sociology & Social Welfare* 29, no. 2: 125–142.

Borovoy, Amy. 2005. *The Too-good Wife: Alcohol, Codependency, and the Politics of Nurturance in Postwar Japan.* Berkeley: University of California Press.

Brandes, Stanley. 2002. *Staying Sober in Mexico City.* Austin: University of Texas Press.

Bunting, Chris. 2011. *Drinking Japan: A Guide to Japan's Best Drinks and Drinking Establishments.* London: Tuttle Publishing.

Cain, Carole. 1991. "Personal Stories: Identity Acquisition and Self-understanding in Alcoholics Anonymous." *Ethos* 19, no. 2: 210–253.

Campbell, Nancy. 2007. *Discovering Addiction: The Science and Politics of Substance Abuse Research.* Ann Arbor: University of Michigan Press.

Carr, E. Summerson. 2011. *Scripting Addiction: The Politics of Therapeutic Talk and American Sobriety.* Princeton: Princeton University Press.

Castro-Vázquez, Genaro, and Izumi Kishi. 2007. "Silence, Condoms, and Masculinity Heterosexual Japanese Males Negotiating Contraception." *Men and Masculinities* 10, no. 2: 153–177.

Chenhall, Richard. 2007. *Benelong's Haven: Recovery From Alcohol and Drug Abuse Within An Aboriginal Australian Treatment Centre.* Melbourne: Melbourne University Publishing.

Chenhall, Richard, and Tomofumi Oka. 2006–2007. "An Initial View of Self-help Groups for Japanese Alcoholics: Danshūkai in Its Historical, Social, and Cultural Contexts." *International Journal of Self Help and Self Care* 5, no. 2: 111–152.

——— 2014. "Self-Help Groups for Alcoholics in Japan: Models of 'Recovery'." In *Internationalising Japan: Discourse and Practice*, eds. Jeremy Breaden, Stacey Steele, and Carolyn Stevens. Melbourne: Routledge.

Christensen, Paul. 2010. *The Fragility of Sobriety: Alcoholism and Masculinity in Japan.* Ph.D. Dissertation. Honolulu: University of Hawai'i at Mānoa.

——— 2012. "Real Men Don't Hold Their Liquor: The Complexity of Drunkenness and Sobriety in a Tokyo Bar." *Social Science Japan Journal* 15, no. 2: 239–254.

——— 2014. "Connoisseurship and Drunkenness in Tokyo." *International Journal of Drug Policy* 25, no. 4: 804–809.

Clammer, John. 2013. *Difference and Modernity: Social Theory and Contemporary Japanese Society.* London: Routledge Library Editions.

Clifford, James. 2001. "Indigenous Articulations." *The Contemporary Pacific* 13, no. 2: 467–490.

Connell, R. W. 1995. *Masculinities.* Berkeley: University of California Press.

——— 2000. *The Men and the Boys.* Berkeley: University of California Press.

Courtwright, David, Herman Joseph, and Don Des Jarlais. 1989. *Addicts Who Survived: An Oral History of Narcotic Use in America Before 1965.* Knoxville: University of Tennessee Press.

Dasgupta, Romit. 2000. "Performing Masculinities? The Salaryman at Work and Play." *Japanese Studies* 20, no. 2: 189–200.

——— 2013. *Re-reading the Salaryman in Japan: Crafting Masculinities.* New York: Routledge.

Dennett, Andrea. 1996. "The Dime Museum Freak Show Reconfigured as Talk Show." *Freakery: Cultural Spectacles of the Extraordinary Body*, ed. R. G. Thomson, 315–26. New York: NYU Press.

Doi, Takeo. 2002 [1971]. *The Anatomy of Dependence.* Tokyo: Kodansha International.

Douglas, Mary. 1987. *Constructive Drinking: Perspectives on Drink From Anthropology.* New York: Psychology Press.

Durrant, Russil, and Jo Thakker. 2003. *Substance Use and Abuse: Cultural and Historical Perspectives.* London: Sage.

Edwards, Walter. 1989. *Modern Japan Through Its Weddings: Gender, Person, and Society in Ritual Portrayal.* Palo Alto: Stanford University Press.

Fingarette, Herbert. 1988. *Heavy Drinking: The Myth of Alcoholism As a Disease*. Berkeley: University of California Press.

Foucault, Michel. 1994. *The Birth of the Clinic: An Archaeology of Medical Perception*. New York: Vintage Books.

——— 1995. *Discipline and Punish: The Birth of the Prison*. New York: Vintage Books.

Fowler, Edward. 1996. *San'ya Blues: Laboring Life in Contemporary Tokyo*. Ithaca: Cornell University Press.

Frühstück, Sabine. 2007. *Uneasy Warriors: Gender, Memory, and Popular Culture in the Japanese Army*. Berkeley: University of California Press.

Garcia, Angela. 2010a. *The Pastoral Clinic: Addiction and Dispossession Along the Rio Grande*. Berkeley: University of California Press.

——— 2010b. *How Dion Died: The 2-year-old Fell Victim to the Reality of Drug Abuse*. The Los Angeles Times, Op-Ed., July 17.

Garriott, William. 2011. *Policing Methamphetamine: Narcopolitics in Rural America*. New York: New York University Press.

Gill, Tom. 2001. *Men of Uncertainty: The Social Organization of Day Laborers in Contemporary Japan*. Albany: SUNY Press.

——— 2003"When Pillars Evaporate: Structuring Masculinity on the Japanese Margins." In *Men and Masculinities in Contemporary Japan: Dislocating the Salaryman Doxa*, eds. James Roberson and Nobue Suzuki. London: RoutledgeCurzon: 144–161.

Gordon, Andrew. 2008. *A Modern History of Japan: From Tokugawa Times to the Present*. New York: Oxford University Press USA.

Gordon, Colin, Graham Burchell, and Peter Miller. 1991. *The Foucault Effect: Studies in Governmentality*. Chicago: University of Chicago Press.

Gupta, Akhil, and James Ferguson. 1992. "Beyond Culture: Space, Identity, and the Politics of Difference." *Cultural Anthropology* 7, no. 1: 6–23.

Gusfield, Joseph. 1996. *Contested Meanings: The Construction of Alcohol Problems*. Madison: University of Wisconsin Press.

Heath, Dwight. 1958. "Drinking Patterns of the Bolivian Camba." *Quarterly Journal of Studies on Alcohol* 19, no. 3: 491–508.

Heine, Steven. 2012. *Sacred High City, Sacred Low City: A Tale of Religious Sites in Two Tokyo Neighborhoods*. New York: Oxford University Press.

Hendry, Joy. 1994. "Drinking and Gender in Japan." In *Gender, Drink, and Drugs*, ed. Maryon McDonald. New York: Berg Publishers, 175–190.

——— 1996 [2000]. *Understanding Japanese Society*. London: Routledge.

Higuchi, Susumu, and Hiroaki Kono. 1994. "Early Diagnosis and Treatment of Alcoholism: The Japanese Experience." *Alcohol and Alcoholism* 29, no. 4: 363–373.

Higuchi, Susumu, Sachio Matsushita, and Yoneatsu Osaki. 2006. "Drinking Practices, Alcohol Policy and Prevention Programmes in Japan." *International Journal of Drug Policy* 17, no. 4: 358–366.

Higuchi, Susumu, Sachio Matsushita, Hitoshi Maesato, and Yoneatsu Osaki. 2007. "Japan: Alcohol Today." *Addiction* 102, no. 12: 1849–1862.

Higuchi, Susumu, Hitoshi Maesato, Atsushi Yoshimura, and Sachio Matsushita. 2014. "Acceptance of Controlled Drinking Among Treatment Specialists of Alcohol Dependence in Japan." *Alcohol and Alcoholism* July/August 49, no. 4.

Hobsbawm, Eric. 1996 [1975]. *Age of Capital: 1848–1875*. New York: Vintage.

Holter, Øystein. 2005. "Social Theories for Researching Men and Masculinities: Direct Gender Hierarchy and Structural Inequality." In *Handbook of Studies on Men and Masculinities*, eds. Michael Kimmel, Jeff Hearn, and R. W. Connell. London: SAGE Publications.

Hunt, Geoffrey, and Judith Barker. 2001. "Socio-cultural Anthropology and Alcohol and Drug Research: Towards a Unified Theory." *Social Science & Medicine* 53, no. 2: 165–188.

Ivy, Marilyn. 1995. *Discourses of the Vanishing: Modernity, Phantasm, Japan*. Chicago: University of Chicago Press.

Iwata, Yuya and Yoji Inoue. 2008. "Dansei Danshū Keizokusha ni okeru Inshū no Shūkanka kara Arukōru Izonsho Chiryō Akusesu made no Purosesu oyobi Shakaiteki Shien ni kansuru Shitsuteki Kenkyū" (The Process between the Formations of Drinking Habits to the Treat-

ment from the Perspective of Abstinent Alcoholics in Japan). *Shakai Igaku Kenkyū* (Bulletin of Social Medicine) 26(1): 65–75. Available at http://ergo.itc.nagoya-u.ac.jp/shakai-igakukai/report/no26/26-08.pdf (accessed August 13, 2013).
Japan Times, The. 2007. Prince uses speech to talk about his alcohol problem. July 8.
——— 2008. Cases for abetting drunken driving exceed 1,200. October 10.
——— 2009. Alcoholism Remains a Taboo Issue. April 17.
——— 2010. Prince Tomohito Again in Rehab. January 13.
Jarrad, Jeffrey. 1995. "The Brazilianization of Alcoholics Anonymous." *The Brazilian Puzzle: Culture on the Borderlands of the Western World*: 209–236.
Jellinek, Ervin. 1960. *The Disease Concept of Alcoholism*. Berkeley: University of California Press.
Johnson, David. 2003. "Getting in and Getting along in the Prosecutor's Office." In *Doing Fieldwork in Japan*, eds. Theodore Bestor, Patricia Steinhoff, and Victoria Lyon Bestor. Honolulu: University of Hawai'i Press.
Kasai, Kenta. 2008. Danshū ga tsukuridasu kyodosei [Collectivity created through abstinence]. Tokyo: Sekai Shissha.
Katō, Junji. 1995. *Nemoto Sho den* (Biography of Sho Nemoto). Sendai: Ginga Publishing.
Katsuno, Hirofumi, and Christine Yano. 2002. "Face to Face: On-line Subjectivity in Contemporary Japan." *Asian Studies Review* 26, no. 2: 205–232.
Kazama, Takashi, and Kazuya Kawaguchi. 2003. "HIV Risk and the (Im)Permeability of the Male Body." In *Men and Masculinities in Contemporary Japan: Dislocating the Salaryman Doxa*, eds. James Roberson and Nobue Suzuki.
Kimura, N., T. Shirasaka, Y. Sasaki, C. Kawazoe, and T. Saito. 2013. "A Survey of Alcoholics and Their Families on Controlled Drinking As a Treatment Goal: Discussions on New Treatment Approaches." *Nihon Arukōru Yakubutsu Igakkai zasshi* (*Japanese Journal of Alcohol Studies & Drug Dependence*) 48, no. 1: 76–84.
Kingsberg, Miriam. 2013. Methamphetamine Solution: Drugs and the Reconstruction of Nation in Postwar Japan. *The Journal of Asian Studies* 72(1): 141–162.
Kitanaka, Junko. 2011. *Depression in Japan: Psychiatric Cures for a Society in Distress*. Princeton: Princeton University Press.
Kobayashi, Tetsuo. 1990. *Matsumura Harushige: Danshukai Shodai Kaicho*. Tokyo: *ASK Publishing*.
Kondo, Chiharu, Tsutomo Iimuro, Kiyohito Iwai, Kazuhiko Kurata, M Kouda, Hisanaga Tachikawa, K Nakashima, and Tsunetsugu Munakata. 2000. "A Study of Recovery Factor About Drug Addiction Recovery Center 'DARC'." *Nihon Arukoru Yakubutsu Igakkai zasshi* (*Japanese Journal of Alcohol Studies & Drug Dependence*) 35, no. 4: 258–270.
Kondō, Hiroshi. 1996. *The Book of Sake*. Tokyo: Kodansha International.
Koob, George, and Nora Volkow. 2009. "Neurocircuitry of Addiction." *Neuropsychopharmacology* 35, no. 1: 217–238.
Kownacki, Richard, and William Shadish. 1999. "Does Alcoholics Anonymous Work? The Results From a Meta-Analysis of Controlled Experiments." *Substance Use & Misuse* 34, no. 13: 1897–1916.
Laudet, Alexandre. 2003. "Attitudes and Beliefs About 12-step Groups Among Addiction Treatment Clients and Clinicians: Toward Identifying Obstacles to Participation." *Substance Use & Misuse* 38, no. 14: 2017–2047.
——— 2007. "What Does Recovery Mean to You? Lessons From the Recovery Experience for Research and Practice." *Journal of Substance Abuse Treatment* 33, no. 3: 243–256.
LeBlanc, Robin. 2010. *The Art of the Gut: Manhood, Power, and Ethics in Japanese Politics*. Berkeley: University of California Press.
Lebra, Takie. 1976. *Japanese Patterns of Behavior*. Honolulu: University of Hawai'i Press.
Leheny, David. 2006. *Think Global, Fear Local: Sex, Violence, and Anxiety in Contemporary Japan*. Ithaca: Cornell University Press.
Levine, Harry. 1978. "The Discovery of Addiction; Changing Conceptions of Habitual Drunkenness in America." *Journal of Studies on Alcohol and Drugs* 39, no. 1: 143.
Lie, John. 2001. *Multiethnic Japan*. Cambridge: Harvard University Press.

Light, Richard. 2003. "Sports and the Construction of Masculinity in the Japanese Education System." In *Asian Masculinities: The Meaning and Practice of Manhood in China and Japan,* eds. Kam Louie and Morris Low. London: Routledge.
Lin, Ho Swee. 2012. "Tokyo at 10: Establishing Difference through the Friendship Networks of Women Executives in Japan." *Journal of the Royal Anthropological Institute* 18(1): 83–102.
Linhart, Sepp. 1986. "Sakariba: Zone of 'Evaporation' Between Work and Home." *Journal of Asian Studies* 29(3): 617–632.
Lock, Margaret. 1984. *East Asian Medicine in Urban Japan: Varieties of Medical Experience.* Berkeley: University of California Press.
Louie, Kam, and Morris Low. 2003. *Asian Masculinities: The Meaning and Practice of Manhood in China and Japan.* London: Routledge.
MacAndrew, Craig, and Robert Edgerton. 2003 [1969]. *Drunken Comportment: A Social Explanation.* New York: Percheron Press.
Mäkelä, Klaus. 1996. *Alcoholics Anonymous As a Mutual-help Movement: A Study in Eight Societies.* Madison: University of Wisconsin Press.
Mathiasson, John. 1987. "A Higher Power of Their Own Understanding: Recovery in Alcoholics Anonymous as a Shamanistic Journey." Unpublished ms.
Markel, Howard. 2012. *An Anatomy of Addiction: Sigmund Freud, William Halsted, and the Miracle Drug Cocaine.* New York: Random House.
Marshall, Mac. 1979. *Weekend Warriors: Alcohol in a Micronesian Culture.* New York: Mayfield Publishing Company.
Marshall, Mac, Genevieve Ames, and Linda Bennett. 2001. "Anthropological Perspectives on Alcohol and Drugs at the Turn of the New Millennium." *Social Science & Medicine* 53, no. 2: 153–164.
Marutani, Miki, and Misako Miyazaki. 2010. "Culturally Sensitive Health Counseling to Prevent Lifestyle-related Diseases in Japan." *Nursing & Health Sciences* 12, no. 3: 392–398.
Matsumoto, T., and O. Kobayashi. 2008. "What Is the Japanese Mental Health Service Lacking for Drug Dependence Rehabilitation?." *Nihon Arukōru Yakubutsu Igakkai zasshi (Japanese Journal of Alcohol Studies & Drug Dependence)* 43, no. 3: 172.
McIntire, Don. 2000. "How Well Does AA Work? An Analysis of Published AA Surveys (1968-1996) and Related Analyses/comments." *Alcoholism Treatment Quarterly* 18, no. 4: 1–18.
McLelland, Mark. 2000. *Male Homosexuality in Modern Japan: Cultural Myths and Social Realities.* Oxon: RoutledgeCruzon.
Meyer, Roger. 1996. "The Disease Called Addiction: Emerging Evidence in a 200-Year Debate." *The Lancet* 347, no. 8995: 162–166.
Miller, William. 1998. "Researching the Spiritual Dimensions of Alcohol and Other Drug Problems." *Addiction* 93, no. 7: 979–990.
Miller, William, and Ernest Kurtz. 1994. "Models of Alcoholism Used in Treatment: Contrasting AA and Other Perspectives with Which It Is Often Confused." *Journal of Studies on Alcohol and Drugs* 55, no. 2: 159.
Miller, William, and Stephen Rollnick. 2012. *Motivational Interviewing: Preparing People to Change Addictive Behavior.* New York: Guilford Press.
Mitchell, Timothy. 2004. *Intoxicated Identities: Alcohol's Power in Mexican History and Culture.* New York: Routledge.
Moeran, Brian. 1998. "One over the Seven: Sake Drinking in a Japanese Pottery Community." In *Interpreting Japanese Society: Anthropological Approaches*, ed. Joy Hendry. London: Routledge: 243-258.
——— 2005. "Drinking Country: Flows of Exchange in a Japanese Valley." In *Drinking Cultures: Alcohol and Identity*, ed. Thomas Wilson. New York: Berg Publishers, 25–42.
Morjaria, Asesha, and Jim Orford. 2002. "The Role of Religion and Spirituality in Recovery From Drink Problems: A Qualititative Study of Alcoholics Anonymous Members and South Asian Men." *Addiction Research & Theory* 10, no. 3: 225–256.
Moynihan, Clare. 1998. "Theories in Health Care and Research: Theories of Masculinity." *British Medical Journal* 317, no. 7165: 1072.

Nakane, Chie. 1970. *Japanese Society*. Berkeley: University of California Press.
New York Times, The. 2007. A Font of Commentary Amid Japan's Taciturn Royals. October 20.
O'Barr, William. 1994. *Culture and the Ad: Exploring Otherness in the World of Advertising, Institutional Structures of Feeling*. Boulder: Westview Press.
O'Brien, Rosaleen, Graham Hart, and Kate Hunt. 2007. "Standing Out From the Herd: Men Renegotiating Masculinity in Relation to Their Experience of Illness." *International Journal of Men's Health* 6, no. 3: 178–200.
Ohnuki-Tierney, Emiko. 1984. *Illness and Culture in Contemporary Japan: An Anthropological View*. Cambridge: Cambridge University Press.
——— 1993. *Rice As Self: Japanese Identities Through Time*. Princeton: Princeton University Press.
Oka, Tomofumi. 2011. "The 'New Life' Model of a Japanese Self-Help Group for Alcoholics." *Sophia University Studies in Social Services, 35, 16-35.*
Oka, Tomofumi, and Richard Chenhall. 2014. "Spirituality and Japanese Self-Help Groups for Alcoholics: Zen Buddhism for Abstinence" (http://www.inter-disciplinary.net/critical-issues/wp-content/uploads/2014/02/okaspirpaper.pdf).
Oka, Tomofumi, Sachiko Tanaka, Hidehiko Ake, and Shōko Kuwabara. 2011. "Self-Help Groups for Family Survivors of Suicide in Japan: For Empowerment, Not Grief Care." Proceedings of the 21st Asia-Pacific Social Work Conference (http://pweb.sophia.ac.jp/oka/papers/2011/17-po-e-16.pdf).
Oka, Tomofumi, and Mikihiro Hayashi. 2010. "Do Members of Self-help Groups in Japan Consider the Medicalisation of Their Problems and Conditions to Have Liberated Them or Pathologised Them? Three Case Studies." In *Joint World Conference on Social Work and Social Development: The Agenda, Hong Kong*. (http://133.12.138.67/oka/papers/2010/oka_hayashi_20100509.pdf)
Ortner, Sherry. 1996. *Making Gender: The Politics and Erotics of Culture*. Boston: Beacon Press.
Osaki, Yoneatsu, Sachio Matsushita, Tomonobu Shirasaka, Hisanori Hiro, and Susumu Higuchi. 2005. "Nationwide Survey of Alcohol Drinking and Alcoholism Among Japanese Adults]." *Nihon Arukōru Yakubutsu Igakkai zasshi* (*Japanese Journal of Alcohol Studies & Drug Dependence*) 40, no. 5: 455.
Osaki, Yoneatsu, Takeo, Tanihata, Takashi Ohida, Hideyuki Kanda, Kenji Suzuki, Susumu Higuchi, Yoshitaka Kaneita, Masumi Minowa, and Kenji Hayashi. 2009. "Decrease in the Prevalence of Adolescent Alcohol Use and Its Possible Causes in Japan: Periodical Nationwide Cross-Sectional Surveys." *Alcoholism Clinical and Experimental Research* 33(2): 247–254.
Ōyama, Shirō. 2000. *San'ya Gakeppuchi Nikki* (*A Man with No Talents: Memoirs of a Tokyo Day Laborer*). Tokyo: Kadokawa Shuppan.
Partanen, Juha. 2007. "Spectacles of Sociability and Drunkenness: On Alcohol and Drinking in Japan." *Contemporary Drug Problems*. 33: 177.
Peralta, Robert. 2007. "College Alcohol Use and the Embodiment of Hegemonic Masculinity Among European American Men." *Sex Roles* 56, no. 11–12: 741–756.
Pine, Adrienne. 2008. *Working Hard, Drinking Hard: On Violence and Survival in Honduras*. Berkeley: University of California Press.
Prussing, Erica. 2007. "Reconfiguring the Empty Center: Drinking, Sobriety, and Identity in Native American Women's Narratives." *Culture, Medicine and Psychiatry* 31, no. 4: 499–526.
——— 2011. *White Man's Water: The Politics of Sobriety in a Native American Community*. Tucson: University of Arizona Press.
Reinarman, Craig. 2005. "Addiction As Accomplishment: The Discursive Construction of Disease." *Addiction Research & Theory* 13, no. 4: 307–320.
Rimke, Heidi Marie. 2000. "Governing Citizens Through Self-help Literature." *Cultural Studies* 14, no. 1: 61–78.
Roberson, James. 1998. *Japanese Working Class Lives: An Ethnographic Study of Factory Workers*. New York: Routledge.

———2005. "Fight!! Ippatsu!!: 'Genki' Energy Drinks and the Marketing of Masculine Ideology in Japan." *Men and Masculinities* 7, no. 4: 365–384.
Roberson, James, and Nobue Suzuki. 2003. *Men and Masculinities in Contemporary Japan: Dislocating the Salaryman Doxa.* New York: RoutledgeCruzon.
Robertson, Jennifer. 1994. *Native and Newcomer: Making and Remaking a Japanese City.* Berkeley: University of California Press.
Room, Robin. 2001. "Intoxication and Bad Behaviour: Understanding Cultural Differences in the Link." *Social Science & Medicine* 53(2): 189–198.
Rose, Nikolas. 1996. *Inventing Our Selves: Psychology, Power, and Personhood.* Cambridge: Cambridge University Press.
——— 1999. *Governing the Soul: The Shaping of the Private Self.* London: Free Association Books.
Rosenberger, Nancy. 1994. *Japanese Sense of Self.* Cambridge: Cambridge University Press.
Saito, S., and N. Ikegami. 1978. "KAST (Kurihama Alcoholism Screening Test) and Its Applications." *Japan Journal of the Study of Alcohol* 13: 229–237.
Schnell, Scott. 1997. "Sanctity and Sanction in Communal Ritual: A Reconsideration of Shintō Festival Processions." *Ethnology* 36, no. 1: 1–12.
——— 1999. *The Rousing Drum: Ritual Practice in a Japanese Community.* Honolulu: University of Hawai'i Press.
Scott, Joan. 1986. "Gender: A Useful Category of Historical Analysis." *The American Historical Review* 91, no. 5: 1053–1075.
Singer, Merrill, and Hans Baer. 1995. "Confronting Juan Garcia's Drinking Problem: The Demedicalization of Alcoholism." In *Critical Medical Anthropology*, eds. Merrill Singer and Hans Baer. Amityville: Baywood Publishing Company, 301–328.
Smith, Stephen R. 1988. "Drinking and Sobriety in Japan." Ph.D. Dissertation. Columbia University.
——— 1998. "Good Old Boy Into Alcoholic: Danshūkai and Learning a New Drinking Role in Japan." In *Learning in Likely Places: Varieties of Apprenticeship in Japan,* ed. John Singleton. Cambridge: Cambridge University Press.
Song, Jesook. 2009. *South Koreans in the Debt Crisis: The Creation of a Neoliberal Welfare Society.* Durham: Duke University Press.
Soko ga Shiritai (Let's find out). 1993. Tokyo: Tokyo Broadcasting System.
Steinhoff, Patricia. 2003. "New Notes from the Underground: Doing Fieldwork Without a Site." *Doing Fieldwork in Japan,* eds. Theodore Bestor, Patricia Steinhoff and Victoria Lyon Bestor. Honolulu: University of Hawai'i Press.
Stevens, Carolyn. 1997. *On the Margins of Japanese Society: Volunteers and the Welfare of the Urban Underclass.* New York: Routledge.
Stewart, Kathleen. 1996. *A Space on the Side of the Road: Cultural Poetics in An "Other" America.* Princeton: Princeton University Press.
Strate, Lance. 1992. "Beer Commercials: A Manual on Masculinity." In *Men, Masculinity, and the Media,* ed. Steve Craig. Thousand Oaks: SAGE Publications: 78-92.
Stromberg, Peter. 1990. "Ideological Language in the Transformation of Identity." *American Anthropologist* 92, no. 1: 42–56.
Strutz Sreetharan, Cindi. 2004. "Japanese Men's Linguistic Stereotypes and Realities: Conversations from the Kansai and Kanto Regions." *Japanese Language, Gender, and Ideology: Cultural Models and Real People,* eds. Shigeko Okamoto and Janet Shibamoto Smith. New York: Oxford University Press.
Suwaki, Hiroshi. 1979. "Naikan and Danshūkai for the Treatment of Japanese Alcoholic Patients." *British Journal of Addiction to Alcohol & Other Drugs* 74, no. 1: 15–19.
Swora, Maria Gabrielle. 2001. "Commemoration and the Healing of Memories in Alcoholics Anonymous." *Ethos* 29, no. 1: 58–77.
Takakura, Minoru. 2011. "Does Social Trust at School Affect Students' Smoking and Drinking Behavior in Japan?" *Social Science & Medicine* 72(2): 299.
Tengan, Ty P. Kāwika. 2008. *Native Men Remade: Gender and Nation in Contemporary Hawai'i.* Durham: Duke University Press.

Tiger, Rebecca. 2013. *Judging Addicts: Drug Courts and Coercion in the Justice System*. New York: New York University Press.

Turner, Victor. 1974. *Dramas, Fields, and Metaphor: Symbolic Action in Human Society*. Ithaca: Cornell University Press.

——— 1987. "Betwixt and Between: The Liminal Period in Rites of Passage." In *Betwixt & Between: Patterns of Masculine and Feminine Initiation,* eds. Mahdi, Louise Carus, Steven Foster, and Meredith Little. La Salle, Ill.: Open Court Publishing.

Vaillant, George. 2005. "Alcoholics Anonymous: Cult or Cure?" *Australian and New Zealand Journal of Psychiatry* 39, no. 6: 431–436.

Valverde, Mariana. 1998. *Diseases of the Will: Alcohol and the Dilemmas of Freedom*. Cambridge: Cambridge University Press.

Valverde, Marian, and Kimberley White-Mair. 2001. "'One Day at a Time' and Other Slogans for Everyday Life: The Ethical Practices of Alcoholics Anonymous." *Sociology* 33, no. 2: 393–410.

Vaughn, Michael, Frank Huang, and Christine Ramirez. 1995. "Drug Abuse and Anti-Drug Policy in Japan: Past History and Future Directions." *British Journal of Criminology* 35(4): 491–524.

White, Merry. 1994. *The Material Child: Coming of Age in Japan and America.* Berkeley: University of California Press.

Wilcox, Danny. 1998. *Alcoholic Thinking: Language, Culture, and Belief in Alcoholics Anonymous.* Greenwood Publishing Group.

Wilson, Thomas. 2005. *Drinking Cultures: Alcohol and Identity.* New York: Berg.

Yano, Christine. 2002. *Tears of Longing: Nostalgia and the Nation in Japanese Popular Song.* Cambridge: Harvard University Asia Center.

Index

About the Author

Paul Christensen is an assistant professor of anthropology in the department of Humanities and Social Sciences at the Rose-Hulman Institute of Technology in Terre Haute, Indiana. He received his Ph.D. from the University of Hawai'i at Mānoa in 2010. From 2011–2014 he was a visiting assistant professor of anthropology at Union College in Schenectady, New York. He joined the faculty at Rose-Hulman in 2014.